The Word took bodily form
so that we might receive the Holy Spirit:
God became the bearer of a body
so that men might be bearers of the Spirit.

ATTRIBUTED TO ATHANASIUS

TITLES IN THIS SERIES

THE
HOLY
SPIRIT

SINCLAIR B. FERGUSON

CONTOURS *of*

CHRISTIAN

THEOLOGY

GERALD BRAY
General Editor

InterVarsity Press
Downers Grove, Illinois

InterVarsity Press
P.O. Box 1400, Downers Grove, IL 60515-1426
World Wide Web: www.ivpress.com
E-mail: email@ivpress.com

InterVarsity Press® is the book-publishing division of InterVarsity Christian Fellowship®, a movement of students and faculty active on campus at hundreds of universities, colleges and schools of nursing in the United States of America, and a member movement of the International Fellowship of Evangelical Students. For information about local and regional activities, write Public Relations Dept., InterVarsity Christian Fellowship, 6400 Schroeder Rd., P.O. Box 7895, Madison, WI 53707-7895, or visit the IVCF website at <www.intervarsity.org>.

All Scripture quotations, unless otherwise indicated, are taken from the British edition of the HOLY BIBLE, NEW INTERNATIONAL VERSION®. NIV®. Copyright ©1973, 1978, 1984 by International Bible Society. Used by permission of Zondervan Publishing House. All rights reserved.

ISBN 978-0-8308-1536-4

Printed in the United States of America ∞

green press INITIATIVE *InterVarsity Press is committed to protecting the environment and to the responsible use of natural resources. As a member of the Green Press Initiative we use recycled paper whenever possible. To learn more about the Green Press Initiative, visit <www.greenpressinitiative.org>.*

Library of Congress Cataloging-in-Publication Data

Ferguson, Sinclair B.
  The Holy Spirit/Sinclair B. Ferguson.
    p. cm.—(Contours of Christian theology)
  Includes bibliographical references.
  ISBN 0-8308-1536-8 (alk. paper)
  1. Holy Spirit.   I. Title.   II. Series.
  BT121.2.F38 1997
  231'.3—dc20

                                                                96-43163
                                                                CIP

P	34	33	32	31	30	29	28	27	26	25	24	23	22	21	20
Υ	28	27	26	25	24	23	22	21	20	19	18	17	16	15	14

To
Bill and Barbara
Edgar

With gratitude

Contents

Series Preface

Contours of Christian Theology covers the main themes of Christian doctrine. The series offers a systematic presentation of most of the major doctrines in a way which complements the traditional textbooks but does not copy them. Top priority has been given to contemporary issues, some of which may not be dealt with elsewhere from an evangelical point of view. The series aims, however, not merely to answer current objections to evangelical Christianity, but also to rework the orthodox evangelical position in a fresh and compelling way. The overall thrust is therefore positive and evangelistic in the best sense.

The series is intended to be of value to theological students at all levels, whether at a Bible college, a seminary or a secular university. It should also appeal to ministers and to educated lay-people. As far as possible, efforts have been made to make technical vocabulary accessible to the non-specialist reader, and the presentation has avoided the extremes of academic style. Occasionally this has meant that particular issues have been presented without a thorough argument, taking into account different positions, but when .this has happened, authors have been encouraged to refer the reader to other works which take the discussion further. For this purpose adequate but not extensive notes have been provided.

The doctrines covered in the series are not exhaustive, but have been chosen in response to contemporary concerns. The title and general presentation of each volume are at the discretion of the author, but final editorial decisions have been taken by the Series Editor in consultation with IVP.

In offering this series to the public, the authors and the publishers hope that it will meet the needs of theological students in this generation, and bring honour and glory to God the Father, and to his Son, Jesus Christ, in whose service the work has been undertaken from the beginning.

Gerald Bray
Series Editor

Preface

The Holy Spirit! It was commonplace in my student days for authors, lecturers and preachers to begin their comments on the subject of the Holy Spirit with some such statement as, 'The Holy Spirit has been until recently the forgotten person of the Godhead.' No-one writing on this topic today would employ such language. Such has been the widespread impact of Pentecostalism and the charismatic movement that literature on the Holy Spirit is now of such proportions that the mastery of the corpus would be beyond the powers of any individual.

The Holy Spirit is no longer thought of as the 'forgotten person' of the Godhead, and insofar as this is true, Christians of all persuasions should rejoice. Indeed, it might be thought that the pendulum has swung so far in the direction of an obsession with the powers of the Spirit that a moratorium on books on the Holy Spirit is a great desideratum; only the exigencies of a series would seem to justify the writing of yet another study on a now well-worn theme.

Yet the assumption which became virtually an article of orthodoxy among evangelicals as well as others, that the Holy Spirit had been discovered almost *de novo* in the twentieth century, is in danger of the heresy of modernity, and is at least guilty of historical short-sightedness. It forgets that it was with good reason that the Reformation pastor-theologian John Calvin was described as 'the theologian of the Holy Spirit'.[1] Moreover, each century since his time has witnessed events which were ascribed to the unusual working of the Holy Spirit. Even in the late twentieth century, the two *opera magna* on the Holy Spirit remain the extensive studies by the seventeenth-century Puritan John Owen, Vice-Chancellor of the University of Oxford, and by the great Dutch theologian-politician, Abraham Kuyper, founder of the Free University of Amsterdam. Looking back even further, the assumption that the twentieth century had recovered truth lost since the first two centuries displays a cavalier attitude to the material unearthed by H. B. Swete in his valuable series of studies on the Spirit begun more than a century ago. These richly demonstrate the attention which much earlier centuries gave to honouring him along with the Father and the Son.

The assertion that the Holy Spirit, once forgotten, is now forgotten no longer needs rephrasing. For while his *work* has been recognized, the Spirit *himself* remains to many Christians an anonymous, faceless aspect of the divine being. Even the title 'Holy Spirit' evokes a different gamut of emotions from those expressed in response to the titles 'Father' and 'Son'. Perhaps the facts of the situation would have been better stated by describing him as the *unknown* rather than the *forgotten* (or even 'shy', as has recently been done) person of the Trinity.

The demands of a doctrinal series require contributors to cover the basic ground of the locus assigned to them. In this volume in the *Contours of Christian Theology* series, the focus of the concern is to trace the revelation of the Spirit's identity and work in a biblico-theological and redemptive-historical manner. This is not to say that historical theology is bankrupt, and certainly not to reject the apostolic principle that we understand the riches of the gospel in concert with the whole church (Eph. 3:18–19). My interest in and sense of indebtedness to the church's understanding of the Spirit will, I hope, be evident.

12

According to Thomas Aquinas, theology comes from God, teaches about God and leads us to God (*a Deo docetur, Deum docet, ad Deum ducit*). That is true in a special sense of the theology of the Holy Spirit. The great desideratum in all our reflection on the Spirit is surely the goal of personal and intimate communion with him by whom we are brought to worship, glorify and obey the Father and the Son. This marriage of theology and doxology is normative in the pages of Scripture, and it is for that reason that the pages which follow trace the work of the Spirit in a biblico-theological way.

It will be clear in what follows that I have taken the canon of the Old and New Testaments at their face value, believing that here we find God's word, and that the form in which it has come to us (undoubtedly by various means) is the only reliable foundation on which to build a theology of the Holy Spirit. But, in keeping with the general concerns of the *Contours of Christian Theology* series, along with the Pilgrim Father John Robinson, I share the conviction that there is still fresh light breaking out on the church from the word of God.

The person and work of the Holy Spirit continue to be an area of controversy among Christians. In this respect, some readers, perhaps many, will believe that they themselves see light where I do not. It is a remarkable fact of recent church history that convictions which were controversial in my student days in the 1960s and 70s have now become so broadly adopted that it is the mainstream views of those days which are now regarded as controversial. That notwithstanding, I have tried to keep in mind both the apostolic injunction to maintain the unity of the Spirit in the bond of peace, and my own ordination vows to maintain a spirit of brotherhood to all the Lord's people. My hope and prayer is that the opinions expressed in areas of controversy touched on in this book will not prejudice fellow-Christians against the whole.

This volume stands in the *Contours of Christian Theology* series between the study of *The Work of Christ* and *The Church*; it therefore includes some discussion of elements of soteriology (the application of Christ's work) and ecclesiology (the gifts of the Spirit to the body of Christ). It thus serves as a bridge between these companion studies and, it is hoped, will be read in conjunction with them.

I wish to thank Gerald Bray, the General Editor of this series, for the invitation to contribute the volume on *The Holy Spirit*. I am grateful to David Kingdon, Theological Books Editor of IVP, both for his friendship and for his patience with a procrastinating author, seasoned with only the occasional pinch of cajoling! The completion of these pages represents a downpayment on two further debts: first to the Board of Trustees of Westminster Theological Seminary, Philadelphia, for granting me sabbatical leave in the Fall Semester of 1994; and chiefly to my wife Dorothy, who more than anyone has encouraged me to complete this work.

Sinclair B. Ferguson
Westminster Theological Seminary
Philadelphia, Pennsylvania

1

THE HOLY SPIRIT &
HIS STORY

What, or who, is the Holy Spirit? Most Christians readily and warmly respond to the description of Jesus as the Son of God not only because of his humanity (Jesus), but also because the designation 'Son' indicates a relational identity (son–father) with which we are familiar. In addition, when, in Christ, we learn to call God 'Father', that name conveys a rich kaleidoscope of images which helps us to understand and respond to him as the one who governs, guides, provides for, guards and loves his children.

But the name 'Holy Spirit', or worse (at least at the emotional and psychological levels) 'Holy Ghost', tends to convey a cold, even remote image. After all, what is 'Spirit'? Yet, perhaps the older 'Holy Ghost', with its connotations of vagueness, mystery and insubstantiality, did in fact express what many Christians experience: the Holy Spirit is seen to be distant and impersonal by comparison with the Father and the Son. 'We know not what spirits are, nor what our own spirit is,' wrote Abraham Kuyper.[1]

How much less capable are we of comprehending the Spirit of God?

What, or who, then, is the Holy Spirit?

Holy *ruach*

The root significance of the biblical term 'holy' (Heb. *qāḏôš, qōḏeš*; Gk. *hagios*) has been long debated, but there is general consensus that it connotes such ideas as to be cut off or separate from; to be placed at a distance, and hence to be set apart in order to belong to God. Employing this spatial language metaphorically, the Old Testament underlines the 'otherness' of the Spirit's being. The classic illustration of this, Isaiah's devastating encounter with the Holy One of Israel (Is. 6:1ff.), exemplifies the way in which spatial imagery is employed to convey moral distance. God is 'high', while Isaiah is low; 'lifted up' (RSV, AV) and 'exalted' (NIV), while Isaiah is thrust down. God's presence ('the train of his robe') fills the temple, while Isaiah shrinks back into a corner. God's holiness is the seering purity of his eternal and infinite being. By comparison, Isaiah feels himself to be unclean and undone.

The biblical words for 'spirit' (Heb. *ruach*;[2] Gk. *pneuma*) are onomatopoeic terms, both their physical formation and their sound conveying a sense of their basic meaning: the expulsion of wind or breath, the idea of air in motion. 'Spirit' expresses, in its most fundamental form ('the breath of life'), power, energy and life.

In the world of Hellenistic philosophy, which provided the wider intellectual environment of the later biblical period, *pneuma* was thought of as a kind of deeply refined and purified matter (matter itself being thought of as fallen and evil by definition). In the philosophy of the Stoics, for example, it was thought of as the stuff of the soul, a kind of 'vital nervous fluid' which extends from the soul throughout the person, endowing him or her with energy and life.[3]

Although often understood as near-immateriality, in fact the Old Testament term *ruach* more particularly underlines the presence of energy and activity. While air, or wind, could well serve as an analogy for highly refined matter, this is not the focus of attention in the biblical use of *ruach* (or, for that matter, *pneuma*). In the Old Testament, *ruach* ordinarily implies air in motion, often manifested in the natural order as a powerful wind or storm (*e.g.* Jb. 1:19, and in perhaps more than a quarter of the Old Testament instances), or in the life-breath of the individual. Thus, for example, the marvels of Solomon's wisdom and achievements left the Queen of Sheba breathless (1 Ki. 10:4–5: 'she was overwhelmed' is how NIV puts it, 'she had no more *ruach*' is what the text tells us!). Indeed, in human activity, *ruach* can refer not merely to breathing out but to snorting (*e.g.* 2 Sa. 22:16; Jb. 4:9). Energy rather than immateriality is what is in view.

While in the natural order *ruach* may occasionally denote a gentle breeze (as in some translations of Gn. 3:8), the dominant idea in the Old Testament is that of power. The parallelism in Micah 3:8 well illustrates this: 'But as for me, I am filled with *power*, with the *Spirit of the Lord*.'[4] When used of God (around one third of the Old Testament uses), therefore, *ruach* does not connote the idea of divine immateriality (spirit, not matter), although doubtless that is implied in the general biblical perspective. The emphasis is, rather, on his overwhelming energy; indeed one might almost speak about the violence of God. 'Divine Spirit' thus denotes 'the energy of life in God',[5] as in the striking parallelism of Isaiah 31:3: 'The Egyptians are men and not God; their horses are flesh and not spirit.' The emphasis lies in the contrast between weakness and power, not in the contrast between material and immaterial. Spirit here contrasts with flesh whose 'characteristic is inertia, lack of power, such as can only be removed by the Spirit of God'.[6]

The results of the activity of *ruach* are in keeping with its nature. When the *ruach Yahweh* comes on individuals they are caught up in the thrust of an 'alien' energy and exercise unusual powers: the faint are raised into action; exceptional human abilities are demonstrated; ecstasy may be experienced. Yahweh's *ruach* is, as it were, the blast of God, the irresistible power by which he accomplishes his purposes, whether creative or destructive. By his *ruach* he creates the host of heaven (Ps. 33:6), gives power to judge–saviours like Othniel and Samson (Jdg. 3:10; 14:6), snatches up prophets, lifts them and places them elsewhere (as, for example, Ezk. 3:12, 14; 11:1; *cf.* 1 Ki. 18:12). Those who are the subjects of the activity of the divine *ruach* act in supernatural ways, with supernatural energy and powers.

God's *ruach*, therefore, expresses the irresistible force, the all-powerful energy of God in the created order. He cannot be 'tamed' by men. Instead, through his *ruach* he is able to 'tame' or subdue all things to fulfil his own purpose.

This almost violent dimension of the Spirit is vividly portrayed by Isaiah: 'He will come like a pent-up flood that the breath [*ruach*] of the LORD drives along' (Is. 59:19); 'The grass withers and the flowers fall, because the breath [*ruach*] of the LORD blows on them' (Is. 40:7).

Already, however, it is clear from the various biblical references above that *ruach* denotes more than simply the energy of God; it describes God extending himself in active engagement with his creation in a personal way. This raises a question to which we must later give attention: are these references to the Spirit to be thought of merely as describing the mode of God's presence in the world, or as denoting hypostatic (personal) distinctions within the being of God, adumbrating the diversity in God which would be expressed in the later church doctrine of the Trinity?

In pursuing this theme, we must first follow through the strands of Old Testament teaching on the Holy Spirit.

Creator Spiritus?

Scripture hints that God's Spirit has been engaged in all of his works from the beginning. In early Christian theology this was traced back to the work of creation.[7] When 'the earth was formless and empty, darkness was over the surface of the deep . . . the Spirit of God [*ruach elohim*] was hovering over the waters' (Gn. 1:2).

Ruach elohim here has often been understood as a reference to the Spirit of God and translated accordingly. While there has never been unanimity on this point, more recently, within the Christian tradition of exegesis, this view has been vigorously challenged, largely it would seem on the presupposition that behind the traditional interpretation lies a misplaced hermeneutical desire to find an early, or at least embryonic, hypostatization of the Spirit, and (within Christian exegesis) a corresponding embryonic trinitarianism, in the opening words of Genesis.

18

In addition, the way in which the idea of the wind features in Near Eastern creation myths, particularly the Phoenician creation narrative, seems to some scholars to suggest that wind, rather than the divine Spirit, is probably in view.[8] The text is therefore often read as describing the gloomy chaos of the nascent creation. The emptiness of the wasteland, the darkness and the *ruach* thus belong together as the inchoate mass of existence which must be overcome and transformed into the order and fullness which Genesis 1 will later describe. The fact that no further allusion is made to the activity of the *ruach* is taken as indicating that it belongs to the chaos rather than to the creating agent. Thus, while some, like Gerhard von Rad, are still prepared to translate *ruach elohim* as 'God's storm', others yet more radically sever *ruach* altogether from divine actions and translate *ruach elohim* as an 'almighty wind'.

Such reservation and hesitation to see any hint of hypostatization, far less trinitarianism, in the opening verses of the Bible are, of course, by no means new. Already in the sixteenth century, Calvin (not himself one to find the doctrine of the Trinity under every Old Testament text) was familiar with them but described them as 'too frigid to require refutation'.[9]

Yet the context of Genesis 1:2 suggests that the *ruach elohim* does not stand in antithetical relationship to the creating agent. Rather, what is in view is cosmic order being established by the *ruach elohim*. The further clear references (Gn. 1:1, 3) to the activity of *elohim* as creative divine activity suggest that the most natural reading of *ruach elohim* in verse 2 is in terms of divine activity. The verb translated 'hovering' (*rāḥap*) conveys the idea of shaking or fluttering. It is used in only two other places in the Old Testament. In Jeremiah 23:9 it is used of the shaking of bones. Despite suggestions to the contrary,[10] shaking would surely be an unusual way to describe the activity of the wind.

Furthermore, we find a significant series of (deliberate) connections later in Scripture between the creation, the Exodus and the Spirit. Isaiah 63:7–14 clearly identifies the Spirit as the executive of the Exodus. But earlier, in Deuteronomy, the executor of the Exodus is one who protects the people in 'a barren and howling waste . . . like an eagle . . . hovers over its young' (Dt. 32:10–11). This is the only other instance of the use of the word *tōhû* ('formless') in the Pentateuch (although its use again in Je. 4:23 is instructive). It cannot be accidental that, here in Deuteronomy 32:10–11, as in Genesis 1:2, it occurs in conjunction with the verb *rāḥap*. An analogy (surely deliberate) is thus drawn in the Old Testament between the 'hovering' of the *ruach elohim* over the inchoate creation and the presence of the Spirit of God in the as-yet-incomplete work of redemption. This suggests that already *ruach elohim* in Genesis 1:2 was intended to denote the divine Spirit.

Other more general Old Testament reflections on the Genesis narrative, as they celebrate God's work in the created order, suggest that the earliest interpreters of Genesis 1 (*i.e.* later biblical authors) also detected the presence of the divine Spirit in the work of creation. Thus Psalm 104:30 records: 'When you send your Spirit [*ruach*], they are created.' This stands in parallel with 'When you hide your *face*, they are terrified; when you take away their breath, they die and return to the dust' (104:29). Here again there seems to be a deliberate echo of Genesis 1:2 and 2:7. The *ruach* of God and the face of God are complementary ideas, both indicative of personal divine presence. Clearly, *ruach* stands on the side of God, not on the side of chaos.

Job 33:4 points in the same direction: 'The Spirit [*ruach*] of God has made me; the breath of the Almighty gives me life.' While the second half of the verse echoes Genesis 2:7, the first half appears to echo Genesis 1:2. Here *ruach* means more than wind or storm.

In the light of this tradition of exegesis within the Old Testament itself, *ruach* in Genesis 1:2 is best understood as a reference to the activity of the divine Spirit, not the impersonal activity of the wind. Pannenberg's contention that to translate *ruach* in Genesis 1:2 as 'storm' or 'hurricane' is 'grotesque' may seem over-reactionary; but in the light of the fact that elsewhere *ruach elohim* is assumed to mean Spirit of God, he is surely right to suspect the intensity of the effort to reject that meaning in Genesis 1:2.[11] At the very least, in the light of the Old Testament's own reflections, the hovering and the blowing of Genesis 1:2 must be taken as indices of the presence of the power of the Spirit.[12] Indeed, while generally unnoticed in the exposition of Genesis 1, it can be argued that recognizing the presence of the divine Spirit in Genesis 1:2 would provide the 'missing link' in the interpretation of the 'Let *us* make . . .' in Genesis 1:26–27. The Spirit of God would then be the only possible referent of this address *within the structure of the account itself.*[13] In this case, the engagement of the Spirit in the work of creation would mark the beginning and end of a literary *inclusio* in Genesis 1.

This is not to claim that the Old Testament provides a detailed analysis of the role of the Spirit of God in creation, or that the enigmatic statement in Genesis 1:2 alone is adequate to ground the idea that the Spirit of God is a distinct divine hypostasis. Much remains opaque. What is of interest is that the activity of the divine *ruach* is precisely that of extending God's presence into creation in such a way as *to order and complete what has been planned in the mind of God.* This is exactly the role the Spirit characteristically fulfils elsewhere in Scripture. In the New Testament the Spirit undertakes this role in the accomplishment of redemption: the Father sends, the Son comes, the Spirit vindicates (1 Tim. 3:16); the Father plans, the Son sacrifices and rises, the Spirit applies (*e.g.* 1 Pet. 1:1–2).

Alongside the (admittedly scanty) references to the work of the Spirit as the executive in ordering creation there lies another fundamental strand of Old Testament teaching: the Spirit of God is the executive of the powerful presence of God in the governing of the created order.

Governing presence

Ruach expresses the idea of wind or air *in motion.* As such it serves well as a bridge term to describe the outgoing of the Creator to the creation.

The divine *ruach* is the mode of God's power-presence among his people. Ezekiel suggests an intimate relationship between the Spirit of God and the face or presence of God: 'I will no longer hide *my face* from them, for I will pour out *my Spirit* on the house of Israel, declares the Sovereign LORD' (Ezk. 39:29; see Ezk. 37 for the outpouring in view; *cf.* also Pss. 104:29–30; 139:7).

The Lord's power-presence is revealed in his Spirit with a view to fulfilling a variety of goals in redemptive history. He not only carries individuals beyond their normal physical capacities; he gives them abilities which extend beyond their native wit. Thus

21

he distributes gifts of statesmanship and craftsmanship. Joseph and Daniel, the two leading figures with *savoir faire* in the Old Testament, were men in whom 'the spirit' of another world was seen to dwell in unusually great measure (Gn. 41:38; Dn. 4:8–9; 5:11–14). Both displayed the characteristics which would be fully expressed in the activity of the messianic Spirit later described in Isaiah 11:1–5, especially the wisdom and understanding which are the fruit of knowing and fearing God.

Similarly, Moses was endued with the divine Spirit to enable him to govern, and this in turn was shared with the seventy elders who undertook with him the burden of administration and rule among God's redeemed people (Nu. 11:25). Just as the Spirit produced order and purpose out of the formless and empty primeval created 'stuff' (Gn. 1:2), so, when the nation was newborn but remained in danger of social chaos, the Spirit of God worked creatively to produce right government, order and direction among the refugees from Egypt (*cf.* Is. 63:7–14).

In pursuing his purposes among his called-out people, God's Spirit also granted gifts of design and its execution to men like Bezalel and Oholiab (Ex. 31:1–11; 35:30–35). Again there is a significant theological pattern operative here. The beauty and symmetry of the work accomplished by these men in the construction of the tabernacle not only gave aesthetic pleasure, but a physical pattern in the heart of the camp which served to re-establish concrete expressions of the order and glory of the Creator and his intentions for his creation. A hint was thus given that the work of 're-creation' must begin with the chosen people. Among them stood earthly reflections of the dwelling-place of God. As Calvin rightly says, 'The tabernacle was a sort of visible image of God.'[14] Here, already in the Exodus narrative, we find the principle which will emerge with full clarity only later in the New Testament: the Spirit orders (or re-orders) and ultimately beautifies God's creation. In the Garden of Eden, the tabernacle and the temple the worshipper discovers the beauty of holiness, which is but a reflection of the beauty of God himself (1 Ch. 16:29; Ps. 96:9). In the final temple, the man filled with the Spirit, Jesus (Jn. 2:19–22), this pattern will reach its apex. But already, from the beginning, the ministry of the Spirit had in view the conforming of all things to God's will and ultimately to his own character and glory.

Spiritus recreator

The ministry of the Spirit is not limited to gifts which serve the national establishment of God's people. His work is also moral and redemptive. Already in the Old Testament the Spirit of God is *holy* Spirit. Whatever objective and cultic orientation 'holiness' may have, it also involves moral and ethical characteristics. Thus, in Psalm 51:11, David confesses that his relationship to God's Spirit as holy has been jeopardized by moral failure.

Isaiah 63:7–14, to which reference has already been made, is particularly illuminating in this respect, serving as it does as a commentary on the Exodus narrative. As God became their Saviour:

> In his love and mercy he redeemed them . . .
> Yet they rebelled
>   and grieved his Holy Spirit . . .
>
> Then his people recalled the days of old,
>   the days of Moses and his people . . .
> Where is he who set
>   his Holy Spirit among them,
> who sent his glorious arm of power . . .?
> . . . like cattle that go down to the plain,
>   they were given rest by the Spirit of the LORD.

Here God's Spirit is seen to have been actively present in the wilderness wanderings (God 'set his Holy Spirit among them', 63:11). The people were guided by the Spirit (63:13–14). But they rebelled and 'grieved his Holy Spirit' (63:10).

Here we come as near as the Old Testament anywhere does to an explicit hypostatization of the Spirit. Not only is a distinction suggested between God transcendent and immanent, but to 'grieve' is an *inter-personal* activity. It is scarcely convincing to deny this on the grounds that while the text attributes to the people the causing of grief, it does not attribute 'being grieved' to the Spirit.[15] When it is said that one grieves another, all ordinary canons of interpretation imply that the other is grieved.

But we may take even this a stage further. The Spirit is the

23

executive of the saving activity of God. Isaiah 63:7–14 clarifies this with its reflections on the Exodus, the great paradigmatic redemptive act of the Old Testament.

(1) The Spirit is associated with the activity of Moses in working miracles (see Ex. 8:19; note the similarity here with Jesus and the apostles, Lk. 11:20; Heb. 2:1–4). He is the divine witness-bearer to the redemptive activity of God (Is. 63:11–12).

(2) The Spirit leads and guides the people into the benediction of covenant fulfilment: 'like cattle that go down to the plain, they were given rest by the Spirit of the LORD' (Is. 63:14). What, in the New Testament, Christ gives through the work of the Spirit (Mt. 11:28–30), in the Old Testament God gives proleptically in the figure (type) of the Exodus and the entrance into the land through the same Spirit.

(3) The Spirit is the executive of the Exodus-redemption wrought by God the Saviour (Is. 63:8). It is God who saves, and it is against him that the people thereafter rebel. But in rebelling against God, it is specifically God *as Holy Spirit* that they grieve – a phrase that is taken up and expounded by Paul in a profoundly soteriological context in Ephesians 4:30, suggesting that the New Testament understood the Isaianic statement in personal terms.

The Spirit's ministry in the Old Testament, then, cannot be limited to the creation of a political entity, a theocracy in the external sense. It includes the moral ordering of the people. This is confirmed in a deeply personal manner in the great lamentation of Psalm 51. David's fear of losing the Spirit involves more than that his adultery has disqualified him from the high office for which he has been anointed. His prayer 'Do not . . . take *your Holy Spirit* from me' (51:11) is exegeted within the psalm itself by his cry not to be cast from the Lord's *presence* but rather to have the joy of *salvation* restored to him. Only by possessing the Spirit can his own heart be pure and joyful and his own spirit be kept steadfast and willing (Ps. 51:10, 12). David may indeed fear that he is on the brink of experiencing the fate of Saul, and being removed from royal office (1 Sa. 16:14). But on his lips the prayer has a personal-subjective-soteriological, and not merely an official-objective-theocratic, orientation. It is personal fellowship with God, not merely the security of his monarchy, that concerns him here. For David, the presence of the Spirit and the possession of salvation and its joy are correlative.

Any biblical theology of the Spirit's work must recognize the progressive and cumulative character of historical revelation. But systematic or logical considerations invite the conclusion that the Spirit's activity in the Old Testament epoch involved personal renewal of a moral and spiritual nature.

In the New Testament's understanding of salvation, certain moral and spiritual characteristics are produced exclusively by the Spirit. But these (*e.g.* the fruit of the Spirit in Galatians 5:22–23) are already exemplified by Old Testament believers. Moreover, these believers are set before New Testament believers not only as examples of justification by faith (*e.g.* Abraham in Rom. 4), but also of the life of faith (*e.g.* Heb. 11:1ff.; Jas. 2:14–26; 5:17–18) or of what it means to walk by the Spirit. Hence, Christian believers can turn to the Psalms not only to find their own experiences of sorrow, doubt, fear and even despair mirrored there, but, as is commonly confessed, to find examples of wholehearted adoration and devotion that exemplify what it means to worship God by the Spirit. Such exhibitions of the presence of the saving fruit of the Spirit argue for the presence of his soteriological ministry in the old covenant as well as in the new.

In this connection, it is sometimes stated that there is a major dichotomy between the Spirit's ministry in the old and in the new covenants. Thus, for example, it is sometimes questioned whether Old Testament believers were regenerated. Nicodemus' inability to understand Jesus' teaching on the necessity of regeneration is often taken to underline this (Jn. 3:4).

In the New Testament, the new birth or regeneration may well connote to a specifically new covenant activity of God, inaugurated by the work of Christ in his death, resurrection, ascension and the sending of his own Spirit (*cf.* Jn. 3:12–15). Even the least in the kingdom is greater than John the Baptist (Mt. 11:11). But the drift of John 3 indicates that Nicodemus should have been able to understand the need for a work of renewal, and the promise of a new covenant in which it would be effected, from his Hebrew Bible (Jn. 3:7). He should not have been surprised. Already in the old covenant the Lord circumcised the hearts of the people (Dt. 30:6); new life from God's hand was a reality in the old covenant, even if it only foreshadowed the reality of participating in the resurrection life of Christ.

This notwithstanding, one of the temptations of a theology of the Spirit which recognizes the deep-rooted continuity of revelation in the Bible is so to stress the continuity of the Spirit's ministry that we are in danger of flattening the contours of redemptive history, and of undermining the genuine diversity and development from old to new covenants. Paul's teaching in 2 Corinthians 3 indicates that there is an epochal development from the old to the new, precisely in terms of the ministry of the Spirit. This will become clearer when we later give extended attention to the significance of the coming of the Spirit at Pentecost (in chapter 3).

Spirit and word

Not until the pages of the New Testament do we find a more systematic reflection on the work of the Spirit in the giving of the Old Testament (for example in 2 Tim. 3:14–17, although even here the emphasis is on the function of Scripture). When the New Testament authors address this subject, however, it is clear that they see themselves as simply exegeting the Old Testament. The conviction that the Old Testament prophets were 'carried along by the Holy Spirit' (2 Pet. 1:21) reflects the prophets' own claim to inspiration: 'the hand of the Lord' was upon them; their oracles were 'the word of the Lord' (*e.g.* Je. 1:2, 8, 15, 19, *et passim*).

Jeremiah records what is in fact the paradigm for such inspiration: 'my [God's] words in your [Jeremiah's] mouth' (Je. 1:9). Isaiah specifically conjoins the Spirit with God's words, in both inspiration and illumination: ' "As for me, this is my covenant with them," says the LORD. "My Spirit, who is on you, and my words that I have put in your mouth will not depart from your mouth, or from the mouths of your children, or from the mouths of their descendants from this time on and for ever" ' (Is. 59:21).

The doctrine of inspiration is, therefore, not invented but inherited by the New Testament writers. It is epitomized by David's last prophetic words: 'The Spirit of the LORD spoke through me; his word was on my tongue' (2 Sa. 23:2).

The written record of God's mighty deeds and interpretative words is the fruit of the ongoing activity of the Spirit among the redeemed people. It is the word which proceeds from God's mouth. It is *theopneustic*, coming on the divine breath as it were (Mt. 4:4), and is given through men borne by his Spirit (2 Pet. 1:20–21). All Scripture is thus seen to be God-breathed and serves the purpose of instructing, convincing, healing and equipping God's people (2 Tim. 3:16–17).

As to *how* this divine out-breathing and Spirit-bearing influence the production of Scripture, little is said or claimed. God reveals himself in various ways: dreams, visions, individual illumination and research, as well as ordinary and extraordinary divine providences, are involved in the process. The authors of Scripture display an interest in the product rather than the process. The mode of the operation of the divine Spirit on the human spirit remains as mysterious as his activity in creation and re-creation (*cf.* Ps. 139:7–16, Lk. 1:35; Jn. 3:8–9). It is clear that the activity of God does not minimize the individuality of the human authors. In fact the reverse is the case, since the personalities of the human authors appear to be stamped all over the finished product. Simultaneously, like all divine revelation, the revelation which is given in Scripture is *autopistic* in character: it contains and expresses its own testimony to its divine authorship. In the New Testament we find this idea a little more clearly systematized, and, as we shall see, the Spirit is given to the apostles partly with their role as penmen of Scripture in view. But nowhere is the *modus operandi* of the Spirit's activity fully explained. The words of Ecclesiastes are as true here as elsewhere: 'As you do not know the path of the wind, or how the body is formed in a mother's womb, so you cannot understand the work of God, the Maker of all things' (Ec. 11:5).

Throughout the Old Testament, then, the activity of the Spirit is identified with the being of God. In places this activity is described in less than personal terms, as an expression of the apparently violent, naked power of God falling or rushing on individuals and seizing their lives for a divine function (*e.g.* Jdg. 3:10; 11:29; 14:6, 9). But the Old Testament witness goes beyond this. More personal terms are employed. Thus, when the Spirit comes, he clothes himself with those on whose lives he descends (Jdg. 6:34; 1 Ch. 12:8; 2 Ch. 24:20). He forges an ethical (*i.e.* a holy and personal) bond between himself and the redeemed people; he may be 'grieved' by their behaviour as he was during the Exodus.

Hypostatic Spirit?

The Spirit of God, therefore, is not merely a synonym for the power of God. But the question remains: are we to think of the Spirit as a mode of God's presence, or (as trinitarian orthodoxy would later do) in personal (hypostatic) terms?

Since the post-apostolic age, there has been within the Christian tradition a tendency, and even an anxiety, to detect the hypostatic presence of the Son or the Spirit already in the Old Testament. That was understandable in the context of the Christian apologetic in the face of Judaism. If the triune character of God is a biblical idea, should it not already be evident in the Old Testament? Thus, in Genesis 1, the use of the plural form *elohim* for God and the enigmatic words 'Let *us* make . . .' (1:26–27) were often seen as indications of a threefold hypostatization in God's being.[16]

A more sober approach to biblical theology emerged in the Reformation's historical reading of the text and its principle that doctrine be drawn from the text of Scripture only by 'good and necessary consequence'. But later critical scholarship tended to destroy confidence in the possibility of a unified systematic theology built on the basis of Scripture; and this has led many biblical scholars to doubt that the Old Testament gives any hint of a distinct hypostatic existence for the Spirit.[17]

The wisest approach to this question is to break it down into its fundamental parts by asking:

(1) Is the activity of the Spirit *divine* activity? The answer is certainly affirmative.

(2) Is the activity of the Spirit *personal* activity? Again the answer is, surely, affirmative. The Spirit directs the people of God. It is axiomatic that only a personal Spirit could engage in high-level rational activity in relationship to other persons.

This brings us to the third and crucial question:

(3) Is the activity of the Spirit *hypostatically distinct*? The action of the Spirit in creation, Exodus and kingdom-governing is certainly both personal and divine; but is the Spirit merely a

mode of God's being – the divine viewed from the perspective of his immanence in the created order in distinction from his transcendent self-sufficiency – and thus akin to such expressions as 'the arm of the Lord'? Are we to think of God's Spirit, therefore, as extension rather than hypostatization? Or can we, on the basis of 'good and necessary consequence' from the Old Testament evidence, go a stage further?

It should be axiomatic in all Christian theology that the Holy Spirit (as indeed the Father) is fully revealed to us only in and through Jesus Christ. This much is already anticipated under the old covenant. It is recognized that there is a partial character about the work of the Spirit which will reach its fullness only in the Messiah (Is. 11:1ff.), and therefore in the inner and widespread experience of the Spirit (Ezk. 36:25–27; Joel 2:28ff.). We therefore ought to expect a strong element of the enigmatic about the Old Testament witness to the Spirit parallel to what the authors of messianic prophecy discovered in their own prophecies about Christ (cf. 1 Pet. 1:10–11). Only through the revelation of the Spirit in the Messiah does the enigmatic testimony of the Old Testament come into its true light, so that the Spirit's activity is seen to have been more than merely an extension of the presence of God.

B. B. Warfield's measured comment on the revelation of the Trinity in general may be taken as an equally wise approach to the revelation of the hypostatic Spirit in particular:

> The Old Testament may be likened to a chamber richly furnished but dimly lighted: the introduction of light brings into it nothing which was not in it before; but it brings out into clearer view much of what is in it but was only dimly or not at all perceived before. The mystery of the Trinity is not revealed in the Old Testament; but the mystery of the Trinity underlies the Old Testament revelation, and here and there almost comes into view. Thus the Old Testament revelation of God is not corrected by the fuller revelation which follows it, but is only perfected, extended and enlarged.[18]

The wisdom of this statement becomes clear when we examine the many Old Testament references to the Spirit of

God. No doubt, from the perspective of the New Testament, the relationship between the work of the Spirit in the Old and in the New is one of continuity. No doubt, too, the nature of the Spirit's ministry in the Old adumbrates the hypostatization which emerges in the New. But it is doubtful whether we are justified in holding that the Old Testament unequivocally clarifies that the *ruach Yahweh* is a distinct hypostasis within a trinitarian being. Augustine's famous *bon mot* is as true here as it is elsewhere:

Novum Testamentum in Vetere latet,
et in Novo, Vetus patet.[19]

(The New is in the Old concealed,
and in the New, the Old revealed.)

So there is an incompleteness about the Old Testament's revelation of the Spirit, just as there is in its revelation of the Son (*cf.* Heb. 1:1–2; 11:39–40; Eph. 3:1–13), and for that matter of the Father (Jn. 1:18; 14:6). As in the revelation of Christ (*cf.* 1 Pet. 1:10–12), the prophets of the Old Testament epoch were conscious of this. The Spirit had been active among God's people; but his activity was enigmatic, sporadic, theocractic, selective and in some respects external. The prophets longed for better days. Moses desired, but did not see, a fuller and universally widespread coming of the Spirit on God's people (Nu. 11:29). By contrast, in the anticipated new covenant, the Spirit would be poured out in a universal manner, dwelling in them personally and permanently (*cf.* Joel 2:28ff.; Ezk. 36:24–32).

There is more to this principle than may appear at first glance. For it is not only *because of Christ* that we come to know the Spirit more fully, but actually *in Christ*. Indeed, it is apparently a principle of the divine Spirit's working that he declines to disclose himself in any other way (Jn. 16:13–15). He will not be known as he is in himself apart from Christ. Before the Spirit rests permanently on all the faithful children of God, he first must rest on the uniquely faithful Son of God (*cf.* Jn. 1:33).

In the pages of the New Testament, the personal deity of the

Spirit at last becomes clear. He engages in divine activity, possesses divine knowledge of divine things (1 Cor. 2:10–11) and exercises divine prerogatives (Rom. 15:19; 1 Cor. 12:11). But perhaps the most impressive testimony to the Spirit as hypostatically distinct yet fully divine is found in his frequent presence alongside the Father and the Son in the apostolic writings. The 'benediction' (2 Cor. 13:14) is but one of a series of passages in Paul's letters in which the Spirit is joined fully and equally with the Father and the Son in the outworking of salvation; 'the grace of the Lord Jesus Christ, the love of God, and the fellowship of the Holy Spirit' is an impoverished blessing if interpreted in modalistic or Arian terms! It is the unstudied coherence of such statements which makes them such a compelling witness to the divine dignity and personal authority of the Spirit. This point could be argued at length, but is at its most persuasive if the testimony of Scripture is allowed to speak for itself (as, for example, by reading through the following sections in Paul: Rom. 14:17–18; 15:16, 30; 2 Cor. 1:21–22; Gal. 3:11–14; 4:6; Eph. 2:20–22; 3:14–16; Phil. 3:3).

In this light, arguments against the hypostatic nature of the Spirit which derive from the use of the neuter pronoun in relation to his activity are unimpressive, in view of the fact that the Greek word *pneuma* is neuter gender. This is to confuse rules of grammar with principles of theology. But on the contrary, the use of the demonstrative pronoun in the masculine form to represent the Spirit (*cf.* Jn. 14:26; 15:26) is surely expressive of a sense of the Spirit's personal being.

The Christian church has often rightly pointed in this context to the words of the Great Commission (Mt. 28:18–20) as the *locus classicus* for the role of the Spirit within the triune Godhead. Here, as Athanasius pointed out in the Arian controversy, we are bound to see both the hypostatic character of the Spirit and his full deity; for otherwise baptism takes place in the name of God and two of his creatures. What emerges, then, at the climax of the history of redemption, is a portrait of the Spirit in which possession of divine attributes and participation in the divine nature are manifested in a manner which is hypostatically distinct from the Father and the Son.

Classical orthodoxy has spoken of the Spirit as the third 'person' of the Trinity. It is commonplace to note in this connection that the Latin term *persona* does not mean 'person' in the modern sense. Nevertheless, as J. N. D. Kelly points out, as early as Tertullian 'it connoted the concrete presentation of an individual as such' even if 'the idea of self-consciousness nowadays associated with "person" and "personal" is not prominent'.[20] It is perhaps not surprising that Karl Barth, with his earlier stress on the infinite qualitative difference between God and man, found himself uncomfortable with the use of the classical term. It was, however, both open to serious misunderstanding and quite unnecessary to prefer the term 'modes' of God's being in speaking of the Father, the Son and the Spirit. Not only did this lead to Barth being accused, inevitably if inaccurately, of modalism; it was also to ignore a theological axiom which would have reorientated much of his theology: the God who, from one point of view, is *totaliter aliter* ('wholly other') has, nevertheless, created man as his image. There is a created analogy of the divine. If the *imago Dei* is person, it is in a manner analogous to the personal in God. It is on the basis of this principle that we may rightly use any human language to describe God, and thus speak about the Holy Spirit in personal terms.

But all of this awaits the unfolding of the redemptive revelation of God in Christ. This being the case, it must be said that the story of the Spirit remains an incomplete one when limited to the pages of the Old Testament. The Gospel of John makes this clear: 'Up to that time the Spirit had not been given, since Jesus had not yet been glorified' (Jn. 7:39). The entire Old Testament revelation has a 'not yet' written over it as it looks forward to its goal in Christ.

This was highlighted for those who lived before the coming of Christ by the silencing of the prophetic voice during the centuries prior to the restoration, betokened in the events surrounding the births of John the Baptist and Jesus. The central promises of the new covenant still awaited their fulfilment: 'I will put my Spirit in you . . .' (Ezk. 36:27). The long-expected day promised through Joel was 'not yet': 'And *afterward*, I will pour out my Spirit on all people. Your sons and daughters will prophesy . . .' (Joel 2:28). Thus, in the Old Testament period, the great Day of the future would be the Day of the Spirit. The Day when the Messiah would come, filled with the Spirit (Is. 11:1ff.; 42:1ff.; 61:1ff.), had not yet arrived.

It is all the more significant, therefore, that Luke's Gospel begins with the announcement of John the Baptist as one who will be filled with the Spirit from birth (= prophecy restored, Lk. 1:15); with the overshadowing of Mary by the Spirit (= the beginning of the new creation, Lk. 1:35); and with Elizabeth and Zechariah being filled with the Spirit (Lk. 1:41, 67). Simeon, in whose life the Holy Spirit was present though before the time, understood the inner significance of the coming of the Messiah. Salvation had dawned in the Christ-child. The promised Messiah had come, the One on whom the Spirit, at last, would *rest* (Is. 11:2).

In the coming of Jesus, the Day of the Spirit had finally dawned.

2

THE SPIRIT OF
CHRIST

The most concentrated teaching in the Gospels on the ministry of the Spirit is to be found in Jesus' farewell discourse (Jn. 13 – 16). Here the significance of the Spirit's coming is announced in programmatic terms: 'When the Counsellor comes, whom I will send to you from the Father, the Spirit of truth who goes out from the Father, he will testify about me. And you also must testify, for you have been with me from the beginning' (Jn. 15:26–27).

The witness-bearing of the church to Jesus Christ has become such a central part of the Christian vision that we are apt to lose sight of the redemptive-historical and theological significance of this statement. The language is legal in nature, and continues a motif which runs through John's Gospel: Jesus is on trial.

In the first half of the Gospel of John, the 'book of signs' (chapters 1–12), various 'witnesses' appear and give their testimony. Eventually the author will indicate that the function of his Gospel has been to act as a witness-document to Christ's identity: 'these are written that you may believe that Jesus is the Christ, the Son of God' (Jn. 20:31). It is no surprise, then, that the language of witness and testimony appears more frequently in this Gospel than in the rest of the New Testament combined.

In this ongoing trial, the reader is being presented with evidence about Jesus and challenged to reach his or her own verdict (*cf.* 20:30–31). Moreover, this will be a continuing process; Jesus means to send the apostles into the world to be his witnesses ('you also must testify', Jn. 15:27; *cf.* Mt. 28:18–20; Lk. 24:48; Acts 1:8). Within this context, however, we now learn that the chief witness for Christ will be the Holy Spirit whom he will send from the Father (Jn. 15:26). He is the *paraklētos*.

The Paraclete

Much attention has been devoted in Johannine studies to the meaning and identity of the *paraklētos*. A compound of *kaleō*, 'to call', and *para*, 'alongside', the term denotes someone who is called to one's aid or defence. A paraclete is, in the older sense of the word, a 'comforter' (Lat. *cum forte*), *i.e.* someone who comes to strengthen. It is now more generally recognized, however, that in John the term has a forensic connotation. The Spirit is the witness-advocate who testifies to Christ.

The apostles are also witnesses, and it is important to notice what qualifies them, indeed impells them, to be so: 'you also must testify, *for you have been with me from the beginning*' (Jn. 15:27).

John's love for the *double entendre* suggests an analogy here between the apostles and the Spirit. They share the same activity, namely witness-bearing, and the same qualification for it: they have been with Christ from the beginning of his ministry just as the Spirit has been with him 'from the beginning'. The disciples and the Spirit share the essential qualification for authoritative witness-bearing.

In our Lord's culture, trials were conducted not by lawyers acting for the prosecution and the defence, but by a judge eliciting the truth from witnesses who came forward with evidence (*cf.* Dt. 17:6). In such a context the 'advocate' or 'defence counsel' sought by an accused person was not a highly-trained professional, but someone who would vindicate him or her by telling the truth. An eye-witness and/or a character-witness was what was required; someone whose relationship to the accused enabled him to speak with authority; an intimate friend rather than a person professionally trained in the law.

Against this background, the Spirit is ideally suited to be the chief witness for Christ because he was the intimate companion of Jesus throughout his ministry. As the great Cappadocian Father, Basil of Caesarea (c. 330–379), put it, the Holy Spirit was Christ's 'inseparable companion . . . all the activity of Christ was unfolded in the presence of the Holy Spirit . . .'.[1] That is why his witness is so important, potent and reliable. From womb to tomb to throne, the Spirit was the constant companion of the Son. As a result, when he comes to Christians to indwell them, he comes as the Spirit *of Christ* in such a way that to possess him is to possess Christ himself, just as to lack him is to lack Christ.

This relationship is implied in Paul's words in Romans 8:9–10, where the Spirit and Christ are virtually interchangeable terms, pointing to their economic equivalence while recognizing their personal distinctions:

> You, however, are controlled not by the sinful nature but by the Spirit, if the *Spirit of God lives in you.* And if anyone does not *have the Spirit of Christ*, he does not belong to Christ. But if *Christ is in you,* your body is dead because of sin, yet your spirit is alive because of righteousness.

Here, clearly, the statements 'Spirit of God lives in you', 'have the Spirit of Christ' and 'Christ is in you' are three ways of describing the single reality of the indwelling of the Spirit. This complex, multi-layered phenomenon indicates that there is an economic identity between Christ and the Spirit. The Spirit possesses this identity precisely because he was with Christ 'from the beginning' (Jn. 15:27).

This aspect of the Spirit's ministry has suffered considerable neglect in the history of theology, despite noteworthy exceptions. Abraham Kuyper was right when he wrote that 'the Church has never sufficiently confessed the influence the Holy Spirit exerted upon the work of Christ'.[2]

As early as the Isaianic portrait of the Messiah, he had been viewed as the Man of the Spirit *par excellence* (Is. 11:1, 42:1; 61:1). Moreover, the New Testament pointedly refers to the Spirit's ministry throughout the life of Jesus, from his mother's womb to the garden tomb and beyond. A survey of the way in which this unfolds will enhance our knowledge of the Spirit and help to remove the anonymity of his identity. Three distinct 'stages' can be traced.

Stage I: Conception, birth and growth

The return of the long-silent Spirit of prophecy was heralded by his preparatory activity in connection with the birth of Jesus. Mary was 'with child through the Holy Spirit'. She conceived because the Holy Spirit 'overshadowed' her and the power of the Most High 'came upon' her (Lk. 1:31, 35).

There is little obvious theological reflection on or explanation of this within the New Testament. Nevertheless, the birth narratives provide hints of the significance of the Spirit's ministry in the incarnation.

(1) The Holy Spirit 'came upon' Mary the virgin (Lk. 1:35). Luke here underlines the continuity between the ministry of the Holy Spirit in the Old Testament period and now in the incarnation by using a standard Old Testament expression to describe his activity (*e.g.* 1 Sa. 10:6, 10; 16:13). When the Spirit 'comes' on an individual, he 'clothes himself' with that person's life, conforming it to his own purposes. Furthermore, in keeping with a long-established divine pattern emphasizing the monergistic activity of God in redemptive history, a 'barren' woman is made fruitful (*cf.* Gn. 17:15–19; 18:9–14; Jdg. 13:1–24; 1 Sa. 1:1–20; Is. 32:15). Indeed, here we meet the climactic illustration of this principle. When the Spirit comes to mark the dawning of the new messianic era, not merely a barren woman, but *a virgin* woman, is with child (Is. 7:14; Mt. 1:23).

(2) The 'power of the Most High will overshadow [*episkiasei*]' Mary.

In the Septuagint, the verb *episkiazō* translates the Hebrew *sākak*, which is used of the hovering of the cloud of God's glory-presence (Ex. 40:35, 29, LXX). In Psalm 91:4 (LXX, 90:4), it describes the protective hovering of God over his people, reminiscent of the glory-cloud of his presence which guarded and guided the people through the wilderness.

We have already noticed the connection between the Spirit of God hovering, bird-like, over the waters at the original creation and the Lord hovering, eagle-like, over his people in the Exodus-cloud (pp. 19–20). The One who led the people through the wilderness as a pillar of cloud and fire (Ex. 13:21) is the Holy Spirit (Is. 63:10–11). That cloud – the cloud of the glory of the Spirit – reappears in the cloud representing the presence of the glory of God at the tabernacle (Ex. 40:34–38) and in the temple (Is. 6:1–4). It is what came to be spoken of as the *shekinah*. In one of the most dramatic of Ezekiel's visions, he witnessed the shekinah-glory of God departing from the temple (Ezk. 10:1–22). Only in the emergence of the new temple would it return (Ezk. 43:1–5).

The glory of God represented by the *shekinah* cloud was one of the features lamented as being absent in connection with the building of the second temple. Yet the Lord promised that his glory would be seen there (Hg. 2:7–9), and indeed would suddenly return (Mal. 3:1–5).

According to the New Testament, Jesus Christ is that promised glory. From the beginning of his life the Spirit of God's glory overshadowed him. The glory was hidden within the temple (*cf.* Jn. 2:19–22). Only occasionally was it made visible (Jn. 1:14), as on the mount of transfiguration where, significantly, the cloud overshadowed the disciple band and the voice of God was heard again. Clearer indication that we have a continuation of the Old Testament motif could scarcely be given. But Luke underlines this by the only other use in his Gospel of the verb *episkiazō* (Lk. 9:34) to describe the overshadowing of the cloud as well as by describing the topic of conversation between Jesus and Moses and Elijah as the *exodus* (lit.) which he was to 'bring to fulfilment' (Lk. 9:31).

These echoes of both creation and Exodus suggest that the work of the Spirit in the incarnation should be interpreted in a two-fold light.

First, it is a divine work of new *creation*. As in the original creation, the Spirit's work is *de novo*, but it is not *ex nihilo*. Rather, he works on already existent materials (the humanity of Mary) in order to produce the 'second man' and through him restore true order, just as he brought order and fullness into the formlessness and emptiness of the original creation.

Second, it is the beginning of the work of redemption, the new *exodus*. The Spirit hovered over the true Son of God throughout his temptations in the wilderness and for the whole of his life and ministry (*cf.* Lk. 4:1; 22:28). The care of God for the son he called out of Egypt, so elequently expressed throughout the Old Testament (*cf.*, for example, Dt. 8:1ff.; Ezk. 16:1ff.), is here continued in the care of the Spirit for the Son incarnate (whom he also called out of Egypt, Mt. 2:15) even in the embryonic state.

No doubt, too, there is an element of mystery, one might almost say theological chastity, in this expression. If, as David acknowledged (Ps. 139:13), God brings into being the finest of his works in the darkened chamber of a mother's womb, it is especially fitting that the assumption of our weak humanity by the strong Son of God should be hidden from view and from comprehension by the overshadowing of the Spirit.

The major question surrounding the testimony of Matthew and Luke in relation to the birth of Christ concerns the historicity of the virgin conception–birth. This is widely seen in modern scholarship as a midrashic or mythological tradition echoing Isaiah 9:7, and not as part of the earliest kerygma; it embellished the first witness to the identity of Jesus (a resurrected Lord required a supernatural mode of entry into the world). Such scholarship rejects the Augustinian notion that a virginal conception was necessary to maintain our Lord's sinlessness, and regards the witness of the early creeds to the virgin birth as in need of reinterpretation.

This scepticism has been answered frequently enough.[3] Our interest here lies exclusively in asking what function the Holy Spirit is seen to play in this strand of the New Testament's teaching.

The promise given to Mary of the 'coming upon' and 'overshadowing' of her by the Spirit had one specific purpose in view: 'So the holy one to be born will be called the Son of God' (Lk. 1:35). The function of the Holy Spirit was to maintain the holiness, the sinlessness, of the one who was to be born.

The New Testament nowhere suggests that this was achieved merely by the absence of the male progenitor. The notion that sinfulness is the result of intercourse, or is passed on through the male rather than the female line, finds no support in

Scripture. It is often therefore assumed that the doctrine of the virgin conception–birth is superfluous.

In fact, however, five things are in view:

(1) The action of the Holy Spirit (coupled with the absence of conception 'by the will of man', Jn. 1:13) points to the sovereign newness of the work that God is accomplishing.

An early patristic textual tradition, found in the late second century in Irenaeus and Tertullian, reads John 1:13 as referring to Jesus as the one 'born not of human decision or a husband's will, but born of God'.[4] The evidence in the textual traditions for this is slight, but some scholars have vigorously defended this patristic reading on the ground that it is earlier than the extant manuscript evidence.[5] But even if these words refer to the Christian's rebirth, it can be argued that the Johannine *double entendre* makes it likely that the author was conscious of the parallel between the birth of Christ and the exercise of divine sovereignty in the new birth of the Christian. As Abraham Kuyper reasoned: 'St John . . . undoubtedly borrowed this glorious description of our higher birth from the extraordinary act of God which scintillates in the conception and birth of Christ.'[6] While Mary is involved in the virgin conception she is completely passive in it, because it is the direct result of the mysterious action of the Holy Spirit. Here, as Barth underlined, over against the place given to Mary by Roman Catholic theology, the active contribution of humanity in providing salvation is nullified.

Five mothers are mentioned in the genealogy of Jesus. Whereas Perez and Zerah are *ek tēs Thamar* ('whose mother was Tamar', Mt. 1:3), Boaz *ek tēs Rachab* and Obed *ek tēs Routh* (1:5), and Solomon *ek tēs tou Ouriou* ('whose mother was [the wife] of Uriah', 1:6), the conception and birth of Jesus (1:16) require further qualification. This conception is uniquely *ek pneumatos hagiou* ('from the Holy Spirit'; 1:18, 20).

(2) The human nature which was assumed by the Son of God was not created *ex nihilo*, but was inherited through Mary. It is *our* human nature, 'addicted to so many wretchednesses', as Calvin vividly puts it.[7] Subject to the pains and temptations of this life, his human nature needed to be acted upon by the Holy Spirit in order to be sanctified. While the New Testament nowhere further unravels what this involved, it is the central

implication of the Spirit's work. Only by the work of the Spirit could the divine person of the Logos assume genuine human nature, come 'in the likeness of sinful man' (Rom. 8:3), and yet remain 'holy, harmless, undefiled' (Heb. 7:26, AV), 'the holy one' (Lk. 1:35).

(3) The revelation of the virgin conception by the Spirit forbids any adoptionist Christology. There is no room for the notion that the man Jesus of Nazareth becomes the Son of God by adoption. The reverse is true: the Son of God becomes the man Christ Jesus by incarnation through the power of the Spirit. The virgin conception therefore underlies Jesus' words in John 8:23, 'I am from above.' His birth also is 'from above' (cf. Jn. 3:3, 5). The modern addiction to a Christology exclusively 'from below' is a reversal of the biblical understanding of Christ. But it represents a truncated pneumatology as well as a deformed Christology.

(4) The conception of Jesus by the Spirit underlines both his identification with our frailty (he assumes our nature at its smallest and weakest) and his essential distinctiveness, not in relation to the reality of his humanity but in relation to his liability to guilt. He is 'the last Adam', the 'man from heaven' (1 Cor. 15:45, 47–49). The work of the Spirit preserves both the reality of his union with us in genuine human nature, and his freedom from the guilt and curse of Adam's fall (Rom. 5:12–21). Since his *person* is not of Adamic stock, he does not share in the guilt and condemnation of Adam (Rom. 5:12–14). Since he assumed human nature through the Spirit who sanctified this union from the moment of his conception, he was one of us and was capable of bearing others' guilt as one who was not personally liable for it. Were his origin 'from the earth', he would share in the guilt and condemnation of 'the earthly man' (1 Cor. 15:48).

Thus, as the inaugurator of the new humanity, the 'second man' is brought into the world by the Spirit's agency. His virgin conception is therefore essential to our salvation and was, fittingly, brought to pass by the Spirit who is the executive of that salvation.

(5) The conception of Jesus by the Holy Spirit is the mode by which the Father's sending of the Son is effected. As such, it underlines the principle that, in the work of redemption which

Christ spearheads, each person of the Trinity is engaged. The patristic maxim that all persons of the Trinity share in all external acts of God (*opera ad extra trinitatis indivisa sunt*, 'the external works of the Trinity are undivided') is here (as in the resurrection) perfectly illustrated; yet, in the language of the older theology, there is an appropriation of the conception of the Son of God by the Holy Spirit. The execution of the counsel of the Father and the Son is once more seen to be the great characteristic of his work.

The relative silence of the Gospels on the development of Jesus through childhood and adolescence into adulthood is well known. Luke records at the conclusion of the temple visit of the twelve-year-old Jesus, he 'grew in wisdom and stature, and in favour with God and men' (Lk. 2:52). This follows the astonishment of the teachers at the understanding that Jesus already possessed.

This narrative does not stand on its own. It reflects the fulfilment of several Old Testament themes. The person who meditates on, loves and knows God's Word may have greater insight than his teachers and more understanding than his elders (Ps. 119:99–100). Such wisdom is the evidence of the work of the messianic Spirit, and in this sense Luke 2:52 is the fulfilment and application of Isaiah 11:1–3a:

> A shoot will come up from the stump of Jesse;
>> from his roots a Branch will bear fruit.
> The Spirit of the LORD will rest upon him –
>> the Spirit of wisdom and of understanding,
>> the Spirit of counsel and of power,
>> the Spirit of knowledge and of the fear of the LORD –
> and he will delight in the fear of the LORD.

If we ask how the Spirit produced this in the life of Jesus, a partial answer would be along the lines of the words of the third Servant Song in Isaiah:

> The Sovereign LORD has given me an instructed tongue,
>> to know the word that sustains the weary.
> He wakens me morning by morning,
>> wakens my ear to listen like one being taught.

> The Sovereign LORD has opened my ears,
>   and I have not been rebellious.
> (Is. 50:4–5)

Hidden behind this is the earlier identification of the Servant:

> Here is my servant, whom I uphold,
>   my chosen one in whom I delight [*cf.* Luke's comment
>   that Jesus increased in favour with God];
> *I will put my Spirit on him.*
> (Is. 42:1)

The picture is one of daily, constant communion with God, manifested in the new and virtually unparalleled sense of intimacy with God expressed in Jesus' words, 'Did you not know that I must be in *my Father's* house?' (Lk. 2:49, RSV).[8]

The convergence of these various strands of the Old Testament suggests that the ministry of the Spirit to Jesus during the 'hidden years' was intimately related to his understanding of God's word and his sensitivity and obedience to it as he came to recognize its significance for his own life. Luke specifically draws attention to this (Lk. 2:47) in terms of the fulfilment of Isaiah 11:2 in Jesus' life and therefore of the presence of the messianic Spirit on him.

Jesus' intimate acquaintance with Scripture did not come *de caelo* ('from heaven') during the period of his public ministry; it was grounded no doubt on his early education, but nourished by long years of personal meditation. Later, in his public ministry, it becomes evident that he was intimately familiar with its contents (as his use of Dt. 8 in combating the wilderness temptations makes clear), and also possessed in his human nature a knowledge of God by the Spirit which lent freshness, authority and a sense of reality to his teaching (Mt. 7:28–29).

There is a continuing ministry of the Spirit in the life of Jesus ('filled', *plēroumenon*, in Lk. 2:40 indicates experience which was progressive as well as passive). We may assume, from Luke's comment that Jesus 'increased in wisdom and in stature, and in favour with God and man' (Lk. 2:52, RSV), that he gave expression to the appropriate fruit of the Spirit at each period of his human development. As Irenaeus stated so eloquently,

44

albeit in the context of his distinctive recapitulatory Christology:

> He passed through every stage of life. He was made an infant for infants, sanctifying infancy; a child among children, sanctifying childhood, and setting an example of filial affection, of righteousness and obedience; a young man among young men, becoming an example to them, and sanctifying them to the Lord.[9]

Stage II: Baptism, temptations and ministry

If Jesus was full of the Spirit from conception, what is the significance of the coming of the Spirit at his baptism?

(1) Jesus was anointed by the Spirit (Acts 10:38). The Spirit came upon him while he was praying, following his baptism (Lk. 3:21). In Luke's writings, the Spirit is given regularly in response to prayer and in connection with the advance of the kingdom (see Lk. 11:13; Acts 1:4; 2:1–4; 4:23–31).

This event marks Jesus' public entrance into and consecration to his messianic ministry, as he later explained in his synagogue sermon in Nazareth, when he identified himself with the figure of Isaiah 61:1ff. (Lk. 4:16–21). He comes on the scene as the long-awaited prophet of God (Dt. 18:18; Jn. 1:21, 25). In addition, Luke's reference to Jesus being about thirty years of age (Lk. 3:23) probably reflects the age of entry into priestly service.[10] Jesus is thus also viewed as an anointed priest. Just as the High Priest prepared for his atonement-day ministry by washing and anointing, so Jesus received the washing of this baptism and the anointing of the Spirit with a view to his own priestly ministry. In his water-baptism he consecrates himself by prayer to his coming death-baptism (cf. Jn. 17:19). The heavenly voice he hears echoes the words of enthronement from Psalm 2:7, underlining that Jesus is entering into the ministry of the universal king. The coming of the Spirit therefore is an anointing for the three-fold messianic office prefigured by prophets, priests and kings.

This is a new stage of service for Jesus. He enters into the public arena. In the frailty of human flesh he stands in need of a fresh and greater endowment of the Spirit, in order that, through his death, resurrection and ascension, he may become the One who enters into such unmeasured possession of the Spirit that he himself will be able to baptize with the Holy Spirit (*cf.* Jn. 1:33–34). Jesus, who has been borne by the Spirit through the first thirty years of his life, now increasingly expresses his relationship with the Spirit in accomplishing our redemption. He receives him without measure. Just as those who were baptized by John placed their whole lives under his baptism for repentance (and were summoned to life-long repentance), so Jesus was baptized with the Spirit and lived under his lordship. So also do those who in turn receive Christ's baptism in order that they might be conformed to Christ.

Significantly, the contrast that John the Baptist draws between his own ministry and that of Christ is in terms of two baptisms. It might be thought that the fundamental contrast should be between John as witness and Jesus as Saviour, and that therefore a reference to Christ's sacrificial work would be central. While it is present by implication (in John's reference to the Lamb of God, Jn. 1:29), more striking is the emphasis on baptizing with the Spirit as the *telos* of Christ's presence among men.

(2) Heaven opens, signifying a divine revelation (Mk. 1:10); a revelatory voice speaks. The opening of heaven is a character-istically apocalyptic phenomenon, and prepares us for new revelation (*cf.* Rev. 4:1). Here the descent of the Spirit takes place visibly, as he alights on Jesus in the bodily form of a dove. God speaks from heaven, identifying him as his beloved Son (Mk. 1:11).

Jesus is here being equipped for conflict, indicated by the fact that in each of the Synoptic Gospels the baptism narrative is followed immediately by the wilderness temptations.

In Jesus' experience, the word of God and the Spirit of God co-operate to produce an impregnable assurance of his own identity and ministry as Son of God and Suffering Servant– Messiah. The physical manifestation of the Spirit and the audible voice are a 'seal' to him (*cf.* Jn. 6:27). The voice exegetes the significance of the Spirit's manifestation. It means: 'You are my Son, whom I love; with you I am well pleased' (Mk. 1:11; the allusions are to Ps. 2:7 and Is. 42:1, combining a messianic and a Servant passage in confirming Jesus' identity and office). In this sense, the descent of the Spirit, and Jesus' new experience of him, serve to assure Jesus of the Father's love (essential if he is to be sustained through the forthcoming conflict), and of the reality of the Sonship which he is to express in his willingness to suffer as the Servant of the Lord (an essential principle for him to grasp if he is to withstand the attacks of Satan, who seeks to persuade him that Sonship and suffering are mutually exclusive ideas, *cf.* Mt. 4:3, 6).

For Jesus, then, the Spirit is a Spirit of Sonship and assurance, who will bear witness with his spirit that he is the Son of God and who will enable him, even in Gethsemane, to call God '*Abba*! Father!' (*cf.* Rom. 8:15–16). The Spirit thus seals and confirms the bond of love and trust between the Father and the incarnate Son.

While dogmatic certainty about the precise significance of the Spirit appearing in dove-form may not be attainable, all of the possible biblico-theological nuances point in a common direction.

There may be a general echo here of the work of the Spirit hovering, bird-like, over the waters in the first creation (Gn. 1:2). Possibly the allusion is to the Flood narrative, and the descent of the dove on the 'new creation' which arose out of the 'destruction' of the earth under God's judgment (Gn. 8:12, 21). Both echoes may in fact be present, underlining that Jesus is the 'second man' and 'last Adam' who will become life-giving spirit (1 Cor. 15:45–47), the new Noah who will, at last, fulfil the hopes of the faithful for one who will bring rest to a cursed world (*cf.* Gn. 5:29; Is. 63:14; Mt. 11:28–30).

It may also be relevant that in Jewish tradition the dove served as a symbol of Israel. Christ, the new Adam, is also the new Israel, the true Servant of the Lord. In addition to this background, it may be that the dove-like appearance is intended to trigger off thoughts of the function of the dove as the sin-offering for the poor in the levitical sacrificial system (Lv. 5:7; *cf.* Jn. 2:14, 16).

Thus the Spirit comes on Christ as the head of the new creation; but that creation will emerge only out of the costly sacrifice of himself as a sin-offering on Calvary (*cf.* 2 Cor. 5:21).[11]

Central to the entire event, however, is the fact of the Spirit's coming. This is the evidence that 'the time has come' (Mk. 1:15). The promised dawn had arrived, the final year of Jubilee (Lk. 4:18ff.) which will usher in the kingdom and triumph of

God, and during which the Old Testament promises of the coming age will be fulfilled. Jesus is anointed 'with the Holy Spirit and power' for his ministry (Acts 10:38). In this sense, the baptism of Jesus and his reception of the messianic Spirit without measure (Jn. 3:34) constitute the essential prelude to his baptizing the church with the Spirit on the Day of Pentecost when the disciples, in their turn, would receive power (Acts 1:8).

For the New Testament, these events, separated in time, are interwoven theologically. A similar interconnection exists between Jesus' reception of the messianic Spirit and his temptations.

Jesus was 'led by the Spirit' into the wilderness to be tempted by the devil (Mt. 4:1; Lk. 4:1). Whereas Luke uses a relatively innocuous verb (agō, 'to lead'), Mark's account is markedly more vigorous: the Spirit 'drove out [ekballei] Jesus' (Mk. 1:12). He soon employs it again of the exorcism of demons (Mk. 1:34). Matthew uses the same verb when he records Jesus' urging of his disciples to pray that labourers will be thrust out into the spiritual harvest field (Mt. 9:38).

These further uses give colour to the significance of the Spirit's ministry here: 'driving out' expresses the energy and power of the Spirit as the Lord who advances the kingdom of God into enemy-occupied territory. This is precisely the ambience of Jesus' wilderness ministry.

It has been commonplace to interpret Jesus' temptations as analogous to, almost a model for, the tempting of the Christian: Christ was tempted as we are, but resisted; therefore we should resist in similar ways. But this leads to a partial and negative interpretation of his experiences. His temptations constitute an epochal event. They are not merely personal, but cosmic. They constitute the tempting of the last Adam.[12] True, there is a common bond between his temptations and ours: he is really and personally confronted by dark powers. But the significance of the event does not lie in the ways in which our temptations are like his, but in the particularity and uniqueness of his experiences. He was driven into the wilderness as an assault force. His testing was set in the context of a holy war in which he entered the enemy's domain, absorbed his attacks and sent him into retreat (Mt. 4:11, and especially Lk. 4:13). In the power of the Spirit, Jesus advanced as the divine warrior, the God of battles who fights on

THE SPIRIT OF CHRIST

behalf of his people and for their salvation (*cf.* Ex. 15:3; Ps. 98:1). His triumph demonstrated that 'the kingdom of God is near' and that the messianic conflict had begun.

The Lukan narrative bridges the gap between the baptism in Jordan and the temptations in the wilderness with a genealogical table tracing Jesus' lineage back to Adam (Lk. 3:23–38). Here the *inclusio* of the whole of human history between Adam and Jesus suggests that the temptation and victory of the latter are to be interpreted in the light of the testing and defeat of the former with all its baneful entail. The second man–Son thus undid what was done by the first man–son; he obeyed and overcame as the last Adam, and now no further representative figure is needed.

The conflict in which Jesus engaged is, therefore, to be seen as a re-run of Eden. Like Adam before him, Jesus was incited to 'be as God' and to reject his word. But he chose the way of God-glorifying obedience and suffering instead. His resistance and faithfulness contrast also with the forty years of wandering and testing in which the people grieved the Spirit rather than conformed to his guidance (*cf.* Is. 63:7–14). They rebelled against the Spirit who drove them out of Egypt and grieved him; on the contrary, Jesus, anointed with the Spirit, was carried obediently and overcomingly through the test of the wilderness's evil day.

Thus, in the power of the Spirit, in the inhospitable desert which the world had become through the first Adam's sin, the second man, the eschatological Adam (*ho eschatos Adam,* 1 Cor. 15:45), regained enemy-occupied territory. The immediate consequence is that Jesus was able sovereignly to dismiss the devil ('Away from me, Satan!' Mt. 4:10), who was forced to depart until he could find 'an opportune time' (Lk. 4:13). The longer-term consequence was that, having beaten back Satan on his 'own territory', Jesus was now in a position to strike fear into his legions and cast them out.

Mark's record of the temptations ends more abruptly, and contains no record of either their content or their conclusion. He thus indicates that there is a further perspective on the event: it is the opening gambit in a battle which will proceed throughout the whole course of Jesus' ministry. In various ways the entire Gospel gives expression to this conflict motif.

The Spirit's role in Jesus' ministry is now evident. He serves as the heavenly cartographer and divine strategist who maps out the battle terrain and directs the Warrior-King to the strategic point of conflict. He is Christ's adjutant-general in the holy war which is waged throughout the incarnation.

Thus Jesus, Roman-general-like, returns from his hidden conquest 'to Galilee in the power of the Spirit' (Lk. 4:14). The immediate effect of the fact that 'God anointed Jesus of Nazareth with the Holy Spirit and power' was that 'he went around doing good and healing all *who were under the power of the devil*, because God was with him' (Acts 10:38; *cf.* 4:37). For Luke, the whole of Jesus' ministry following his baptism is exercised in the power of the messianic Spirit. He has been anointed to engage in a power-conflict. But in him the final year of Jubilee has now come; there is freedom (Lk. 4:18–19; *cf.* Lv. 25:8–55). The result is that his preaching has authority (Lk. 4:32), his word has exorcising and liberating power (Lk. 4:33–37), and his touch heals 'all' (Lk. 4:40). Nothing is outside of his dominion. The wonders he performs are accomplished in the energy and by the presence of the Holy Spirit (*cf.* Mt. 12:28). That is why they serve as signs of the coming messianic age in which the Spirit's power will be fully manifested and all nature will be healed.

The presence of the Spirit in this work of recapitulation marks the dawning of the Day of the Lord. In the coming of the kingdom, prophecies of the Old Testament find a proleptic fulfilment:

> In that day the Lord will punish
> the powers in the heavens above
> and the kings on the earth below.
> They will be herded together
> like prisoners bound in a dungeon;
> they will be shut up in prison
> and be punished after many days.
> The moon will be abashed, the sun ashamed;
> for the Lord Almighty will reign
> on Mount Zion and in Jerusalem
> and before its elders, gloriously.
> (Is. 24:21–23)

Such fulfilment takes place in Christ, not at the end-point of history, but in advance, unexpectedly. None are more taken aback than the demonic powers who ask Jesus, 'Have you come here to torture us *before* the appointed time?' (Mt. 8:29).

All this is evidence that the promised Coming One is in fact Jesus and that in him the Spirit has come in power. This helps to explain why, while blasphemy against the Son of Man may be forgiven, that against the Spirit will not. The latter involved not just a personal reaction to Jesus, but a rejection of the Spirit's ministry and therefore of the evidence that the kingdom has come and the new age has dawned (*cf.* Mt. 12:25–29; Lk. 10:21).

K. Rengstorf underlines the seriousness of the issue: 'This sin is committed when a man recognizes the mission of Jesus by the Holy Spirit but defies and resists and curses it. The saying shows the seriousness of the situation. It is the last time, in which the lordship of God breaks in.'[13] In this sense, the blasphemy against the Spirit of which Jesus speaks belongs to the hour immediately before God's judgment clock strikes midnight and the day of salvation is brought to an end. The last hour has now arrived.

Thus far we have focused on the ministry of the Spirit in the work and actions of Jesus, on which the Gospels make specific comment.

Less specific, yet no less important, observations are made on the relationship between the Spirit and the character of Jesus. When he returned to Galilee after the temptations it was 'in the power of the Spirit' (Lk. 4:14). Luke's words preface the account of Jesus' sermon in the Nazareth synagogue on the fulfilment of Isaiah 61:1ff., 'The Spirit of the LORD is on me . . .'. The whole pericope concentrates not on Jesus' works but on his words. The effect of his presence is significant: 'He taught in their synagogues, and everyone praised him . . . all spoke well of him and were amazed at the gracious words [words of grace] that came from his lips' (Lk. 4:15).

Set in the wake of Luke 2:52 and 3:22 (with its allusion to the Servant Song in Is. 42:1ff.), this points us to the personal characteristics which the Spirit produced in Jesus' life. He had grown in wisdom and in other qualities which evoked the favour of both God and man. Later, Isaiah 42:1ff. is specifically cited of

Jesus (Mt. 12:18–21): '. . . he will proclaim justice . . . He will not quarrel or cry out . . .'.

Here we find reference to his meek and gracious spirit in the pursuit of righteousness. He does not break the bruised reed or quench the dimly burning wick; he does not draw attention to himself or parade his own abilities. This is the consequence of the divine gift, 'I will put my Spirit on him' (Is. 42:1). What Paul will describe as 'walking in the Spirit' and bearing 'the fruit of the Spirit' (Gal. 5:22–26) finds its prototype in Jesus himself, as does Paul's rich description of love as the first and most essential mark of the Spirit (1 Cor. 13:1ff.)

The fact that Jesus was the Man of the Spirit is, therefore, not merely a theological categorization; it was a flesh-and-blood reality. What was produced in him was fully realized human holiness. He was the incarnation of the blessed life of the covenant and of the kingdom-beatitudes which are its fruit (Mt. 5:1ff.; *cf.* Ps. 1).

Similarly, Jesus grew in the wisdom from above which was both pure and peace-loving, considerate, submissive, full of mercy and good fruit (Jas. 3:17). He was the wise man who shows his wisdom by his good life and by deeds done in the humility that comes from wisdom (Jas. 3:13). This is what it meant for him to live in the power and grace of the Spirit.

But what of Jesus' experience of the presence and gifts of the Spirit? That he worked miracles lies on the surface of the text of the Gospels. That he spoke in tongues is sometimes suggested[14] but is nowhere stated and, as we shall see, given the distinctive function of tongues-speaking in redemptive history, is a gratuitous assumption. That he exercised the manifold word-gifts of the Spirit is evident throughout his teaching, as is the fact that through the Spirit he enjoyed intimate fellowship with God, and on occasion exulted in his presence and power (Lk. 10:21). The fact that the expression of his exultation is occasional rather than constant, spasmodic rather than permanent, underlines the fact that his communion with the Spirit took place within the whole gamut of human emotions. But the predominant interest of the New Testament lies not in his experience of these gifts, or in his emotions as such, but in the true knowledge of God that he possessed in communion with the Spirit and his consequent exemplification of the fruit of the Spirit.

52

Stage III: Death, resurrection and ascension

The Gospels suggest that the whole of Jesus' ministry was conducted in the Spirit's power. Yet the only reference to the Spirit's ministry during Jesus' sufferings and death is in Hebrews 9:14: 'Christ, who through the eternal Spirit offered himself unblemished to God . . .'. A strong case can be made for understanding the *pneuma* in which Jesus offered himself as referring to the divine Spirit.[15]

No further exposition is offered us at this juncture to answer questions which may arise in our minds, and speculation would be misplaced.

Similarly brief, if less cryptic, are the New Testament's reflections on the role of the Spirit in Jesus' resurrection. Here again we find an illustration of the patristic maxim *opera ad extra trinitatis indivisa sunt* ('the external works of the Trinity are undivided') – even if these *opera* are 'appropriated' to one or other person of the Godhead.

The resurrection, while chiefly attributed to the Father (Acts 2:32; 17:31; Rom. 8:11; 1 Cor. 15:15), is also seen to be an action of the Son (Jn. 2:19–21; 10:17–18). But, according to Paul, it is also 'through the Spirit of holiness' that Jesus 'was declared with power to be the Son of God, by his resurrection from the dead' (Rom. 1:4). This, coupled with the 'faithful saying' that Jesus was 'vindicated by the Spirit' (a reference to the resurrection as his 'justification', 1 Tim. 3:16), and Peter's words 'He was put to death in the body but made alive by the Spirit . . .' (1 Pet. 3:18), underlines the Spirit's role in the resurrection.

In the power of the Spirit Jesus was raised from the dead – 'by the glory of the Father' (Rom. 6:4). Paul has in view the radical transformation of the very nature of Christ's bodily existence. It has become a body of glory (Phil. 3:21). The resurrection body may be identified with the body that has died, but it is certainly not identical in properties, as is obvious from the behaviour of our Lord's body following the resurrection. Its attributes contrast strongly with its previous ones; it is powerful and no longer weak and subject to death. It is a *spiritual* body, one brought into being and appropriate to the lordship of the Spirit. Such is the fullness of the Spirit into which Jesus entered at the resurrection that Paul is able to say that 'the last Adam [became] a life-giving spirit' (1 Cor. 15:45).

This last statement, 'the last Adam [became] a life-giving spirit' (1 Cor. 15:45), is as significant as it is extraordinary. Here the NIV translation may fail us, for 'spirit' in this context probably refers to the Holy Spirit, and should be capitalized.[16] Christ on his ascension came into such complete possession of the Spirit who had sustained him throughout his ministry that *economically* the resurrected Christ and the Spirit are one to us. He is *alter Christus*, another Christ, to us; ministerially he is indeed *allos paraklētos*.

Paul is here explaining the nature of the resurrection body. Christ's resurrection body is the firstfruits and prototype of a new humanity. Not only so, but Christ as life-giving Spirit is the source of our resurrection existence. He gives life suited to the Spirit. He is saying even more than this, however: Christ, as 'Son of God with power' (by contrast to 'Son of God in weakness') has become life-giving Spirit.

Clearly we cannot regard this as a statement of ontological fusion (*i.e.* as a denial of the distinction in personal existence between the Son and the Spirit). Paul constantly employs a trinitarian formulation in describing the work of God and recognizes the permanence of the distinction of the three persons (*e.g.* Rom. 8:14–17; 15:30; 2 Cor. 13:14). But Paul's view of the relationship between Christ and the Spirit has clear parallels with the idea present in the Johannine witness: the Son and the Spirit share an identity of ministry. The Son is *paraklētos*, the Spirit is *allos paraklētos*. Both function as paracletes, and do so successively in the earthly realm, the Spirit being another of the same kind as the Son (*cf.* Jn. 14:16, where 'another' [*allos*] certainly conveys the notion 'another of the same kind', even if the classical distinction between *allos* and *heteros* is not always sustained).[17]

Thus, to have the Spirit is to have Christ; to have Christ is to have the Spirit. Not to have the Spirit of Christ is to lack Christ. To have the Spirit of Christ is to be indwelt by Christ (Rom. 8:9–11). There is clear ontological distinction, but economic or functional equivalence. In this sense, through the resurrection and ascension, Christ 'became life-giving Spirit'.

The explanation for this is found in a further remarkable

statement: 'Now the Lord [the antecedent is "Christ", 2 Cor. 3:13] is the Spirit, and where the Spirit of the Lord is, there is freedom. And we, who with unveiled faces all reflect the Lord's glory, are being transformed into his likeness with ever-increasing glory, which comes from the Lord, who is the Spirit' (2 Cor. 3:17–18).

This last phrase 'from the Lord, who is the Spirit' translates three Greek words: *apo* (from), *kyriou* (Lord, genitive case following the preposition *apo*) and *pneumatos* (Spirit, also in the genitive case). The statement is amenable to more than one interpretation: (1) 'from the Spirit of the Lord'; (2) 'from the Lord who is the Spirit'; (3) 'from the Lord of the Spirit'. The third option may, at first glance, seem to be the least likely, but it is the most natural rendering and one that is highly illuminating theologically. Paul is then saying that the Lord Jesus Christ is Lord of the Spirit. There is no ontological confusion here, but an economic equivalence; nor is there an ontological sub-ordinationism, but rather a complete intimacy of relationship between Jesus and the Spirit.

In effect, Paul is teaching that through his life and ministry Jesus came into such complete possession of the Spirit, receiving and experiencing him 'without limit' (Jn. 3:34), that he is now 'Lord' of the Spirit (2 Cor. 3:18). With respect to his economic ministry to us, the Spirit has been 'imprinted' with the character of Jesus.[18] This is precisely what it means for Jesus to send him as *allos paraklētos*.

The great Dutch theologian Herman Bavinck finely expressed this New Testament emphasis:

> This taking possession of the Holy Spirit by Christ is so absolute an appropriation that the apostle Paul can say of it in 2 Corinthians 3:17 that the Lord (that is, Christ as the exalted Lord) is the Spirit. Naturally Paul does not by that statement mean to obliterate the distinction between the two, for in the following verse he immediately speaks again of the Spirit of the Lord (or, as another translation has it, of the Lord of the Spirit). But the Holy Spirit has become entirely the property of Christ, and was, so to speak, absorbed into Christ or assimilated by him. By the resurrection and ascension

> Christ has become the quickening Spirit (1 Cor.
> 15:45). He is now in possession of the seven Spirits
> (that is, the Spirit in His fulness), even as He is in
> possession of the seven stars (Rev. 3:1).[19]

The clearest hints of this identification of ministries are found in John's Gospel, particularly in the farewell discourse. There, however, the identification is underlined to assure the disciples that the ministry of the Spirit stands in total continuity with that of the Son. Like Jesus, the Paraclete is sent by the Father and comes from the Father. Jesus is the truth, the Paraclete is the Spirit of truth who leads Christians into the truth (Jn. 14:6, 17; 15:26; 16:13); Jesus is the teacher of his disciples (14:23, 26); the Paraclete comes to teach them further. Jesus is the witness God has sent; the Paraclete is sent into the world to be a witness (18:37; 15:26). The world does not know or accept Jesus (5:43; 12:48); nor does the world recognize the Paraclete (14:17). In all of these senses the Paraclete is the one who 'takes what belongs to Jesus' (cf. 16:14).

Thus, when Jesus announces his departure from the disciples but assures them that 'I will come [back] to you' (14:18), he is speaking neither about his resurrection reappearance (20:14, 19), nor about his anticipated final return, but about his 'coming' in the gift of the Spirit. So complete is the union between Jesus and the Paraclete that the coming of the latter is the coming of Jesus himself in the Spirit.

The significance of this will become clearer when we turn, as we must now do, to consider the meaning of the coming of the Spirit at Pentecost.

The ministry of the Spirit in this increasing identification with Jesus is in order that, being 'shaped' as messianic Spirit by the life and ministry of Jesus, he may come to us thus qualified to reshape us to be 'like Christ', from one degree of glory to another (2 Cor. 3:17–18). This is the central function of the Holy Spirit in the life of the Christian believer.

3

THE GIFT OF
THE SPIRIT

During the period between his resurrection and his ascension, Jesus continued to teach his disciples in the power of the Holy Spirit (Acts 1:2). Instructions were given to them for the period immediately following the ascension: 'Do not leave Jerusalem, but wait for the gift my Father promised, which you have heard me speak about . . . in a few days you will be baptised with the Holy Spirit . . . you will receive power when the Holy Spirit comes on you . . .' (Acts 1:4–5, 8; *cf.* Lk. 24:49). The fulfilment of these promises began on the Day of Pentecost. But what is the meaning of Pentecost?

Pentecost publicly marks the transition from the old to the new covenant, and signifies the commencement of the 'now' of the day of salvation (2 Cor. 6:2). It is the threshold of the last days, and inaugurates the new era in which the eschatological life of the future invades the present evil age in a proleptic manner. Thus, from the New Testament's standpoint, the 'fulfilment [or "end", *ta telē*] of the ages has dawned' (lit.) on those who, through the gift of the Spirit, are 'in Christ' (1 Cor. 10:11). That which is 'new' in the new covenant ministry of the Spirit is therefore inextricably related to the significance of the Pentecost event.

The New Testament provides two distinct, yet harmonious, major strands of interpretation for the events of Pentecost: the Lukan and the Johannine.

The Lukan testimony

The New Testament views Pentecost, like Calvary, as an event with multi-faceted significance. A variety of tributaries of biblical theology flow into it. Central to interpreting it is the way in which it is understood as an aspect of the work of Christ.

Jesus' relationship to the Spirit in Luke–Acts may be traced through the three stages we have already noted. The first stage is in his conception by Mary through the power of the Spirit. The second commences with his baptism, when he received the messianic anointing as the new Adam (*cf.* Lk. 3:22–23 with 4:37), the Man of the messianic age, full of the Spirit (Lk. 4:1, 18–21). Anointed with the Spirit, he went around doing good, *i.e.* proclaiming that the kingdom is now present, and showing evidences of its presence in his mighty works (*cf.* Acts 10:38). The third stage began with his resurrection and ascension, when he who was himself baptized with water by John baptized with the Holy Spirit (Lk. 3:16; Acts 1:5; 11:16) and clothed his disciples 'with power from on high' (Lk. 24:49). The one who earlier received, was filled with and was borne along by the Spirit, then entered a new stage of relationship, in which the promise of the Father was fulfilled (Lk. 24:49), and he now possessed the prerogative of sending the Spirit.

Spirit and fire

The baptism that Jesus received in Jordan and the baptism that he initiates at Pentecost are epochally different, yet intimately related. John announced that Jesus' baptism would be with the Spirit and with fire, bringing in the messianic age through cataclysmic destruction.

Jesus understood that, in bestowing the Spirit upon his people and ushering in the new age, he himself would experience the reality which his baptism in Jordan intimated, namely a baptism of fire. His whole emotional life was geared to that event as his own words testify: 'I have come to bring fire on the earth, and how I wish it were already kindled! But I have a baptism to undergo, and how distressed I am until it is completed' (Lk. 12:49–50). What John the Baptist could not understand clearly was that the 'fire' of which he spoke would fall upon the Messiah himself, in the judgment-dereliction of the cross. In fact, later John expressed his doubts about the significance of Jesus' ministry, apparently because it lacked 'fire' (Lk. 7:18–23).

Luke's researches were not lacking then, when, in his record of Jesus' post-resurrection words to the disciples about being baptized with the Holy Spirit, he makes no mention of fire. Its flames had been exhausted in Christ. Part of the symbolism of the 'tongues of fire' which the disciples saw on the Day of Pentecost (Acts 2:3) may well lie in the hint that this is a baptism of gracious rather than of destructive power because of the judgment which Christ had vicariously borne in his passion.[1]

Promise fulfilled

In his Pentecost sermon, Simon Peter takes us momentarily behind the events of history to give us a glimpse of a transaction between the Father and the Son–Mediator to give us further insight into the significance of Pentecost: 'Exalted to the right hand of God, he [Christ] has *received* from the Father the *promised* Holy Spirit and *poured out* what you now see and hear' (Acts 2:33).

There are two aspects to this promise. The gift of the Spirit is a central element in the new covenant promise that God had given to his people (*cf.* Ezk. 36:27), and the inner essence of the promise given to Abraham (*cf.* Gal. 3:14). But another aspect emerges, for the gift of the Spirit was promised *to Christ* in order to fulfil the messianic promises: 'so will he sprinkle many nations, and kings will shut their mouths because of him . . . I will give him a portion among the great, and he will divide the spoils with the strong' (Is. 52:15; 53:12). It is through the gift of the Spirit to Christ and the bestowal of the Spirit by Christ that the Father's promise to his Son in Psalm 2:8 is fulfilled: 'Ask of me, and I will make the nations your inheritance . . .' The fulfilment of the Great Commission takes place in the power of the Spirit. The hidden reality revealed publicly by Pentecost is that the ascended Christ had now asked the Father to fulfil his promise, had received the Spirit for his people, and had now poured him out on the church so that the messianic age begun in the resurrection of Christ might catch up in its flow those who are united to him by participation in the one Spirit. Thus, in Abraham's seed all the nations of the earth would now be blessed (Gn. 12:3; Gal. 3:13–14).

New creation

The physical and visible accompaniments of the Spirit's coming help to shed further light on its multi-layered significance, since they carry echoes of various Old Testament themes. The 'sound like the blowing of a violent wind' echoes the imagery of the powerful operation of the *ruach elohim* of creation (Gn. 1:2), suggesting that the event about to take place marks the beginning of a new world order.

Judgment reversed

On the morning of Pentecost, the disciples began to speak in other tongues so that visitors to Jerusalem heard the message of the gospel in their own language (Acts 2:4). Luke's statement here is accompanied by a 'table of nations' (Acts 2:8–12), just as the Genesis record of the confusing of human language is accompanied by a 'table of nations' (Gn. 10:1–32). Part of the answer to the question 'What does this mean?' (Acts 2:12), therefore, seems to be that here we have the reversal of Babel, the founding of the community of the reconciled. I. H. Marshall has pointed out that the number 120 (Acts 1:15) was the minimum number of men required 'to establish a community with its own council', so that these early Christians were able to 'form a new community'.[2] On the Day of Pentecost that new community became the sphere in which the eschatological reversal of the effects of sin began to appear in a reconciled people consisting of both Jew and Gentile, possessing one Lord, one faith and one baptism (Eph. 4:1ff.), united by the Spirit.

The effects of Babel were thus arrested. Now the word of reconciliation will be preached in many languages, since the disciples have received the promised power of the Spirit to enable them to be witnesses to Christ all over the world (Lk. 24:48; Acts 1:4).

There is, however, another dimension to this unusual phenomenon of speaking in tongues, if the tongues in view here and
in the church at Corinth were in the nature of foreign
languages. In discussing the question of tongues-speaking in 1
Corinthians 14, Paul cites Isaiah 28:11–12 ('Through men of
strange tongues and through the lips of foreigners I will speak to
this people, but even then they will not listen to me') and
indicates that tongues are 'a sign, not for believers but for
unbelievers' (1 Cor. 14:21–22).

The context of these words in Isaiah is one of covenant
rejection. On account of the immaturity of his people's
behaviour patterns, God will speak in an unwelcome accent:
'Very well then, with foreign lips and strange tongues God will
speak to this people' (Is. 28:11). Here, as elsewhere, the hearing
of foreign tongues is a sign of God's promised judgment on his
covenant people (cf. Dt. 28:49; Je. 5:15), an indication that the
kingdom is being taken from them and given to a people who
will produce fruit appropriate to it (Mt. 21:43). The universalism
of Pentecost also has its dark side: Israel began to experience a
partial hardening until the 'fullness' of the Gentiles is brought
in (Rom. 11:25).

Pentecost and Sinai

By the time of the first century, the Day of Pentecost seems to
have been associated with the giving of the law at Sinai. By the
time of the second century, this was thought to have taken place
in the seventy languages of the world, and this tradition may
have already been commonplace.[3] But even if that association in
Judaism is questioned, a Sinai–Pentecost parallel is established
in the New Testament itself. The revelation of God to Moses at
Sinai had been accompanied by fire, wind and a divine tongue
(Heb. 12:18–21). Moses had ascended the mountain. When he
descended he had in his possession the Ten Commandments,
the law of God. Christ too had recently ascended. At Pentecost
he comes down, not with the law written on tablets of clay, but
with the gift of his own Spirit to write the law in the hearts of
believers and by his power to enable them to fulfil the law's
commands. Thus the new covenant promise begins to be
fulfilled (cf. Je. 31:31–34; Rom. 8:3–4; 2 Cor. 3:7–11).

61

The significance of prophecy

In Peter's exposition of the significance of the events of Pentecost, the words of prophecy in Joel 2:28–32 are central:

> 'In the last days, God says,
>   I will pour out my Spirit on all people.
> Your sons and daughters will prophesy,
>   your young men will see visions,
>   your old men will dream dreams.
> Even on my servants, both men and women,
>   I will pour out my Spirit in those days,
>   and they will prophesy.'
>
> (Acts 2:17–18)

The term 'prophecy' has proved to be an elusive one in biblical studies.[4] But what is clear in this context is that Peter understood the prophesying to which Joel referred to be fulfilled in the phenomenon of the speaking in tongues in a manner that the people could understand. Peter thus regarded tongues, when understood naturally by the hearers or interpreted for them, as the functional equivalent of prophecy.

The elapse of the Spirit was the fulfilment of Joel's prophecy of the last days. The long-looked-for Day of the Lord had arrived; the powers of the age to come were now released. The characteristic feature of this was a distinction in the distribution of the Spirit. He was now 'poured out' by Christ in unrestrained measure, and distributed without geographical and ethnic limitation, 'on all people'.

Implied in this is the principle that the divinely given, but temporary, distinguishing features of the Mosaic covenantal economy were now rendered obsolete. This is the thrust of Acts 2:17–18. In the old covenant, the typical effect of the Spirit's coming was prophecy, with its various modes of production (*cf.* Nu. 11:24–29; 1 Sa. 10:10–11). It was, generally speaking, limited to only a few, almost exclusively men. Now, in the new covenant, the boundaries of the Mosaic economy within which the Spirit had, by and large, previously manifested himself are rendered obsolete. Both sons and daughters prophesy; young men have visions, old men have dreams. These were, of course, modes of communicating the knowledge of God under the old covenant. Now, in Christ, the old distinctions are nullified. Now all of the Lord's people possess the knowledge of God formerly experienced only by the prophets. This was exactly what Moses himself had longed for, although it could never have been experienced under the Mosaic economy: 'I wish that all the LORD's people were prophets and that the LORD would put his Spirit on them' (Nu. 11:29). Now it was a reality.

When viewed within this old/new covenantal perspective, the central concerns here are not the specific issues which so fascinate the contemporary church (*e.g.* whether women may preach or prophesy, or whether prophecy is a continuing gift to the church in every age). Here 'prophesy' is a metonymy for sharing the messianic Spirit and experiencing the knowledge of the Lord which only the Spirit of God could give (*cf.* 1 Jn. 2:20, 27). Already in the Old Testament, the 'man of the Spirit' was the prophet (Ho. 9:7), and in the Judaism of this period 'to possess the Spirit of God was to be a prophet'.[5] That which came to the people by and large through official channels in the Mosaic economy (*via* prophets, priests and kings) now belongs to all the Lord's people by Christ through his Spirit. A status (prophet) and relationship (intimate knowledge, *cf.* Am. 3:7) with God, known at first hand only by the few under the old covenant, could now be enjoyed by all.

Now all have received the messianic anointing. This is the sense in which the new covenant promise is fulfilled: 'No longer will a man teach his neighbour, or a man his brother saying "Know the Lord," because they will all know me, from the least of them to the greatest' (Je. 31:34). No longer is an anointed human mediator required to teach us to know the Lord; now all who receive the Spirit of Jesus, the exalted Prophet-Messiah, share the prophetic anointing (*cf.* 1 Jn. 2:20, 27). In Christ, they have immediate personal knowledge of God. All, in this sense, are prophets as well as priests and kings.

Pentecost was the fiftieth day from the Passover. It was the Feast of Firstfruits, celebrating the offering of the harvest (Ex. 23:16; Lv. 23:15–21). There is, therefore, a certain appropriateness in the large number and wide ethnic representation of converts on that day – the firstfruits of the gospel in the new epoch. But Pentecost was also, as we have noted, increasingly viewed as a commemoration of the giving of the law at Sinai. Appropriately for this day, Peter's exposition indicates that the peculiarly Mosaic economy is rendered obsolete. The end of the Mosaic epoch and the universal preaching and reception of the gospel are two sides of the same coin. The coming of the Spirit marks the end of the limitations built into the divinely-ordained impermanence of the Mosaic economy and the beginning of the new era.

Pentecost is thus portrayed by Luke as an event of rich redemptive-historical significance. Just as at Calvary Old Testament patterns and promises find their fulfilment, so it is with Pentecost.

The Johannine testimony

John records an incident from the day of the resurrection which, over the centuries, has caused interpreters of his Gospel considerable difficulty. Jesus appeared to the disciples and said:

> 'Peace be with you! As the Father has sent me, I am sending you.' And with that he breathed on them and said, 'Receive the Holy Spirit. If you forgive anyone his sins, they are forgiven; if you do not forgive them, they are not forgiven.'
>
> (Jn. 20:21–23)

Johannine Pentecost?

It has become commonplace to speak of this event as the Johannine Pentecost, on the assumption that it serves the same function in John's theology as that of Pentecost in the theology of Luke. This implies that theological reconstruction has been given priority over historical accuracy to such an extent that events may be radically recast (or even invented *de novo*) for the purposes of the story. By contrast, although Luke's writings have a definite theological function, he presents them as the fruit of historical research (Lk. 1:1–4).

Is it, then, possible to see the pericope in John's Gospel as a piece of functional theology rather than history? Quite apart from a dogmatic interest (*i.e.* the implications for the doctrine of Scripture), there are good reasons for viewing this event as quite distinct from, although theologically related to, the events of Pentecost. In fact, the focus in John 20 is very different from that in Acts 1.

Within the Johannine framework, the coming of the Spirit is dependent on Christ's ascension and exaltation (Jn. 14:16–17; 16:7). Earlier on the resurrection day, Jesus had indicated to Mary that the ascension had not yet taken place (Jn. 20:17). It would be a remarkable inconsistency in John's thinking if he were, in the same chapter, to portray the events of that evening as the promised sending of the Spirit.

The Johannine record underlines two things, in relation to which Jesus' actions appear to be largely symbolical:[6]

(1) Jesus breathed on his disciples as God breathed the breath of life into Adam (Gn. 2:7). The symbolism is that of the beginning of a new creation. Here, to borrow Pauline terms, the last Adam has now become (eschatological) 'life-giving Spirit'.

(2) Jesus equipped the apostles with his own Spirit for a new stage of their ministry in which they will serve in his absence as his ministerial representatives. Hence, the focus of the narrative is on their commission to forgive sins (Jn. 20:22–23; *cf.* Mt. 16:19), rather than on a coming of the Spirit in which all the people of God are to share. Yet, implied in this is precisely the fulfilment of the promises of the new covenant and the universal gift of the Spirit (Je. 31:33–34; Ezk. 36:25–27).

In this connection, the absence of Thomas from the commissioning was repaired the following week (Jn. 20:26ff.) when he was invited to place his hand in the wounded side of Jesus, from which the blood and water had flowed, probably hinting, as we will see, that the gift of the Spirit comes from Jesus as the one 'lifted up' in crucifixion.

Spirit and cross

Among other passages in John's Gospel which shed light on Pentecost, particularly significant are the words of John 7:37–39:

> On the last and greatest day of the Feast,[7] Jesus stood and said in a loud voice, 'If anyone is thirsty, let him come to me. And let him drink, who believes in me.[8] As the Scripture has said, streams of living water will flow from within him.' By this he meant the Spirit, whom

those who believed in him were later to receive. Up to that time the Spirit had not been given, since Jesus had not yet been glorified.

The Feast of Tabernacles was a spectacular occasion. Its ceremonies looked back to the wilderness wanderings and forward to the days of the Messiah when life-giving water from God would be enjoyed (Is. 43:20; Ezk. 47:1) and the Spirit would be poured out (Ezk. 36:25–27). Water was drawn from the Pool of Siloam and poured out at the temple altar each day except the last day, as a reminder of the blessings God had given the people in the wilderness when Moses had drawn water out of the rock. Through Zechariah 9 – 14, the event became associated with the anticipated triumph of God and the blessing of Jerusalem, and pointed forwards to a time when the great prophecy of Isaiah would be fulfilled:

'Surely God is my salvation;
    I will trust and not be afraid.
The LORD, the LORD, is my strength and my song;
    he has become my salvation.'
With joy you will draw water
    from the wells of salvation.

In that day you will say:
Give thanks to the LORD, call on his name;
    make known among the nations what he has done,
    and proclaim that his name is exalted.
Sing to the LORD, for he has done glorious things;
    let this be known to all the world.
Shout aloud and sing for joy, people of Zion,
    for great is the Holy One of Israel among you.'
(Is. 12:2–6)

On the last day of the celebration (*cf.* Jn. 7:37), the water ceremony was enacted with special drama. On this occasion alone the festive crowd walked around the altar seven times. It appears to have been on this 'greatest day of the Feast' that Jesus spoke of the gift of the Spirit, under the form of living water.

A well-known difficulty is attached to the interpretation of

John 7:37–39, highlighted by the problem of identifying the citation of Scripture. Jesus spoke of the outflowing of streams of living water, 'as the Scripture has said'. But no specific text of the Old Testament is cited. To what, then, did Jesus refer?

Two possible translations and interpretations are open to us, involving different punctuations of the (unpunctuated) Greek text. The choice between them involves the question: Are we meant to understand these streams to flow from within the believer (the so-called Eastern view, following Origen and the Greek Fathers, NIV text), or from within Christ (the Western view, following the Latin Fathers, NIV mg.)? Interpreters remain divided.

Although it is impossible to be dogmatic, the more *theologically* satisfying view is that Jesus himself is the source of living water, the fulfilment of the wilderness rock smitten by Moses (Ex. 17:5–6) from whom living water flows (*cf.* 1 Cor. 10:4), and/or the new temple of God envisaged in Ezekiel 47, from which the waters emerged. If so, then what is in view is the gift of the Spirit coming from Christ to his people. Thus, within the Johannine context, it is through Jesus' death that the Spirit is seen as coming to the church. Christ as crucified will give the Spirit. From his side both water and blood flow; the blood of forgiveness, the water of the Spirit. Only as the crucified one can he give the messianic Spirit.

This note is deeply embedded in the warp and woof of John's Christology, and it comes into view in the penchant for *double entendre* we have already noted in his writing. In John's record, Jesus the Messiah becomes the thirsty one (*cf.* Jn. 19:16) under God's covenant curse (*cf.* Dt. 38:48), so that to those who are thirsty he may hand over his thirst-quenching Spirit (Jn. 19:30). Again, John alone notes that when one of the soldiers pierced Christ's side both blood and water flowed from it (Jn. 19:34; *cf.* 1 Jn. 5:6–8). Christ's death is to be seen both as a sacrifice for sins and as the means by which the water of new life in the Spirit flows to us.

This is exactly what was underlined in John's earlier editorial statement: literally, 'the Spirit *was not yet*, since Jesus had not been glorified'.

A flat grammatical interpretation of these words would be exegetically impossible, since the Gospel already speaks of the person and ministry of the Spirit (*e.g.* 1:32–33). Furthermore, prior to the glorification of Jesus, the Spirit was both present and known (*cf.* 14:17, 'You know him, for he lives with you'). The statement must therefore carry economic, not ontological, significance. What John means may be put like this: until the exaltation of Christ, the Spirit of God could not be received in his specific economic identity as the Spirit of the ascended Christ. By means of Christ's exaltation (which for John seems to include his victorious death), he would be.

A further nuance of this same teaching is found in John 14:17, when Jesus says that the Spirit of truth is 'with' the disciples, and later will be 'in' them. What is in view is not so much a distinction between the Spirit being only 'with' believers in the old covenant, while he dwells 'in' them in the new covenant, although that view has widespread support. Rather, it is that during the days of his humiliation, the Spirit of Christ was on Christ, and therefore, and in this sense, 'with' the disciples. But at the exaltation, Christ would breathe his Spirit on his disciples. He would now indwell them in his identity as the Spirit of the exalted Saviour. He who was 'with' them in Christ's presence would then be 'in' them as the Spirit of the incarnate and exalted Christ. The contrast is located not in the manner of his dwelling so much as in the capacity in which he indwells. The giving of the Spirit thus announces the divine exaltation of Christ to the right hand of the Father. It is the public expression of his coronation (Jesus is now 'glorified'). All this is portrayed in the events of the Upper Room.

John's Gospel serves an explicitly evangelistic function (Jn. 20:30–31). Part of his message is that the crucified Saviour in whom he invites us to believe also gives the Spirit to those who trust him. His focus is on the theological groundwork for the faith-reception of the Spirit, whereas Luke's interest is in the historical unfolding of the redemptive-historical pattern of the Spirit's coming. It is unnecessary therefore to resort to a coalescing of the events of John 20:30–31 with Penteost in order to interpret the testimonies of Luke and John.

Within this context, the discourse in John 14 – 16 points to four aspects of the Spirit's ministry which shed light on who he is and what he is sent to accomplish.

Conviction and conversion

In his farewell sermon, Jesus gave a further prediction of the significance of the Spirit's coming: 'If I go, I will send him [the Holy Spirit] to you. When he comes, he will convict the world of guilt in regard to sin and righteousness and judgment: in regard to sin, because men do not believe in me; in regard to righteousness, because I am going to the Father, where you can see me no longer; and in regard to judgment, because the prince of this world now stands condemned' (Jn. 16:7–11).

Immediate application of these words to the contemporary church shortcircuits their significance. In the first instance, they look forward to a specific event in redemptive history, namely 'when he [the Spirit] comes'. Jesus' words should not be applied to our contemporary situation without first asking what their significance was for those who first heard them. They are, in fact, a specific prophecy about events on the Day of Pentecost and consequently are correlative to the editorial statement of John 7:39. Reading them in a decontextualized manner ('What do these verses tell us about our own experience?') fails to take account of their fundamentally Christocentric and redemptive-historical focus. The coming of the Spirit and the conviction he produces are related directly to the status of Christ which is therein revealed.

There is a close relationship between the promise of John 16:8–11 and the events described in Acts 2:22–24. There, in Peter's first sermon, he bore witness to the exaltation of Christ, the truth of which, by the Spirit's work in the hearers' hearts, convicts them of their sin ('you . . . put him to death'); and of Christ's righteousness ('But God raised him from the dead'; *cf.* Acts 3:13–16); and of judgment, since resurrection from the dead, seen as the condemnation of the Prince of darkness and death and the harbinger of the Day of the Lord and final judgment, had taken place in him ('it was impossible for death to keep its hold on him'). Peter sees the coming of the Spirit not only as the fulfilment of Joel's prophecy but also as the fulfilment of Psalm 16:8–11 and Psalm 110:1, which anticipate the exaltation of the Lord and the ensuing period in which his enemies would be subdued before him.

The result of the Spirit-empowered proclamation of the

exalted Lord illustrates the pattern outlined in John 16:8–11: 'the people . . . were cut to the heart and said . . . "Brothers, what shall we do?"' (Acts 2:37). The work of the Spirit in conviction led to conversion and the baptism of repentance, faith and forgiveness ('Those who accepted his message were baptised, and about three thousand were added to their number that day', Acts 2:41).

Inspiration

The second clue from John 14 – 16 to the significance of the Spirit's coming is connected to the function of the apostles in the writing of the New Testament Scriptures.

Jesus was asked why he planned to reveal himself to the apostles and not to the world (Jn. 14:22). His answer traces his own teaching back to the teaching of the Father, thereby stressing its absolute divine authority and origin (Jn. 14:23–24). His words are tantamount to a claim to the divine inspiration of his teaching. This inspiration, he adds, does not cease with his departure, for when the Counsellor comes he 'will teach you all things and will remind you of everything I have said to you' (Jn. 14:26).

The significance of these words is also commonly short-circuited as though they had immediate application to contemporary Christians. But in fact they constituted a specific promise to the apostles which found its fulfilment in their writing of the New Testament Scriptures. The Gospels contain what they were reminded that Jesus had said and taught; in the letters we find the further illumination they received through the Holy Spirit. Thus, when Jesus spoke later of their joint testimony with the Spirit ('the Counsellor . . . will testify about me. And you also must testify . . .', Jn. 15:26–27), the standing example of this joint activity is found in the pages of the New Testament, which are the work of the Spirit and also, simultaneously, the testimony of the apostles. Further, in John 16:13–14, the promise that the Spirit 'will tell you what is yet to come. He will bring glory to me by taking from what is mine and making it known to you' encompasses the giving of the New Testament Scriptures in both their prophetic aspect and their Christological fullness.

No doubt these words have a continuing significance for Christians today, but not in the direct way in which they are often understood (the Spirit will lead *me* into all truth in an unmediated way). Rather, they indicate that it is by means of the apostolic witness (now inscripturated in the New Testament), not by direct revelation of the Spirit to individual believers or by corporate revelation to teaching officers (the claim which was to be developed in the Roman Catholic magisterium), that Christ's person, his teaching and his future purposes are made known.

Communion

The Spirit's coming inaugurates a communion with Christ in which the Spirit who dwelt on Christ now dwells on and in believers. This element is brought out in the farewell discourse, when Jesus promises the disciples 'another paraclete' who will be his economic equivalent because he is his own Spirit. Jesus himself will come back to them (Jn. 14:18), not only in the resurrection but in this new way.

This perspective illumines the force of what is said in John 16:7: 'I tell you the truth: It is for your good that I am going away. Unless I go away, the Counsellor will not come to you; but if I go, I will send him to you.' The coming of the Spirit is the equivalent of the indwelling of Jesus. This is for the disciples' good, since it implies such a close union with Christ that he dwells *in* them, not merely *with* them. This is why Jesus explains the significance of the coming of the Spirit as follows: 'On that day [*i.e.* the Day when the Father will give them another Counsellor = the day of Pentecost] you will realize that [a] I am in my Father, and [b] you are in me, and [c] I am in you' (Jn. 14:20). The trinitarian union and communion of Father and Son in the Spirit is the analogy for the union and communion between Christ and his people.

We have seen the same point made by Paul in 1 Corinthians 15:45. Christ has become 'life-giving Spirit'. Having the Spirit is the equivalent, indeed the very mode, of having the incarnate, obedient, crucified, resurrected and exalted Christ indwelling us so that we are united to him as he is united to the Father.

It is in this sense that John sees the difference that Pentecost signals in the ministry of the Spirit. Now, as the bond of union to God, the Spirit indwells all who believe *as the Spirit of the Lord Jesus Christ.* This is a development of epochal proportions. The Spirit who was present and active at Christ's conception as the head of the new creation, by whom he was anointed at baptism (Jn. 1:32–34), who directed him throughout his temptations (Mt. 4:1), empowered him in his miracles (Lk. 11:20), energized him in his sacrifice (Heb. 9:14), and vindicated him in his resurrection (1 Tim. 3:16; Rom. 1:4), now indwells disciples in this specific identity. This is the meaning of our Lord's words, otherwise impossible to comprehend: 'It is for your good that I am going away' (Jn. 16:7).

The profound experiential implication of this is summarized by Abraham Kuyper: 'What a redeemed soul needs is human holiness.' Angelic holiness will not serve fallen man. If we are to be holy, that holiness must be wrought out in our humanity. This is what Christ has accomplished. And now the Spirit, out of his union with the incarnate Son, brings those resources to bear upon the lives of believers. Because of his ministry in Christ he can now indwell us to reproduce the same holiness in our lives. And so, adds Kuyper, 'The Holy Spirit finds this holy disposition in its required form, not in the Father, nor in Himself, but in Immanuel, who as the Son of God and the Son of man possesses holiness in that peculiar form.'[9]

Jesus himself puts this ministry of the Spirit in a nutshell when he says: 'He will bring glory to me by taking from what is mine and making it known to you' (Jn. 16:14). In a sense, the various aspects of the application of redemption are simply further biblical answers to the question: How does the Spirit accomplish this work?

Procession

In discussing the revelation of the Spirit in the old covenant, we noted that it is inevitable in progressive, historical, Christocentric revelation that only in the coming of the Son is the Spirit (as well as the Father, Jn. 14:9) fully revealed. We would, therefore, expect that, in the coming of the Son, the relationship of the Spirit to both Father and Son would also be more clearly unveiled.

In the farewell discourse, Jesus sends the Spirit 'from the Father' (*para tou patros*) as the one who 'goes out from [AV "proceeds from"] the Father' (*ho para tou patros ekporeuetai*, Jn. 15:26). This statement pinpoints the trinitarian significance of Pentecost. While it is Jesus who sends the Spirit, this takes place in response to his asking the Father to do so (14:16, 26). The Spirit is therefore sent by the Father and by the Son as Mediator. There is a twin source to his mission. He 'goes' on it 'from the Father and from the Son'. In terms of the economic Trinity we can therefore speak of a 'double sending'.

On this the Christian church soon reached general agreement. But the question arises: Does this same relational structure characterize the essential inner relationships of the persons in the Godhead?

This is, of course, the major theological issue which has divided the Eastern and Western Churches since the time of the Great Schism in 1054.[10]

The landmark Christian Confessions of Nicea (325) and Constantinople (381) affirmed the procession of the Spirit from the Father. While various ways of describing his relationship to the Son were informally employed, the definition of this relationship was not regarded by the universal church as a pressing issue. H. B. Swete neatly summarizes the situation at the dawn of the fourth century:

> The Church has begun to seek an answer to the question, 'Whence is the Spirit of God and of Christ? How is He related to the Father? How to the Son?' Already in North Africa and Alexandria the answer has been substantially given, 'He is from the Father; He is through the Son.' But no Church, no individual teacher has yet ventured to say 'He is from Both'. Nor on the other hand have we heard as yet the faintest mutterings of the retort, 'He is from the Father, and from the Father alone'.[11]

Increasingly among Christians in the Latin tradition, however, the idea of a 'double procession' developed momentum. Around the time of the Third Council of Toledo (589) the formula current among western Christians was enshrined in credal confession, so that the Spirit was said to proceed *a Patre Filioque* (from the Father and from the Son). This was the view which had been favoured by Augustine, arising from his understanding of God's essence as love.[12] The Spirit proceeded from the mutual love between Father and Son, and was himself that love, and therefore the essential bond between Father and Son. Almost inevitably his view became the dominant position among western Christians, although the confession of the *Filioque* in the liturgical use of the Creed did not pass uncontested (*e.g.* by Pope Leo III). Later, after the Great Schism, the fifteenth-century Council of Florence held that the *Filioque* doctrine was integral to right trinitarian thinking, in view of the fact that the only legitimate theological distinction between Father and Son was the paternity of the former and the filiation of the latter. The Council's Decree for the Greeks (1439) expressed this as follows:

> Since the Father has, through generation, given to the only-begotten Son everything that belongs to the Father, except being Father, the Son has also eternally from the Father from whom He is eternally born, that the Holy Spirit proceeds from the Son.[13]

In the East, however, the *Filioque* clause was rejected on ecclesiological as well as theological grounds. It had never been agreed by an ecumenical council. But, just as fundamental to eastern theologians, it appeared to threaten the unity of the Trinity by positing two sources for the Spirit, namely Father *and* Son. This accusation, expressed in a particularly vehement manner by Photius (820–91), the Patriarch of Constantinople (858–67 and 880–86), did not take account of the western insistence that the procession of the Spirit was from the Father and the Son *as one*. Indeed, while Augustine agreed that the procession was *a Patre Filoque*, he held that the Spirit principally proceeds from the Father.[14]

In addition, however, the Eastern Church was profoundly suspicious of the way in which the *Filioque* seemed to provide a theological underpinning for papal supremacy – a suspicion not without foundation in history. The view that the Son was the source of the Spirit appeared to increase further the status of the Vicar of Christ.[15]

Generally speaking, contemporary Protestant Christianity tends to be impatient with subtle theological questions and distinctions such as this. In addition, many modern exegetes hold that the 'western' position was rooted in a faulty exegesis, reading ontological procession out of statements in the New Testament which reflect only the Spirit's temporal mission.

But were eastern theologians right? It is unfortunate that the Western Church adopted a form of the creed which was not shared by the East, although in mitigation it should be remembered that Christian theology had begun to develop in two separate geographical and linguistic traditions. The *Filioque* clause was not so much the cause as the occasion of the fraction.

Given geographical and language barriers it is, perhaps, inevitable that to a certain extent the two traditions tended to talk past each other on the issue, without adequately recognizing presuppositional differences. This was especially evident in the concern of eastern theologians – that a double procession threatened the unity of the Godhead. Eastern theologians were heavily committed to a view of the Trinity in which the Father was seen as the fountainhead of the deity of the whole Godhead (and therefore of the deity of both the Son and the Spirit) and the sole guardian of the unity of the Trinity. The *Filioque* clause endangered this principle in a *prima facie* manner. On the other hand, western theology appears to have lacked sufficient theological consistency to recognize the problem. It was not until the time of Calvin that the heart of the difference was exposed. He affirmed that the Son (and by implication the Spirit) possessed underived deity. He is *autotheos*. As to personal relationships, mutuality exists: Son and Father are mutually dependent notions. But each person of the Godhead shares in one and the same underived deity. There is no room for attribution of origin of deity any more than there is room for subordinationism of essential nature.

The eastern view, by contrast, contains within itself an inherent tendency to subordinationism in the manner in which it sees the deity of both Son and Spirit as derived from the Father. Within that context the *double* procession appears as a threat to the unity of the Godhead.

Conversely, the double procession doctrine appears to provide a two-fold theological advantage. It underlines the principle that God is in his very being what he reveals himself to be, so that the economic Trinity is a true, however accommodated, reflection of the ontological Trinity. It also indicates a relationship between the Son and the Spirit which is more than economical (just as the ideas of the generation of the Son *by*, and the procession of the Spirit *from*, the Father indicate the nature of the relationship between the Father and both the Son and the Spirit).

But does the western view find any direct support in Scripture? As we have noted, in this respect the consensus of New Testament scholarship today is weighted towards a negative answer.

The *crux interpretum* here is usually seen to be John 15:26. The modern consensus is that this refers to the economic activity of the Spirit.

The following reasoning represents the Augustinian view, as that has come down to the church with later refinements (*e.g.* in Anselm of Canterbury and Thomas Aquinas):[16]

(1) The Father sends the Spirit *in the name of the Son* (Jn. 14:26); the Son also sends the Spirit *in the name of the Father* ('from the Father', Jn. 15:26). The Spirit comes, therefore, in the (single) name of both Father and Son. While this sending of the Spirit is economical, it is rooted in the personal ontological relationships of the Trinity ('Father' and 'Son' being seen as more than merely economic nomenclature).

The Son sends the Spirit from the Father. The Spirit who is thus 'sent' from the Father 'proceeds', or 'goes out' (*ekporeuomai*), from the Father (Jn. 15:26).

If these two ideas (being sent and proceeding) belong to the same order of reality, a certain redundancy seems to attach to this statement. Furthermore, a clear distinction in tenses is evident in these words: Jesus *will send* (*pempsō*, future tense); the Spirit *proceeds* (*ekporeuomai*, present continuous tense). This suggests that there is a distinction between the sending and the proceeding, and not only in the sense that the one who is 'passive' with respect to sending is 'active' with respect to proceeding. The sending is a specific future event (and is fulfilled at Pentecost); the proceeding, however, appears to be constantly true of the Spirit. It is his nature to proceed from the Father.

It is axiomatic for the integrity of theology that God is as he reveals himself to be. The sending of the Spirit by the Father in some sense mirrors the procession of the Spirit from the Father. Does this not imply that the sending of the Spirit by the Son mirrors his procession from the Son?

(2) The Spirit is the Spirit *of* the Father, since he proceeds from him. But he is also said to be the Spirit *of* the Son (Gal. 4:6) whom the Father has sent just as he sent the Son himself. As the Spirit is 'of' the Father ontologically, prior to his being sent by the Father economically, should we not also think of him as 'of' the Son ontologically as well as economically? Otherwise, what does it mean that the Spirit who searches the depths of God makes him fully known to us (*cf.* 1 Cor. 2:10–13)?

(3) It is not an unimportant consideration that without the *Filioque* we have knowledge of the Father's *ontological* as well as *economic* relationship to the Son and the Spirit, but knowledge only of the *economic* relationship between the Son and the Spirit. This would leave a *prima facie* lacuna in our knowledge of God as he is in himself, and an area of knowledge of God in which the principle that he is as he reveals himself to be would not pertain. An agnosticism in relationship to God's actual being results.

If the economic relations of the Trinity illumine the ontological relationships within the Trinity (which is the case throughout the New Testament), then, since the Spirit proceeds on his mission from both Father and Son, it is appropriate to think of him as proceeding personally within the Godhead (ontologically in this sense) from both Father and Son.

If we ask further what the procession of the Spirit means, and how it is distinguished from the Son's relationship to the Father, we may well be incapable of a wholly satisfactory (and certainly of a comprehensive) answer. On occasion this, coupled with such questions as 'To where does the Spirit proceed eternally?', have been seen as a *reductio ad absurdum* of the classical western position. But this need not trouble us. The personal, or ontological, 'procession' of the Spirit from the Father may quite acceptably be viewed as 'to the Son', and similarly 'from the Son' to the Father. In this general sense we may agree with Augustine that the Spirit is the bond of love between them.[17] His relationship to each is distinct; yet both experience the Spirit in common in mutual union and communion. This is precisely the implication of Jesus' analogy between the union of Father and Son and the union of the Son and believers (*cf.* Jn. 14:20; 17:20–23) – the one Spirit is common to both.

The mystery of the Spirit's ministry thus points to the glory of the Christian's communion with God. Our fellowship in the Spirit is with the Father and the Son (1 Jn. 1:3).[18]

4

PENTECOST TODAY?

The coming of the Spirit on the Day of Pentecost is to be interpreted, as we have seen, as a Christological event, and its pneumatological significance must be viewed in that light. One question remains, however: Does Pentecost have ongoing implications for the life of the church?

The New Testament explores in some detail the existential significance of all the focal points in the work of Christ, particularly his death, resurrection and exaltation (*cf.* Rom. 6:1ff.; Gal. 2:20; Col. 2:11 – 3:4).The same is true of the epochal event of the outpouring of the Spirit: 'we were all baptised by one Spirit into one body – whether Jews or Greeks, slave or free' (1 Cor. 12:13). This is identical language with that used elsewhere of Pentecost (Lk. 3:16 and parallels; Acts 1:5; 11:16).

Paul's statement is all-inclusive and programmatic in character. What is true of Paul and his companions and, presumably, the Corinthians, is assumed to be true of each believer (it is by Spirit-baptism that we enter the one body to which all believers belong) and of all categories of believers (Jews, Greeks, slave, free).

Several important, if controversial, questions arise here – with significant implications for constructing a theology of the church's present experience of the Spirit:

(1) What is the relation between Pentecost and the disciples' earlier experiences of the Spirit?

(2) What is the relation between Pentecost and the experiences of the Spirit recorded in Acts, in Samaria (Acts 8:4–25), in the home of Cornelius (Acts 10:1ff.), and in Ephesus (Acts 19:1–7) – in the first and last of which the coming of the Spirit appears to follow conversion as a distinct second experience?

(3) What is the relation between Pentecost and the Spirit-baptism of which Paul speaks in 1 Corinthians 12:13?

(4) Which, if any, elements of Pentecost are once for all, and which elements can be viewed as repeatable and even normative in the experience of the church?

Pentecost and the disciples

The disciples who gathered together after the resurrection of Jesus were genuine believers (*cf.* Mt. 16:15–20); they were already 'cleansed' and united to Christ (Jn. 15:1–11). By implication, this is the fruit of the work of the Spirit in their lives. But, clearly, they had not yet received the Spirit-baptism which had been promised (Acts 1:5). Their experience of the Spirit was progressive in character.

It is not possible, however, to argue from this premise to the conclusion that the disciples' experience is paradigmatic for the church, for the obvious reason that they, uniquely, span the period of transition from old to new covenant faith. Their experience is epoch-crossing, and consequently atypical and non-paradigmatic in nature. By necessity their entry into the full measure of the Spirit's ministry took place in two distinct stages, reflecting a pattern of both continuity (the same Spirit) and discontinuity (only at Pentecost does he come in his capacity and ministry as the Spirit of the exalted Christ). This pattern is rooted in the emergence of the new era out of the old. There is, therefore, a singularity about their experience, just as there was about the experience of Jesus.

Caesarea, Samaria, Ephesus

What, then, of the coming of the Spirit in Samaria (Acts 8:9–25), in the home of Cornelius (Acts 10:44–48) and in Ephesus (Acts 19:1–7)?

The most straightforward of these events takes place in the household of Cornelius, and is described in terms which echo Pentecost. Identical language is used in relationship to the Spirit's coming: *outpouring* (Acts 2:17–18, 33; 10:45); *baptism* (Acts 1:5; 11:16); and *gift* (Acts 2:38; 11:17). The phenomenon of speaking in other tongues is repeated (Acts 2:4; 10:6). Furthermore, Peter specifically sees an analogy between the events: 'The Holy Spirit came on them as he had come on us at the beginning. Then I remembered what the Lord had said: "John baptised . . . you will be baptised with the Holy Spirit" . . . God gave them the same gift as he gave us . . .' (Acts 11:15–17).

Peter's interpretation of this incident is that, in keeping with the programme of Acts 1:8, the coming of the Spirit to the household of Cornelius marks the breakthrough of the gospel into the Gentile world. This is confirmed by the Jerusalem church: 'When they heard this, they had no further objections and praised God, saying, "So then, God has granted even the Gentiles repentance unto life"' (Acts 11:18). The event is viewed as epochal, programmatic rather than paradigmatic.

Nevertheless, in the case of the Samaritans and the Ephesians there appears to be a distinct second stage to their experience of the Spirit. The Samaritans 'believed Philip as he preached the good news of the kingdom of God and the name of Jesus Christ' and 'were baptised', but only when Peter and John came was prayer made for them 'that they might receive the Holy Spirit, because the Holy Spirit had not yet come upon any of them; they had simply been baptised into the name of the Lord Jesus. Then Peter and John placed their hands on them, and they received the Holy Spirit' (Acts 8:12, 15–17).

Later, Paul asked the Ephesians, 'Did you receive the Holy Spirit when you believed?' The answer, at this late stage in the narrative of Acts, is startling: 'We have not even heard that there is a Holy Spirit.' After preaching Christ to them, 'When Paul placed his hands on them, the Holy Spirit came on them, and they spoke in tongues and prophesied' (Acts 19:1–7).

It has often been argued, on the basis of the experience of the apostles at Pentecost and of both the Samaritans and the Ephesians, that Luke–Acts suggests a model of two-stage entry into the fullness of the Spirit's blessing. While variously described, these stages are ordinarily thought of as:

(1) Regeneration by the Spirit (conversion-initiation).

(2) Baptism with the Spirit.

Thus, at some point during the period described by the Gospels, the apostles were regenerated. Later, at Pentecost, they experienced a new work of the Spirit: they were baptized and filled with the Spirit and spoke in other tongues as an evidence of this new stage of his activity in their lives. In this, it is claimed, they are to be viewed as models of the Spirit's two-stage, or at least two-dimensional, new covenant work.

In keeping with this perspective, in Samaria and Ephesus we similarly encounter believers (*i.e.* people already regenerated) who have not yet received (in the sense of being baptized with) the Spirit. This second stage is conceptually, and in these cases chronologically, separated and separable from regeneration.

We have already seen that, while the experience of the apostles was undoubtedly two-stage in character, it is not *prima facie* paradigmatic in nature. Yet, does not the two-stage pattern which emerges later in Acts indicate that such a pattern was paradigmatic, or at least commonplace, in the church?

A two-stage view of the Spirit's work is characteristic not only in Pentecostal and charismatic but also in Catholic traditions. In the latter, the individual is confirmed into the communion of the Spirit by the laying-on of hands, usually in the context of a quasi-physical apostolic succession (*cf.* Acts 8:17; 19:6); in the former, baptism with the Spirit with its most common manifestation in the gift of tongues is seen as a further stage in spiritual experience, distinct and separable (even if not necessarily chronologically separated) from conversion.

In Luke–Acts, as we have argued, Pentecost is portrayed as a redemptive-historical event. It is not primarily to be interpreted existentially and pneumatologically, but eschatologically and Christologically. By its very nature it shares in the decisive once-for-all character of the entire Christ-event (Jesus' death, resurrection and ascension). In this context, the Acts of the Apostles is not so much 'the Acts of the Holy Spirit' but 'the [continuing] Acts of Jesus Christ through the Holy Spirit' (the implication of Acts 1:1–4 being that the event promised in Acts 1:5 marks a new epoch in all that Jesus himself as the exalted Lord would do and teach).

Interpreted within this framework – which Acts itself provides for us – the events at Samaria and Caesarea mark the second and third stages of the three decisive points of advance in the spread of the kingdom of Christ outlined in Acts 1:8:

(1) The gospel comes to Jerusalem on the Day of Pentecost.

(2) The gospel comes to Samaria. Acts 8, with its description of the remarkable awakening of faith through Philip's ministry, followed by the visit of Peter and John as an apostolic delegation (Acts 8:14) and the subsequent bestowal of the Spirit, makes best sense when understood within the context of the specific stages of advance of the apostolic gospel promised by Jesus. For that reason, while it may be possible to do so, it is not necessary to argue that the Samaritans were not yet converted.[1]

(3) The gospel comes to Caesarea as representative of the Gentile world ('the ends of the earth', Acts 1:8; *cf.* especially Acts 11:18). The coverage given to this event in Acts (sixty-six verses) indicates its decisive programmatic importance for Luke. It is more than merely a 'narrative of surprising conversions', a paradigm for every age. Rather, it is a specific and strategic development in the entire mission programme of Acts 1:8.

The events at Ephesus do not belong to the same order as those at Samaria and Caesarea. The group which Paul encountered, described as 'some disciples' (Acts 19:1), is deliberately presented as idiosyncratic and atypical. Luke gives us a series of signals which indicate that he did not view these men as Christians in the New Testament sense:

(1) The incident is set within the context of the inadequate understanding of the gospel which marked the early ministry of Apollos; Luke specifically mentions the fact that 'he knew only the baptism of John' (Acts 18:25).[2]

(2) Those who knew only John's baptism may have constituted a distinct group in Ephesus; they are described as '*some* disciples' in a context in which there were possibly larger numbers of Christians. Luke explicitly states there were only twelve men in the group. While called 'disciples', it would be wooden to argue that since this elsewhere describes genuine

Christians all those thus described must have been so. In fact these seem, for all practical purposes, to have been disciples of John the Baptist.

(3) They had not received Christian baptism. It was only in co-ordination with their later Christian baptism and the laying-on of hands that 'the Holy Spirit came on them, and they spoke in tongues and prophesied' (Acts 19:6). The marks of the inbreaking of the new covenant were only then evidenced. Like the first disciples at Pentecost, many of whom had also received John's baptism, these twelve men were thus in transit from the era of expectation to that of fulfilment.

It is sometimes argued against the two-stage doctrine that it is a basic hermeneutical principle that we should not seek to derive doctrine from the Acts of the Apostles any more than we would find from the books of Kings. We are to find doctrine that is already formulated elsewhere *illustrated* in the historical narrat-ives. This is a generally valuable principle. The structure of Christian theology should be rooted in the theological exposition and prescription in Scripture and not derived from historical incidents (which, while factual, are not necessarily normative, and themselves may require further theological interpretation).

But this principle (which has itself been fiercely contested) is, in this case, not germane to the argument. For here, the structure and theological flow of Acts itself indicates that these events are not to be thought of as paradigmatic but, each in its own context, as *sui generis*.

Acts does not hold out to us the two-stage experience of the apostles as normative for future Christians. Here Peter's *apologia* for the incident at Caesarea is illuminating. He specifically identifies the experience of the household of Cornelius with the experience of the disciples on the Day of Pentecost (Acts 11:15, 'The Holy Spirit came on them *as he had come on us at the beginning*') and interprets the event in these terms: 'God gave them the same gift as he gave us, who believed [*pisteusasin*; perhaps better treated as inceptive, "when we believed"] in the Lord Jesus Christ' (Acts 11:17). While the disciples certainly believed in Jesus prior to Pentecost, what was new and distinctive about their faith was the nature of its object: whereas before faith was correlative with Christ in the days of his humiliation, it was now correlative with Christ incarnate in his new status as exalted Lord according to the messianic promise (Ps. 110:1).

What was necessarily effected in the apostles' experience in two stages because of the very nature of redemptive history now becomes a unified reality in the experience of later believers. Saving faith is now absolutely correlative with Christ as Lord; and thus to believe is to enter into the same gift as the first disciples received at Pentecost, namely the Holy Spirit. The tongues and prophecy manifested in Acts 10:46, 19:6 and possibly 8:17 were not evidences of a second and normatively distinct existential experience, but signs of the redemptive-historical breakthrough into the new covenant era reaching a further significant staging-post.

The perspective of the New Testament, therefore, is not that Pentecost (or the Acts as a whole) provides us with a two-stage paradigm for personal experience of the Spirit, but rather that at the point of faith we participate individually in the effect of the outpouring of the Spirit at Pentecost.

Abraham Kuyper provides a graphic analogy to illustrate the comparison between the experience of the Spirit before and after Pentecost, and to explain the outpouring of the Spirit thereafter. For all its limitations, it underlines the fact that Pentecost and the events which follow it require an appropriate grid if they are to be interpreted aright:

> Suppose that a city whose citizens for ages have been drinking each from his own cistern proposes to construct a reservoir that will supply every home. When the work is completed the water is allowed to run through the system of mains and pipes into every house . . .
>
> Suppose that the city above referred to consisted of a lower and an upper part, both to be supplied by the same reservoir . . . the distribution of the water took place but once, which was the formal opening of the waterworks, and could take place but once; while the distribution of the water in the upper city, although extraordinary, was but an after-effect of the former event . . . on Pentecost He [*i.e.* the Spirit] is poured out into the body, but only to quench the thirst of one

85

part, *i.e.* the Jewish . . . hence there is an *original* outpouring in Jerusalem on the day of Pentecost, and a *supplementary* outpouring in Caesarea for the gentile part of the Church; both of the same nature, but each bearing its own special character.

Besides these there are some isolated outpourings of the Holy Spirit, attended by the laying on of the apostles' hands . . . from time to time new connections are made between individual houses and the city reservoir, so new parts of the body of Christ were added to the church from without, into whom the Holy Spirit was poured forth from the body as into new members . . .[3]

What took place in Samaria, in the house of Cornelius, and in Ephesus must be interpreted in terms of the unique historical setting of the early church. Pentecost is not 'repeated' any more than the death or resurrection of Christ is a repeatable event. Rather, we enter into it in such a way that the Spirit is poured out into our hearts through faith in Christ (*cf.* Rom. 5:5). Each one thus drinks of the Spirit for himself or herself (1 Cor. 12:13).

This becomes all the clearer when we view Pentecost as an aspect of the work of Christ, not a Spirit event separate from it and in addition to it. It is the visible manifestation of a coronation. The events of the Day of Pentecost are the public expressions of the hidden reality that Christ has been exalted as the Lord of glory and that his messianic request for the Spirit, made as Mediator on our behalf, has been granted.

As we have already seen in part, Peter's statement in Acts 2:33 draws attention to this fulfilment of the messianic promise of Psalm 2:6–8 ('I have installed my King on Zion, my holy hill . . . Ask of me, and I will make the nations your inheritance, the ends of the earth your possession'). The ascended Christ has now made this request, asking for the Spirit to bring about the fulfilment of the promise which itself came in stages (*cf.* Gal. 3:13–14; Je. 31:31ff.; Jn. 14:16). Christ's request was granted. Pentecost, like the visible manifestations of every coronation, is by its very nature *sui generis*. It is no more repeatable *as an event* than is the crucifixion or the resurrection or the ascension of our Lord. It is an event in redemptive history (*historia salutis*), and should not be squeezed into the grid of the application of redemption (*ordo salutis*).

The coming of the Spirit is, therefore, the evidence of the enthronement of Christ, just as the resurrection is the evidence of the efficacy of the death of Christ as atonement (Rom. 4:24). This is not to say that Pentecost has no existential dimension or contemporary relevance. But it does mean that we should no more anticipate a 'personal Pentecost' than that we will experience a personal Jordan, wilderness, Gethsemane or Golgotha. While such language has often been popularly employed, it is theologically misleading. Pentecost itself is no more repeatable than is the crucifixion, or the empty tomb, or the ascension. To assume that it was would be tantamount to producing a 'pentecostal' form of the medieval mass, repeating what is unrepeatable and consequently diminishing, if not actually denying, its true significance.[4]

Different Spirit-baptisms?

What, then, is the relationship between the Spirit-baptism described in Acts 2 and the Spirit-baptism described by Paul in 1 Corinthians 12:13?

The New Testament heavily underlines the principle that Christ's crucifixion, resurrection and ascension all carry profound implications for our present experience. Believers share in the implications of all redemptive-historical events such as Christ's death, burial, resurrection and reign (Rom. 6:1ff.; Gal. 2:20; Col. 2:9 – 3:4). Thus, while Pentecost is also once for all time in character, implications of the baptism with the Spirit which took place on that occasion overflow the banks of that Day and flow on, down through the centuries. Just as the blood of Christ cleanses men and women from every tribe, tongue, people and nation (Rev. 5:9), so the Spirit flows from the riven side of Christ on Pentecost into Jerusalem, and from there spreads throughout Judea, gathering momentum on to Samaria and indeed to the uttermost parts of the earth (Acts 1:8). All who come to believe in Jesus Christ as Lord receive the same gift as the disciples did. Consequently, believers enter into the implications of Pentecost, just as they enter into the implications of Christ's death, resurrection and ascension: 'We were all baptised by one Spirit [*en heni pneumati . . . ebaptisthēmen*] into one body' (1 Cor. 12:13).

It has frequently been argued that Paul is speaking here about a Spirit-baptism distinct from the Spirit-baptism prophesied by John and Jesus and experienced at Pentecost. In the latter baptism, Christ is the baptizer and the Spirit is the element; in this baptism, the Spirit is the baptizer and the body of Christ is the object into which we are baptized. But as James Dunn notes:

> In the NT *en* with *baptizein* never designates the one who performs the baptism; on the contrary, it always indicates the element in which the baptisand is immersed (or with which he is deluged) – except, of course, when it is part of a fuller phrase . . .[5]

It would be contrary to a natural interpretation to read words elsewhere used as a description of Christ baptizing with the Spirit at Pentecost (Mt. 3:11; Mk. 1:8; Lk. 3:16; Jn. 1:33; Acts 1:5; 11:16) as though they denoted not merely a chronologically different experience but a quite different baptism. Ockham's razor is at times as relevant in biblical theology as it was in medieval philosophy!

In 1 Corinthians 12:13 Paul indicates that all believers are baptized with the Spirit and drink the water of the Spirit. Elements of the Pentecost event are thus reduplicated in believers in every age. But how can we distinguish the redemptive-historical (once-for-all) aspects of Pentecost from its existential and repeatable aspects?

Several elements of Pentecost clearly belong to its significance as a once-for-all event. The waiting of the disciples belongs to this category, as do the physical manifestations of the sound of the rushing wind and the tongues of fire. These are not repeated even within the book of Acts itself.

The outbreak of tongues is, however, repeated in the household of Cornelius (Acts 10:46) and in Ephesus (Acts 19:6). Many commentators assume from the visible character of the Spirit's presence in Samaria (Acts 8:17–18) that tongues were probably in evidence there too. The tongues of Pentecost were, therefore, repeated. But, as we have seen, these three incidents are regarded within Acts itself as idiosyncratic. The phenomenon is not recorded in the case of others (*e.g.* the Ethiopian treasurer, Saul of Tarsus, Lydia, the Philippian jailer). These repetitions are aspects of the distinct significance of the event in which they occur. Samaria and Caesarea are staging-posts in the advance of the programme of Acts 1:8; Ephesus marks a transition from the world of the old covenant and John's baptism, to the world of the new covenant and the Spirit-baptism which comes from Christ. Within the book of Acts itself (whatever else may be true of the rest of the New Testament), the tongues of Pentecost are not thought of as a normally repeated element in the initiation experience of later believers.

But there is a further aspect of Pentecost. Jesus promised his disciples that the coming of the Spirit would bring 'power', as a consequence of which they would be his witnesses throughout the earth (Lk. 24:49; Acts 1:8). On the Day of Pentecost, the disciples were 'filled with the Holy Spirit' as a result of which they spoke in tongues. While the repetition of speaking in tongues is rarely mentioned in Acts, the empowering in which the Spirit filled individuals is repeated on a number of occasions.

Luke–Acts speaks of being filled with or being full of the Spirit as an ongoing condition, but also describes particular occasions when individuals appear to experience distinct fillings. In the case of the former the *plēroō* family of words is used (*e.g.* Lk. 4:1; Acts 6:3; *cf.* Eph. 5:18); in the latter the verb *pimplēmi* is employed (*e.g.* Lk. 1:41, 67; Acts 2:4; 4:8, 31; 9:17). In the former sense, to be filled with the Spirit refers predominantly to exhibiting the fruit of the Spirit in a life that is under the lordship of the Spirit (*cf.* Eph. 5:18). But the latter occasions refer to a special influx of ability and power in the service of the kingdom. This is what is in view in Acts 1:8 and evidenced in Acts 2:4. Interestingly this seems to be invariably related to the speech of those whom the Spirit fills. They receive 'power' to be Christ's witnesses.

This elapse of power at Pentecost and the filling of the Spirit, while extraordinary in itself, is not seen in Acts as an isolated phenomenon, or as tied to the specific programme of Acts 1:8. Its repetition does not follow that pattern. This aspect of the Spirit's work seems therefore to be repeatable.

Revival

A related aspect of Pentecost is mirrored in what we often call 'revival', when professing believers are aroused and non-Christians are brought into the kingdom in large numbers, each with an individual sense of sin and need, but in the context of a widespread sense of the presence and power of the Holy Spirit.

In some respects, Pentecost may be viewed as the inaugural revival of the New Testament epoch.[6] Certainly the description of the conviction of sin experienced, the 'sense of awe' (Acts 2:43) which was evoked, and the detailed model of what church life ought to be (Acts 2:44–47) point in that direction. This is what revival is. To develop further the metaphor of the flow of water, we might say that revival is the unstopping of the pent-up energies of the Spirit of God breaking down the dams which have been erected against his convicting and converting ministry in whole communities of individuals, as happened at Pentecost and in the 'awakenings' which have followed.

In these contexts, duplicating the pattern of the Day of Pentecost, the proclamation of Christians appears to possess a special access of 'power' as the Spirit bears witness to Christ along, with and through the witness of disciples (Jn. 15:26–27; cf. Acts 4:33; 6:8; 10:38). This is evident in Philip's mission in Samaria. Paul's letters indicate that he experienced this in a number of strategic centres in the course of his journeys (e.g. 1 Cor. 2:4; 1 Thes. 1:5).

The powerful coming of the Spirit by no means solved all problems. The spiritual quickenings which took place always seem to have had mixed consequences and even to have been mixed in character, being open to the destructive influences of spiritual pride and wrong-headedness, as in Corinth. That the same is true in later 'awakenings' in the history of the church should therefore not surprise us.

Jonathan Edwards, the New England theologian of revival, may be guilty of no more than over-emphasis in writing that:

> It may be observed that from the fall of man to our day, the work of redemption in its effect has mainly been carried on by remarkable communications of the

> Spirit of God. Though there be a more constant
> influence of God's Spirit always in some degree
> attending His ordinances, yet the way in which the
> greatest things have been done towards carrying on
> the work always has been by remarkable effusions at
> special seasons of mercy.[7]

Such occasions may well be what is in view in Peter's words in
Acts 3:19: 'Repent, then, and turn to God, so that your sins may
be wiped out, *that times of refreshing may come from the Lord*, and
that he may send the Christ . . .'. The order of the clauses here
(forgiveness, refreshing, return of Christ) suggests that seasons
of renewal and revival are in view.

Thus we find two phenomena in the pattern of Acts. We are
given 'case-studies' in the Spirit's activity in personal regeneration and conversion. But it is by the signal empowering of the
Spirit (first exemplified at Pentecost) that monumental
advances take place in the kingdom of Christ. The inaugural
outpouring of the Spirit creates ripples throughout the world as
the Spirit continues to come in power. Pentecost is the
epicentre; but the earthquake gives forth further after-shocks.
Those rumbles continue through the ages. Pentecost itself is not
repeated; but a theology of the Spirit which did not give rise to
prayer for his coming in power would not be a theology of *ruach*!

The goal

We have seen, then, that there are these two dimensions to
Pentecost: the redemptive-historical and the personal-existen-
tial. The former is once for all and unrepeatable; the latter
elements should be viewed as aspects of the ongoing ministry of
the Spirit.

In addition, the Spirit's task is to restore glory to a fallen
creation. As Calvin well says, this world was made as a theatre for
God's glory. Throughout it he displays visibly the perfections of
his invisible nature. Particularly in man and woman, his image,
that glory was to be reflected. But they refused to 'glorify' God
(Rom. 1:21); they defiled the reflector (Rom. 1:28) and fell
short of his glory (Rom. 3:23).

But now, in Christ who is 'the radiance of God's glory' (Heb.

1:3), that glory is restored. Having become flesh for us, he has now been exalted in our flesh yet in glory. The eschatological goal of creation has been consummated in him as its firstfruits. Now he sends his Spirit, the intimate companion of his entire incarnation, to recover glory in us. So it is that 'we, who with unveiled faces reflect the Lord's glory, are being transformed into his likeness with ever-increasing glory, which comes from the Lord, who is the Spirit [or, the Lord of the Spirit]' (2 Cor. 3:18).

The purpose for which the Spirit is given is, therefore, nothing less than the reproduction of the image of God, that is transformation into the likeness of Christ who is himself the image of God. To receive the Spirit is to be inaugurated into the effects of this ongoing ministry.

Receiving the Holy Spirit

The New Testament describes initiation into the fellowship of the Spirit from two basic perspectives: the divine giving, and the human receiving. The Spirit is given by the Father (Lk. 11:13). But he is also *received* by the individual (Jn. 7:39; Acts 19:2; Rom. 8:15; Gal. 3:2).

In the one context in which he reflects on the psychology involved in this reception, Paul indicates that it takes place 'by believing what you heard' by contrast with 'observing the law' (Gal. 3:2, 5). The Spirit is received in the context of coming to faith in Christ the Lord. For Paul, therefore, in the normal pattern of experience in the Gentile world, the Spirit is not received separately from faith-initiation into Christ. It is in believing into Christ that the Spirit of Christ is received. For believing into Christ brings with it the reality of the receiving of Christ and his indwelling. This is one and the same reality as the reception and indwelling of the Spirit, since it is in and by the Spirit that Christ comes to indwell us. As Paul's interplay of the indwelling Christ and the indwelling Spirit in Romans 8:8–9 makes clear, the two realities are economically one and experienced as one by the individual. There is no other mode of receiving the Spirit, then, than by faith's reception of Christ. To have Christ is to have the Spirit. How this takes place, and what its implications are, provide the themes of the chapters which follow.

5

THE SPIRIT OF ORDER

The Spirit of God, poured out on the church at Pentecost, is a Spirit of restoration.[1] As such, he came first on Jesus as the head of the new creation, equipping him for service as the second man and last Adam who would restore a righteous dominion (1 Cor. 15:45–49; Gn. 1:26–28; Ps. 8:3–8). We do not yet see this fulfilled (Heb. 2:8); the creation is still groaning in the labour pains which are harbingers of that day; Christian believers similarly groan inwardly as they long for it (Rom. 8:22–25). In this sense, the present activity of the Spirit, while eschatological in the sense that it marks the inauguration of the last-day glory, is sub-eschatological in the sense that it is marked by incompleteness. That glory, which God has restored in Christ, the head of the new creation, awaits a yet-future event.

The post-Pentecost activity of the Spirit, therefore, spreads through history like concentric ripples in a pool. As in the Old Testament era, so in the New, his activity is soteriological, communal, cosmic and eschatological, and involves the transformation of the individual, the governing of the church and the world, and the bringing in of the new age.

Indications of this pattern are already present in the narrative of the Acts of the Apostles. People are brought to faith in Christ as Redeemer and Lord through the power of the Spirit (Acts 1:8), either in considerable numbers (Acts 2:41; 5:14; 6:7; 8:14; 11:24) or as isolated individuals (Acts 8:26–40, esp. v. 29). The new community is formed and sustained under the governing activity of the Spirit (Acts 6:3, 5; 7:55; 10:19, 44–48; 13:2–4; 15:28; 16:6–10); the powers of the age to come are let loose in the present age through the ministry of the apostles (Heb. 2:4; 2 Cor. 12:12; Acts 3:1–10; 5:12). Jesus thus continues the work of building his church which he began during his incarnation (*cf.* Mt. 16:18; Acts 1:2).

Clearly, if we are to be brought from an inglorious death in sin (Eph. 2:1–4) to share the glory of Christ, there is a long way to travel. How are we to trace the Spirit's path and movements?

Order of salvation

In the history of theology, detailed critical examination of soteriological issues arose only after the issues of theology proper and Christology were settled in some detail. In the patristic period, questions concerning God's being and Christ's person and natures predominated. Even the issue of the deity of the Spirit was settled almost as a secondary implication of the deity of Christ. Thereafter, questions concerning the work of Christ came to the fore with discussions of the so-called classical, Anselmian and Abelardian theories of the atonement. Only in the discussions of the Middle Ages and the Reformation period were more definitive statements on soteriology sought and provided. The Roman Catholic Church's classic exposition of justification was promulgated as late as the Council of Trent (1545–63). Even in this context, some delegates nursed hopes that an evangelical (Lutheran) statement on justification by faith might emerge.

The interpretation of how redemption was accomplished by Christ carries inevitable implications for the nature of its application to the individual. In this context, the leading feature of the theology of the Middle Ages was the linking of saving grace to the sacraments, and therefore to the priestly ministry of the church, in the process of being justified (*processus justificationis*). The work of the Spirit was thus enclosed within the administration of the seven sacraments. Such sacramentalism produced a mechanism which, certainly from the Reformation perspective, denied the sovereign work of the Spirit which was not dependent on the administration of the rites of the church.

Medieval theology was largely committed to a *process* of justification, and therefore placed great weight on the mode of preparation for grace. In the process of prevenient grace moving the will to hate sin and desire justice or justification (*justitia*), the individual was disposed to receive habitual grace. Imperfect sorrow for sin (*attritio*), which lacked the qualities of perfected grief (*contritio*), was compensated for by means of the sacrament of penance. No longer a once-in-a-lifetime rite providing the opportunity to return to the grace of baptism, penance thus became a regular feature in the ongoing process towards *justitia.* At the root of this lay the Augustinian notion that justification meant *to be made righteous (justum facere)*, not (as in the biblical theology of the Reformation) to be declared, or counted, or constituted righteous in God's sight. When justification was confused with internal righteousness and viewed subjectively rather than forensically, short of perfect personal holiness, justification could never be complete. As a result, apart from the rarely granted privilege of special revelation to the individual, the blessings of justification could never be assured; hence the denial of assurance by the Council of Trent and the affirmation of the formidable Jesuit theologian Robert Bellarmine (1542–1621) that assurance was the greatest of all Protestant heresies.[2]

Discussions of justification were to lead, eventually, to the Protestant Reformation. Indeed, in this context, Martin Luther's struggles towards Christ and the Reformation hinged in large measure on the transformation (and in important respects the *reversal*) of the medieval *ordo salutis* that burst on his consciousness through his new understanding of Romans 1:16–17. He now saw that Paul spoke not about his working for the attainment of righteousness, but about God's provision of it in the gospel. A powerful rethinking took place in his understanding of the *ordo salutis*, and the text that he had mis-interpreted by means of his Roman *ordo salutis* now instead became the open gate to Paradise.

It is by no means either an accident or an exaggeration that the French-born second-generation Reformer of Geneva in Switzerland, John Calvin, has been described, as we have noted, as 'the theologian of the Holy Spirit'. Of course, the new understanding of the nature of justification (imputed, not infused, alien, not self-attained, righteousness) was a central feature of the new teaching. But this was accompanied by a de-sacramentalizing of the application of redemption, and a corresponding restoration of the role of the Spirit. Not that the sacraments were denuded of their power, so much as subordi-nated to the joint action of the Word and the Spirit.

In the medieval church, the sacraments acted as milestones on the road to justification. Wherever Tridentine Catholicism later held sway, all the blessings of union with Christ were attributed to and mediated through the instrumental causation of the sacramental system, and especially the mass and eucharist. By contrast, in the Reformation teaching it was emphasized that the Holy Spirit brought the individual directly into fellowship with Christ, of which fellowship the sacraments were seen as signs and seals.

Thus, if the question, 'How is the Spirit related to the Father and the Son?' lay at the heart of the first great divide in Christendom, the question, 'How does the Spirit apply the blessings of Christ to the individual?' came to lie at the heart of the second great divide.

The pattern by which the Spirit works is therefore of great significance. It has come to be discussed under the Latin rubric *ordo salutis*, the order of salvation.[3]

The term is, at least in general, self-explanatory. *Ordo* means a series, a line, an order of succession. Cicero used *ordo* for a row of seats in the theatre, or a bank of oars in a vessel. When applied to the application of redemption, *ordo salutis* denotes the orderly arrangement of the various aspects of salvation in its bestowal on men and women. In particular it seeks to answer this question: 'In what ways are the various aspects of the application of redemption (such as justification, regeneration, conversion and sanctification) related to each other?' Discussions of *ordo salutis* thus attempt to unpack the inner coherence and logic of the Spirit's application of the work of Christ.

This is in fact a more ancient question than medieval discussions of it, and surfaces already in Scripture, for example in the controversies over the relationship between grace and law. Paul explicitly indicates that this soteriological issue is also a pneumatological one when he writes: 'Did you receive the Spirit by observing the law, or by believing what you heard?' (Gal. 3:2).

It is easy to become impatient with certain aspects of the discussion of the *ordo salutis*. For one thing, there is disagreement about the order involved even among theologians who belong self-consciously to the Reformation tradition, and increasingly there has been criticism of the idea itself. Furthermore, it is natural for the Christian enthusiast to feel that theologians have spent too much time talking about the order of salvation instead of proclaiming the gospel! But the antithesis implied in such a reaction (proclamation of the gospel *versus* order of salvation) is flawed. For the way we present the gospel invariably expresses an implicit understanding of the *ordo salutis*. Moreover, the discussion is important in heightening awareness of the logic embedded in our understanding of the way the Spirit works in the individual, as well as clarifying the matrix of thought which governs the way in which the Christian gospel is proclaimed.

Which order?

The motivation in the older classical discussions of the *ordo salutis* was to discover not a chronological arrangement, but a logical one; the order in view was not primarily one of temporal priority, but was focused on logical relationships, on an order of nature.[4]

In the English-speaking tradition, the classic example of an *ordo salutis* is to be found in the work of the early English Puritan William Perkins (1558–1602). In his work *A Golden Chaine*,[5] he traced the causes of all the various aspects of redemption back to their fountain in the person of Christ and the eternal purposes of God. In addition, Perkins produced a visual catechism, which could be followed by those who were unable to read his various expositions.

This formulation was largely dependent on Romans 8:28–30,

and especially Paul's statement that those God predestined he called, justified and glorified. These Perkins saw as distinct elements in an unbreakable sequence, one folding into another in a 'golden chain' of salvation. In fact, Perkins' diagram had something of the appearance of a sequence of links closed in on themselves.

The idea and its execution had a certain pastoral brilliance. In fact, although it was rarely recognized, Perkins' model (the theology of which can be traced back to the influence of Calvin's successor in Geneva, Theodore Beza) came to dominate evangelical thinking over the succeeding centuries. Even where his name was unknown, his Christological centre weakened, and the specifics of his own reformed *ordo salutis* rejected, the model of a chain of causes and effects formed the context for centuries of evangelical discussions and controversies. Disagreement might arise as to whether, for example, the new birth causally preceded faith (as in the Calvinist construction, which emphasizes the necessary priority of the divine activity in view of the depravity of human nature) or whether faith and repentance preceded regeneration (as in the Arminian view, which presupposed that responsibility to believe must entail the natural ability to do so). But it was almost never recognized that some form of Perkins' 'chain' model was the common denominator to both and provided the matrix within which the discussion of the inner work of the Spirit was pursued.

The failure to recognize this meant that it was rarely, if ever, asked whether the model of a causal 'chain' was either biblical or a completely adequate model. In more recent discussions, however, this model has come in for considerable criticism. Such passages as Romans 8:28–30 have been interpreted as reflecting less on an order for the application of redemption, and more on the fullness and richness of the blessing of salvation. In this perspective, to view Paul as though he were analysing an order of events is therefore an exegetical misconstruction. If he were doing so he would surely have included the idea of sanctification. This omission tended to puzzle earlier writers. But for a modern theologian like G. C. Berkouwer, it indicates that Paul did not have an order of discrete elements in view at all. It would be inconceivable in such an order that the element of sanctification could be absent.

THE SPIRIT OF ORDER

Berkouwer's criticism is by no means novel, but in it he has been joined by such influential figures as Karl Barth and Otto Weber.[6] While it might be possible to appeal to the relationship between predestination and conformity to the image of Christ within this context as indicative of the role of sanctification, its absence in what is presumably a programmatic statement is surely significant. Had Paul's theology been shaped here by Perkins-style *ordo salutis* categories, he would surely have included sanctification.

A broader concern is also relevant here. When expressed in terms of the model of a chain of causes and effects, the traditional *ordo salutis* runs the danger of displacing Christ from the central place in soteriology. The fruits of his work may be related *to one another* in the chain of cause-and-effect sequence, rather than viewed fundamentally in relation to the work of the Spirit in bringing us into union and communion with Christ himself. Thus, election is spoken of as the cause of regeneration, which in turn is the cause of faith, of which sanctification and perseverance are the invariable and inevitable effects. The relation of each to Christ himself is thus obscured or even minimized.

The danger here is that the medieval *sacramental* chain of causes and effects has simply been replaced by a post-Reformation chain of *subjective* causes and effects. In both, the ministry of the Spirit of Christ is dislocated from its central role. Luther's problem, that man is by nature *curvatus in se* (turned in on himself instead of outwards in reliance upon the Lord), remains unresolved. The focus of attention is on what has been done *in* us, obscuring the One who is the author and finisher of faith, and our union with him. Thus H. N. Ridderbos writes:

> In Paul's preaching there is no such thing as a systematic development of the *ordo salutis*, a detailed doctrine of the anthropological application of salvation. The cause for this is not only that the character of Paul's doctrine is not 'systematic' in the scientific sense of the word, but above all that his viewpoint is a different one.[7]

These criticisms carry considerable weight, although they are often exaggerated and some of them have been unjustly laid at the feet of William Perkins.[8] Nevertheless, it is true that when it was loosed from the rigorous Christocentric and deeply covenantal structure in which Perkins and others embedded it, the *ordo salutis* could easily slide into an unhealthy subjectivism.

These reservations notwithstanding, however, the real question is not so much whether we employ the notion of *ordo salutis*. We cannot avoid *orderly* thought when it comes to theology. After all, the Spirit is a Spirit of order (1 Cor. 14:33)! As Hendrikus Berkhof wryly comments on Barth's stringent criticisms of the *ordo salutis*, when Barth writes about soteriology in his *Church Dogmatics*, 'he too needs a kind of logical order'![9] No-one, surely, holds that regeneration and conversion, justification and sanctification are randomly related. The question, therefore, is: On what principle or model is the order of the Spirit's work to be construed? A better model will be found in the notion that is central to the whole ministry of the Spirit in the New Testament.

Union with Christ

The central role of the Spirit is to reveal Christ and to unite us to him and to all those who participate in his body. Just as the indwelling of Christ and the indwelling of the Spirit are two aspects of one and the same reality in the New Testament, so to sustain us 'in Christ' (an expression which, with its variants, Paul uses around 160 times) is the heart and soul of the Spirit's ministry.

The implication is that the model we employ for structuring the Spirit's ministry should be that of union with Christ. Every facet of the application of Christ's work ought to be related to the way in which the Spirit unites us to Christ himself, and viewed as directly issuing from personal fellowship with him. The dominant motif and architectonic principle of the order of salvation should therefore be union with Christ in the Spirit.

This lies at the heart of evangelical theology, as is evident from the way in which Calvin opens Book III of his *Institutes*:

> We must now examine this question. How do we receive those benefits which the Father bestowed on his only-begotten Son – not for Christ's own private use, but that he might enrich poor and needy men?

First we must understand that as long as Christ remains outside of us, and we are separated from him, all that he has suffered and done for the salvation of the human race remains useless and of no value for us . . . We also, in turn, are said to be 'engrafted into him' (Rom. 11:17), and to 'put on Christ' (Gal. 3:27); for, as I have said, all that he possesses is nothing to us until we grow into one body with him. It is true that we obtain this by faith. Yet . . . reason itself teaches us to climb higher and to examine into the secret energy of the Spirit, by which we come to enjoy Christ and all his benefits.[10]

Calvin has further illuminating comments in his commentaries in this connection, which underline how deeply rooted in evangelical theology is the principle that union with Christ should serve as the framework within which the ministry of the Spirit is to be considered. Commenting on Romans 6:11 ('Count yourselves dead to sin but alive to God in Christ Jesus') he says:

I prefer to retain Paul's words *in* Christ Jesus, rather than to render with Erasmus *by* Christ Jesus because this conveys more clearly the ingrafting by which we are made one with Christ.[11]

Similarly, commenting on 1 Corinthians 1:5 ('In him you have been enriched in every way – in all your speaking and in all your knowledge') Calvin says:

I preferred to keep the phrase *in* him rather than change it to *by* him because in my opinion it is more vivid and forceful. For we are enriched in Christ because we are members of his body, and we have been ingrafted into him; and furthermore since we have been made one with him, he shares with us all that he has received from the Father.[12]

Calvin is underlining here (and in similar comments elsewhere) that the blessings of redemption ought not to be viewed as merely having Christ as their ultimate causal source but as being ours only by direct participation in Christ, in union with him through the Spirit. This approach better represents the biblical perspective on how the Spirit works. The blessings of salvation become ours through the Spirit, *exclusively, immediately, simultaneously* and *eschatologically* in Christ. In Pauline terms, it is only 'in him' that the blessings of redemption become ours; and it is only by the Spirit that we are 'in Christ'. But in Christ all spiritual blessings are ours here and now (Eph. 1:3ff.), albeit each blessing is capable of its own distinctive consummation.

This approach has several advantages over a 'series', or 'causal chain' model which has tended to dominate expositions of the *ordo salutis.* It means that we cannot think of, or enjoy, the blessings of the gospel either isolated from each other or separated from the Benefactor himself. This promotes a healthy Christ-centredness in Christian living, and also safeguards evangelical teaching from the flaw of isolating the effects of the gospel from faith in Christ himself as both Saviour and Lord. In this sense, Melanchthon's famous anti-scholastic dictum 'To know Christ is to know his benefits' is well taken.[13]

This perspective also obviates the danger of unhealthy and unbalanced subjectivism in Christian experience. It was never a *logically* necessary implication of the Perkinsian model that it would produce unhealthy and anxious introspection. Yet, when severed from Perkins' robust Christocentricity, it could and sometimes did lead to the development of an unhealthy subjectivism in which the location of present experience on the chain of salvation replaced Jesus Christ himself as the focus of attention and faith.

Moreover, when union with Christ is the architectonic principle for interpreting the ministry of the Spirit, the various aspects of the application of redemption retain the vital eschatological dimension (and tension) which features so largely in New Testament thought. Those who live in the Spirit, and thus participate in Christ, also live in this world, dominated as it is by the flesh. For that reason there is always an already/not-yet character to the present experience of salvation. It is doubtful whether the 'chain' model could ever express this fully. Its very form suggests that one link is complete in itself and thus isolated from the others; thus, for example, regeneration is viewed as coming to an end where faith begins. In the New

Testament, by contrast, there remains a yet-to-be-consummated aspect to every facet of salvation.

The chain model for the Spirit's work tends to create the impression that the inaugurated is also the fully realized. But there is an eschatological ('already/not-yet') structure to each aspect of soteriology. Regeneration is a present reality, but it also awaits its consummation (Mt. 19:28). Sanctification already involves a radical, once-for-all-break with the dominion of sin (1 Cor. 6:11; Rom. 6:1–14), but it also develops progressively to its perfection (1 Thes. 5:23). Even glorification, while consummated in the future, has already in a sense begun here and now through the indwelling of the Spirit of grace and glory (2 Cor. 4:18; Rom. 8:28; 1 Pet. 4:13). And while it requires carefully guarded statement, it is also true that justification is an already accomplished and perfect reality, but awaits its consummation – in the same way in which adoption (like justification, a *legal* act in the New Testament) will enter a new stage when we receive that for which we wait eagerly yet patiently, namely 'our adoption as sons, the redemption of our bodies' (Rom. 8:23). Similarly, while believers have already been justified with irreversible finality, they will appear before the judgment seat of Christ to receive what is due to them (2 Cor. 5:10). Then, in his capacity as 'the righteous Judge' (*ho dikaios kritēs*), the Lord will give 'the crown of righteousness' (*ho tēs dikaiosynēs stephanos*) 'to all who have longed for his appearing' (2 Tim. 4:8). Thus, as impeccable a Reformed document as the Westminster Shorter Catechism states that: 'At the resurrection, believers being raised up in glory, shall be openly acknowledged and acquitted in the day of judgment . . .'[14]

Christ as paradigm and source

This perspective of the simultaneity of redemptive blessings in union with Christ by the Spirit is, in fact, deeply-rooted in the eschatological structure of Pauline theology.[15] Followed through carefully, that theology sheds considerable light on our understanding of the application of redemption in Christ. The analysis of this teaching may be broken down into three stages:

(1) Central to the apostle's thinking in this connection is the fact that, for Paul, the foundation of our redemption lies in

participation not only in the death but also in the resurrection of Christ (*e.g.* Rom. 6:3ff.; Eph. 2:5–6; Col. 2:12–13; 3:1). This being raised with Christ took place in representative fashion in Christ's historical resurrection, just as in the same sense when Christ died we died (2 Cor. 5:14–15). But it is realized or existentialized in the believer at regeneration/conversion, which is marked sacramentally by baptism. These two 'moments', Christ's resurrection and ours, belong together logically, although separated by time. Common to both is the ministry of the Spirit.

(2) Paul views the resurrection of Christ from the dead as his 'redemption'. His death is everything that death truly is. In his capacity as the second man, the last Adam, he experienced death as the wages of sin, separation from life, judgment under the wrath of God and alienation from the face of the Father (Rom. 6:10; 2 Cor. 5:21; Gal. 3:13). He died to the sin under whose power he came (Rom. 6:10: 'the death he died, he died *to sin*'). But from death thus conceived Christ was raised, delivered, vindicated or 'saved' through the resurrection (1 Tim. 3:15). In his resurrection he was 'redeemed' and delivered from death by the power of the Holy Spirit. As R. B. Gaffin, Jr., suggests:

> It is, then, not only meaningful but necessary to speak of the resurrection as the redemption of Christ. The resurrection is nothing if not his deliverance from the power and curse of death which was in force until the moment of being raised . . . The resurrection is the salvation of Jesus as the last Adam; it and no other event in his experience is the point of *his* transition from wrath to grace.[16]

(3) In Paul's exposition of the gospel, the categories used to describe the application of redemption to the believer are the categories which explicate the meaning of Christ's resurrection. In other words, the application of redemption to us is rooted in the application of redemption to Christ.

Jesus' resurrection is viewed as his *justification* (1 Tim. 3:16). In it he has vindicated or justified (*edikaiōthē*) by the Spirit. Having been made sin in his death, in his resurrection he was declared *as our representative* to be (what he in fact always was personally) righteous. He did not 'see decay' because he was God's Holy One (Acts 2:27). Dying in our place as the condemned one, he was raised as the justified one.

Paul also implies that the resurrection can be seen as Jesus' *adoption*. As to his human nature, Jesus 'was a descendant of David' but 'through the Spirit of holiness' he 'was declared with power to be the Son of God, by his resurrection from the dead' (Rom. 1:4).

Older interpreters read Romans 1:3–4 within the matrix of classical patristic Christology as a statement of the two natures of Christ. But the contrast in view is not between the two natures but the two states of Christ, and more precisely between the two aeons of his existence: 'according to the flesh' and 'according to the Spirit'; his humiliation and his exaltation. His resurrection thus constitutes him messianic Son of God with power; in it he is adopted as the Man of the new age.[17]

The resurrection may also be viewed as the *sanctification* of Christ. That which is fundamental to our sanctification is found first in Christ himself: he died to sin once for all, and was raised to newness of life in which he lives for ever to God (Rom. 6:9–10).

This perspective will remain alien unless it is recognized that the characteristic Pauline use of the language of sanctification views it in its definitive rather than in its progressive aspects, as a radical deliverance from the dominion of sin which provides the foundation for a progressive deliverance from the influence of sin.[18] In his death Christ came under the dominion of sin; in his resurrection he was delivered from that dominion. This deliverance is the foundation of sanctification, whether in us or in Christ. Hence we may properly speak about Christ's resurrection in the power of the Spirit as nothing less than his sanctification by the Spirit.

Furthermore, the resurrection constituted Christ's *glorification*. As the 'firstfruits of those who have fallen asleep' (1 Cor. 15:20), he was the first whose body was 'sown . . . perishable, . . . raised imperishable; . . . sown in dishonour . . . raised in glory; . . . sown in weakness . . . raised in power; . . . sown a natural body . . . raised a spiritual body' (1 Cor. 15:42–44). By the Spirit's power his bodily existence was transformed into one of glory (*cf.* Phil. 3:21).

To be 'in Christ' means to share in all that Christ has accomplished. More specifically this means that those who are united to the risen Christ share in *his* justification, adoption, sanctification and glorification. Just as in the case of Christ these are all aspects of the single eschatological event of his resurrection and in him are simultaneous and inseparable, so with us. It follows that, in the case of believers, to be united to Christ by the Spirit means to share in his justification, adoption, sanctification and glorification. In Christ these are ours immediately, eschatologically and simultaneously.

Of course, justification, adoption, sanctification and glorification are distinct categories of the application of redemption and should never be confused. But they are not to be viewed as separate events; they are aspects or facets of the one event of our union with Christ in his risen glory, effected by the power of the Spirit and worked out progressively through the Spirit's ongoing ministry.

Within the single union between Christ and his people, it may be possible to trace various levels of orders of nature in which, logically, one element in our union with Christ appears to be the prerequisite for another. But to seek to reduce the elements to a string of causes and effects has the immediate impact of flattening out the dimensions of grace involved.

The application of redemption is the effecting of a two-sided relationship. That, of course, is the pattern already evidenced in the covenant character of salvation in Scripture, where the divine monergism of covenant establishment leads to the mutuality of covenant fellowship in faith and obedience. At the heart of this new covenant lies the work of Christ through whom forgiveness is granted, and the promise of the Spirit through whom renewal and restoration come. New covenant union with God is specifically a union to Christ by the Spirit which brings us the communication of redemptive blessings.

Every element in the classical *ordo salutis* is thus a further perspective on the one reality of the believer's union with Christ. Christ becomes our covenant partner, as the Holy Spirit binds us to him. Everything that is his as the one for us becomes ours. We become one with Christ in the mysterious union of which becoming one flesh in marriage is an analogy (Eph. 5:30–32). The closeness of the union is dependent upon our mutual possession by, and possession of, the Holy Spirit. By him, Christ bestows on us all his goods.

This is given pointed, almost shocking, expression by Paul in 1 Corinthians 6:12–20. Counteracting sexual immorality, he implies that the Christian cannot conveniently place his or her union with Christ in abeyance in order to indulge his or her flesh. No! So close and holistic is the union with Christ that this would be to take Christ's members and draw them into sin. For 'he who unites himself with the Lord is one with him in spirit' (1 Cor. 6:17). A strong case can be made out here for capitalizing 'spirit', in the light of the fact that Paul then goes on to stress that our bodies are temples of the Holy Spirit.[19] The Spirit who made Christ's body a temple dwells within us to fulfil the same function. Christ and we are possessed of one and the same Holy Spirit. He is the bond of an unbreakable union.

Paul's exposition is essentially an outworking of Jesus' teaching in the farewell discourse. The disciples know the Spirit, 'for he lives with you [*i.e.* in Christ himself] and will be in you [*i.e.* after Pentecost]' (Jn. 14:17). But, 'On that day [*i.e.* Pentecost] you will realise that I am in my Father, and you are in me, and I am in you' (Jn. 14:20). The way Christ unites us to himself, the common bond that makes it possible for him to say that he will be in the disciples, is the fact that they will be possessed of the same Spirit as he himself is.

This central doctrine finds expression in the New Testament in a variety of ways, especially in Paul. A century ago scholars in the history-of-religions school traced its origin to the ancient mystery religions. But Paul's theological inheritance in the Old Testament, reinterpreted in the light of Christ, provides an adequate background for the concept. It does not appear *ex nihilo* in Scripture. Hints of it occur in representative figures such as the High Priest, who acts on behalf of the people and is united with them as their representative, and the Suffering Servant, who is portrayed as one who, identified with sinners, bears the sin of others and suffers in their place (Is. 53:4–6, 11–12).

We find the idea present also in the teaching of Jesus. In Matthew 25:31–46 he indicates that to act in relationship to his brothers is to act in relationship to him. Even more obviously the union comes to the fore in the Johannine farewell discourse.

Christ is the vine, his disciples are the branches; they dwell in him and he dwells in them (Jn. 15:1–11). So close is this union, through the Spirit, that Christ is *in* believers and they dwell in him (Jn. 17:26, 21).

Like much in Paul's theology, the seed of this doctrine is found in the revelation surrounding his conversion. While he assumes he is persecuting the church, Saul of Tarsus is arrested by the voice that pointedly asks him why he is persecuting the Lord Jesus. Such is the bond of union between Christ and his people that to persecute them is to persecute him. Significantly, Paul later sees part of his apostolic function as making known to Gentiles this great mystery: 'Christ in you, the hope of glory' (Col. 1:27). Union with Christ by the indwelling Spirit is therefore a central theme in what Paul called 'my gospel' (Rom. 2:16; 16:25).

The various prepositions used to describe the believer's bonding to Christ through the Spirit highlight the closeness and extent of union with him.

(1) Believers are united to Christ in a bond of union so that he may be said to have died 'for' them (*hyper, e.g.* Rom. 5:6, 8; 8:32; 2 Cor. 5:21). Such a relationship of union has been forged between Christ and his people that what he does is theirs.

(2) In the central redemptive moments in Christ's work, believers are so united to him that they may be said to be 'with' him in them, so that these events have lasting implications for their present life.

Sometimes 'with [*syn*] Christ' means 'present with' (*e.g.* in Phil. 1:23). But elsewhere in compound verbs with the prefix *syn* it conveys the idea of participation in (*e.g.* Gal. 2:20, 'crucified with Christ'; Rom. 6:4, 'buried with him'; Rom. 6:8, 'live with him').

(3) Supremely in Paul, and characteristic of his thought, is the use of the phrase 'in Christ' (*en Christō*). It summarizes all that it means to be a Christian, and indeed is used as a virtual synonym for 'Christian' in 2 Corinthians 12:2 ('I know a man in Christ') and Romans 16:7 ('Andronicus and Junias, my relatives who . . . were in Christ before I was').

The strongest clue to appreciating the theological significance of this idea lies in Paul's parallel phrase 'in Adam' (1 Cor. 15:22; *cf.* Rom. 5:12–21). To be 'in Adam' is to be united to him in such a way that all that Adam did in his representative capacity becomes mine, and determines my existence, whether through sin leading to death, or righteousness leading to life. In an analogous way, to be 'in Christ' means that all he has done for me representatively becomes mine actually.

This union with Christ can be viewed from three different but complementary perspectives. We might even say it takes place in three 'moments': the eternal, the incarnational and the existential.

(1) Believers were chosen in Christ before the creation of the world in order that, blessed in covenant union with him, they might be for the praise of his glory (Eph. 1:3–4, 11–12). There is a dimension of this union that transcends our own personal existence and stretches back into the plan and purpose of God in eternity. A sovereign and monergistic determination is in view here, but Paul does not (and perhaps cannot) further clarify the meaning of what he says. Nevertheless, he tells us that God's choice of believers is related to his pre-creation choice of Christ the Mediator.

Christ and his members are what Augustine and others have called *totus Christus*, whole Christ, inseparably joined together by eternal divine determination. What we become in Christ does not rest on what we are, but has the choice of Christ himself as its foundation. Union with Christ, therefore, has the deepest of all possible roots.

(2) Union with Christ is rooted in Christ's incarnation in our flesh. This has two features.

In the power of the Holy Spirit, the Son of God took our flesh in order that in it he might provide the salvation we require, perfectly suited to our needs. He came 'in human likeness' (Phil. 2:7); 'in the likeness of sinful man' (Rom. 8:3). He took our flesh, binding himself to our humanity, in order to bear sins *for us*. Further, he entered our flesh in order to be the *archēgos* of our salvation, the one who accomplished obedience and righteousness in order that these might then be accomplished *in us* through the Spirit (Rom. 8:3–4). 'In bringing many sons to glory, it was fitting that God, for whom and through whom everything exists, should make the author [*archēgos*] of their salvation perfect through suffering. Both the one who makes men holy and those who are made holy are of the same family

109

. . . Since the children have flesh and blood, he too shared in their humanity . . . For this reason he had to be made like his brothers in every way, in order that he might become a merciful and faithful high priest . . .' (Heb. 2:10–17; *cf.* 12:2).

Because our union with Christ is earthed in his flesh, and has his Spirit as its bonding agent, we share in the implications of the great moments of his redemptive work; we are thus crucified, buried, raised and ascended in him (*cf.* Gal. 2:19–20; Rom. 6:1ff.; Eph. 2:6; Col. 2:6 – 3:4). Our lives are no longer determined by what Adam has done, but by what Jesus Christ has done (Rom. 5:12–21; 1 Cor. 15:20ff.).

But we are united to him not only in what he has accomplished in our place, but also in the status into which he, as Mediator, was inaugurated by God. In union with him, our status is thus radically changed. In addition, our personal condition is progressively altered until he transforms us into the final degree of glory when he regenerates our physical existence and conforms it to the blueprint of his own glorious body (Phil. 3:21). Thus, by the Spirit-bond of union with Christ, all that is his as Mediator is bestowed on us by grace. Our true and final life is hidden with Christ in God (Col. 3:3; *cf.* 1 Jn. 3:2).

(3) Furthermore, this union, which as to its ideal aspect has been pre-temporally purposed in the mind of God, and in the space–time continuum is grounded in the incarnation, becomes an existential reality through the indwelling of the Spirit of Christ and its correlate, faith. This determines the whole of life. It is, according to the New Testament, 'in Christ' that we are free; in him we live to the praise of God's glory; in him that we marry and welcome one another; in Christ that we speak and have wisdom; in Christ that we shall die. Even our bodies are, in some sense, members of Christ, since as bodily entities we participate in one Spirit with him (1 Cor. 6:15, 19).

There is also mutuality in this union. While it has a supra-temporal and supra-individual dimension (we were in Christ before the foundation of the world), it is also proper to speak of a 'before' and 'after'. Its full realization takes place in our own existence when the Spirit unites us to Christ by faith. In Paul's idiosyncratic language, we 'believe *into* [*pisteuein eis*] Christ'. Thus, although we may have been chosen in Christ 'before the creation of the world' (Eph. 1:4), until we trust in him we are properly viewed as 'by nature objects of wrath' (Eph. 2:3) and 'separate from Christ' (2:12). Only when we are justified by grace through faith, and the covenantal purpose of God is actualized in us, can we speak of being united to Christ. Consequently, in Romans 16:7, in a striking turn of phrase, Paul speaks about his relatives, Andronicus and Junias, being 'in Christ *before* I was'.

This union brings us into the orbit of the eschatological change effected by Christ in his resurrection-transformation and glory. When anyone is in Christ, says Paul, new creation (not merely 'new creature') is the entail (2 Cor. 5:17). As God's workmanship (Eph. 2:10) we are brought into the sphere of the divine regeneration of all things which has already been inaugurated in Christ's resurrection. Yet, at the same time, the Spirit so engages our whole being that in belonging to Christ there is a 'mutuality', or 'covenantal bond', so that the Spirit's work and the believer's faith are absolutely correlative in the union (as Paul indicates in Gal. 2:17 – 3:4). Indeed, no less vigorous a Reformed theologian than B. B. Warfield is prepared to describe this, daringly, by means of the language of 'synergism':

> But it is a synergism of such character that not only is the initiative taken by God (for 'all things are of God,' 2 Cor. 5:18; *cf.* Heb. 6:6), but the Divine action is in the exceeding greatness of God's power, according to the working of the strength of His might which He wrought in Christ when He raised Him from the dead (Eph. 1:19). The 'new man' which is the result of this change is therefore one who can be described as 'created' (*ktisthenta*) in righteousness and holiness of truth (Eph. 4:24).[20]

It is of the nature of the activity of faith that this synergism, or covenant mutuality, does not compromise the absolute sovereignty and sheer grace of God in our salvation. It is always '*because of him* [God]' that we are 'in Christ Jesus' (1 Cor. 1:30).

What, then, are the implications of viewing union with Christ through faith as the overarching perspective on the work of the Spirit in the application of redemption? Three points may be noted here.

Implications

Firstly, the work of the Spirit is essentially a ministry of uniting us to Christ, and then unfolding to us and in us the riches of God's grace which we inherit in Christ. Calvin, again, captures this in one of his most eloquent passages:

> We see that our salvation and all its parts are comprehended in Christ (Acts 4:12). We should therefore take care not to derive the least portion of it from anywhere else. If we seek salvation, we are taught by the very name of Jesus that it is 'of him' (1 Cor. 1:30). If we seek any other gifts of the Spirit, they will be found in his anointing. If we seek strength, it lies in his dominion; if purity, in his conception; if gentleness, it appears in his birth . . . If we seek redemption, it lies in his passion; if acquittal, in his condemnation; if remission of the curse, in his cross (Gal. 3:13); if satisfaction, in his sacrifice; if purification, in his blood; if reconciliation, in his descent into hell; if mortification of the flesh, in his tomb; if newness of life, in his resurrection . . . In short, since rich store of every kind of good abounds in him, let us drink our fill from this fountain, and from no other.[21]

A second implication, emphasized in various ways in the New Testament, is that while we continue to be influenced by our past life, 'in the flesh', it is no longer the dominating influence on our present existence. We are no longer in the flesh but in the Spirit (Rom. 8:9). Christ's past (if we may so speak) is now dominant. Our past is a past 'in Adam'; our present existence is 'in Christ', in the Spirit. This implies not only that we have fellowship with him in the communion of the Spirit, but that in him our past guilt is dealt with, and our bondage to sin, the law, and death has been brought to an end.

Thirdly, union with Christ by the Spirit is grounded in his union with us in our humanity. It from this that our transformation is resourced through the Spirit. For union with Christ is not deification or mysticism. The Word became flesh in order to become the *archēgos* of a saved humanity. The goal of the Spirit is

112

transformation into the image of God as that is expressed in Christ's humanity, so that believers become progressively more truly and fully human.

This, too, carries further important ramifications which we shall see worked out later when we discuss the Spirit's sanctifying ministry. They are succinctly stated by Louis Berkhof when he writes:

> By this union believers are changed into the image of Christ according to his human nature. What Christ effects in his people is in a sense a replica or reproduction of what took place with him. Not only objectively, but in a subjective sense also they bear the cross, are crucified, die and are raised to newness of life with Christ. They share in a measure in the experiences of their Lord.[22]

6

SPIRITUS RECREATOR

The union with Christ into which the Spirit brings us is multi-dimensional in character. To be 'in Christ', says Paul, is to enter a 'new creation' (2 Cor. 5:17); the old order of sin and death, the age dominated by the flesh and the devil, have given way to a new order of reality in the resurrecton of Christ. Thus the mutual bonding between Christ and his people in the Spirit is the fulfilment of all that was adumbrated in the old covenant bond between Yahweh and his people in the Exodus and entrance into the land of rest; grounded in the work of the Messiah, it is forged through the ongoing work of the Spirit creating a new humanity.

Because it is multi-dimensional, life in union with Christ is necessarily viewed from various perspectives in the New Testament. It involves identification with him in his death, resurrection and ascension; but it also involves a correlation of the action of God with the action of man. As we have seen, Scripture stresses its monergistic roots (God is its author); it is bilateral in

nature, with faith as its other polarity. The threads of regeneration and faith are inextricably intertwined. In both dimensions
of activity the Spirit is active. These strands are capable of
separate analysis (indeed, they ought not to be regarded as
identical), but they cannot be existentially separated from each
other. They belong together in such a way that we cannot mark a
join where the monergistic action of God ends and the activity
of the believer begins. It is significant in this context that *both*
regeneration and the elements of conversion are regarded in
the New Testament as gifts of God.

Regeneration

Union to Christ is inaugurated by the renewing work of the
Spirit in which he begins the transformation into the image of
Christ which will be completed at the eschaton. The ancient
promise is thus fulfilled that God would give his people new
hearts and spirits through the indwelling of his Spirit, resulting
in a new lifestyle (Ezk. 36:24–27).

This transition was marked in the New Testament by the rite
of baptism. By the time of Justin Martyr and Irenaeus in the late
second century AD, regeneration already seems to have become
so closely associated with its symbol of baptism that the two were
thought of as coincident. This link became so refined that the
sign and the thing signified were related in a *sine qua non*
fashion, and a sacramentalist view of regeneration came to
dominate the theology of the church. Even for Augustine, to
whom the Reformers looked as the great theologian of grace,
the idea of regeneration apart from water baptism was unthinkable. The doctrine of the *limbus infantum* for those who died in
infancy unbaptized thus became virtually a dogmatic necessity
for the medieval church.

While the mainstream Reformation thinkers continued to
emphasize the role and necessity of baptism as the sign of
regeneration, they argued that any identification of the two
must be seen as sacramental and not mechanical; the sign and
the thing signified must not be confused, as though the grace
indicated by the sign were contained within it.

Particularly in the teaching of Calvin the term 'regeneration'
was used to denote the renewal which the Spirit effects

throughout the whole course of the Christian life. For him it describes the same reality denoted by 'conversion' and 'repentance' but viewed from a different perspective.[1] Later, in many seventeenth-century writers, effectual calling and regeneration tended to be treated as synonyms. Only in the continuing development of evangelical theology did the term come to be used in the more limited and particular sense of the inauguration of new life by the sovereign and secret activity of God.[2] While this served to focus attention on the power of God in giving new life, when detached from its proper theological context it was capable of being subjectivized and psychologized to such an extent that the term 'born again' became dislocated from its biblical roots.

But what does the New Testament itself mean when it speaks about 'regeneration'? In the structure of evangelical soteriology, regeneration has occupied such a central role that 'second birth' has been regarded as the definitive element of genuine Christian experience. Yet the New Testament term for regeneration, *palingenesia* (from *palin*, 'again', and *genesis*, 'beginning') occurs only twice in the New Testament. In Matthew 19:28, it refers to the 'renewal of all things', the final rebirth of the universe, a meaning that stands in marked contrast with its use in Stoic thought as the periodic restoration of the world.

Palingenesia here is the final resurrection, the realized adoption of God's sons, the redemption of their bodies and of the entire groaning creation (Rom. 8:19ff.), and the establishment of the new heavens and the new earth, the home of righteousness (2 Pet. 3:13). It is cosmic in its effects.

The only other occurrence of *palingenesia* is in Titus 3:5, where Paul speaks of the 'washing of rebirth [*palingenesia*] and renewal by the Holy Spirit'. It is difficult to be dogmatic about the meaning of this phrase. Does the washing *consist* in rebirth, *effect* rebirth, or *symbolize* new birth (through baptism)? Does the statement refer to two actions (washing and renewal), or is it a hendiadys (in which a single idea is denoted by two expressions)?

This latter interpretation seems likely and, if valid, suggests a striking connection between the regeneration of the individual and the dawning of the new age, since Paul's only other use of 'renewal' (*anakainōsis*, Rom. 12:2) serves the function of

117

emphasizing the contrast between the present world order and that of the age to come. Furthermore, as H. N. Ridderbos has pointed out, the outpouring of the Spirit to which Paul refers in this context is 'typical eschatological terminology'.[3] It underlines the fact that Paul sees regeneration within a broader context as a share in the renewal-resurrection which has been inaugurated by the Spirit in Christ. The renewal which is effected in regeneration (and symbolized in baptism) is, therefore, not merely an inner change; it is the incursion of a new order into the present order of reality. Thus regeneration (*palingenesia*) and the cognates (*anagennaō, gennēthēnai anōthen*) denoted not merely the phenomenon of spiritual change from within, from below as it were, but transformation from without and from above, caused by participation in the power of the new age and more specifically by fellowship through the Spirit with the resurrected Christ as the second man, its firstfruits, the eschatological Adam (*ho eschatos Adam*, 1 Cor. 15:45). This is the note which became muted in the teaching of the post-apostolic church but which must be recovered.

New creation – new life

While the term 'regeneration' is not strictly associated with the work of the Holy Spirit in the New Testament, the idea of inauguration into the kingdom of God as a Spirit-wrought new birth is widespread and is in fact foundational in Johannine theology: 'To all who received him [Christ], to those who believed in his name, he gave the right to become children of God – children born of natural descent, nor of human decision or a husband's will, but born of God' (Jn. 1:12–13). That this birth is the work of the Spirit is later underlined by Jesus' words to Nicodemus: 'No-one can enter the kingdom of God unless he is born of water and the Spirit . . . the Spirit gives birth to Spirit . . . So it is with everyone born of the Spirit' (Jn. 3:5–8). Being 'born of God' (*i.e.* through the Spirit) becomes as characteristic a description of being a Christian in Johannine theology as is the expression 'in Christ' in the Pauline corpus (*cf.* 1 Jn. 2:29; 3:9; 4:7; 5:1, 4, 18).

Elsewhere in the New Testament similar language is used of the renewing work of God. While reference to the Spirit is less direct, his sovereign action is nevertheless implied (*e.g.* in Jas.

1:18; 1 Pet. 1:3, 23). Paul views Christians as being like Isaac, children of the promise 'born by the power of the Spirit' (Gal. 4:29).

Regeneration is causally rooted in the resurrection of Christ (1 Pet. 1:3). Like produces like; our regeneration is the fruit of Christ's resurrection. In union with him it is effected here and now, and will be consummated at his return. He is the firstfruits of the resurrection-regeneration of the end time; we will participate in the final harvest, but already, through the bond of union in the Holy Spirit, we share in the firstfruits (Rom. 8:23).

Here then, in the deep structures of New Testament thought, the eschatological nature of regeneration is underscored. The Spirit who has come at Pentecost is the Spirit of the future age; the world into which he brings believers is marked by the powers of the aeon to come (Heb. 6:4–5), as was the ministry of Jesus in the sense that his miracles were themselves confirmatory signs that the anticipated future age of the Messiah and his Spirit had already arrived.

Divine monergism

The New Testament's statements on regeneration emphasize the sovereign, monergistic, activity of the Spirit. The metaphor of birth itself implies not only a radical new beginning, but one which is never autonomous. The divine monergism behind it is spelled out elsewhere in antitheses: we are born, not of our own will, but of God's decision (Jn. 1:12); from above, not from below; of the Spirit, not of the flesh (Jn. 3:3, 5–6); of God, not of man (1 Jn. 2:29; 3:9; 4:7; 5:1, 4, 18); by God's choice, not our own; through his word, not out of the energies of an autonomous will (Jas. 1:18). The priority here is accorded to God, not to man. The reason for this is that man is 'flesh'.

In his conversation with Nicodemus, Jesus says that he ought not to be surprised that he 'must be born again/from above' (Jn. 3:7). This necessity is universal: without the new birth, no-one can either see or enter the kingdom of God (Jn. 3:3, 5). Here the accent is placed heavily on man's inability. The denial of human ability (in the negative of the verb *dynasthai*, 'to be able, to have the power') occurs five times in John 3:3–10. As flesh, man gives birth only to more flesh. He cannot give birth to spirit, or to what is spiritual. Only the Spirit of God can do that (Jn. 3:6). Since the kingdom of God is the kingdom of the Spirit, no flesh has access to it.

It is widely accepted that 'flesh' (*sarx*) probably has a different nuance in John from Paul's characteristic use (*sarx* = human nature debilitated by sin). Since, for John, the eternal Logos became *sarx* (Jn. 1:14), *sarx* must have in view the weakness and frailty, rather than the sinfulness as such, of human nature. E. Schweitzer's comment is representative: 'The nuance of that which is sinful or which entices to sin is quite absent.'[4] Man is thus being viewed apart from and in contrast with God in his inexhaustible spiritual energy.

Such a use of *sarx* does not negate human sinfulness as the root cause of the Spirit-less condition, but it is the effect rather than the cause that is in focus. *Sarx* stands for man viewed apart from God. As flesh we require new birth because we are bereft of the life and energy of the world of the Spirit. If we are to belong to the kingdom, or family, of the Spirit, we must be 'born from above' by the Spirit. Only thus will we be able to 'worship in Spirit' (Jn. 4:23–24).

As flesh, men and women cannot see (*i.e.* experience, Jn. 3:36; 8:51) or enter the kingdom of God (Jn. 3:3, 5). To be flesh is to be blind and insensitive to the realities of the Spirit-governed kingdom of God, and to fail to understand or accept the nature of spiritual reality (*cf.* 1 Cor. 2:14).

Jesus' conversation with Nicodemus provides a striking illustration of this. Nicodemus asks how new birth is possible. He cannot understand Jesus' words. The 'secret of the kingdom of God' is a complete mystery to the man who comes 'at night' (Jn. 3:2); he still needs to come out of the noetic darkness common to all those who do not have the Spirit-given birth (*cf.* Jn. 3:2, 19–21).

This is taken one stage further. Man is not only spiritually blind, but spiritually powerless to enter the kingdom: 'Unless one is born of water and the Spirit, he cannot enter the kingdom of God' (Jn. 3:5, RSV). Leaving aside for the moment the enigmatic phrase 'of water and the Spirit', this statement clearly stresses man's inability. Although in Christ the kingdom has come, man is powerless to enter it by 'the will of the flesh' (*cf.* 3:3: not able to see, *ou dynatai idein*; and 3:5: not able to enter, *ou dynatai eiselthein*). No-one can come to Christ (*i.e.* believe in him) unless drawn (sovereignly) by the Father (Jn. 6:44–45).

As a consequence, regeneration is regarded in John as the *sine qua non* of eternal life. This can be accomplished only from above. Apparently we can no more bring ourselves into the kingdom unaided than we can be conceived and born unaided.

What, then, is involved in the Spirit's work of regeneration?

Aspects of regeneration

What is regeneration? The Spirit's work of radical renewal involves several elements.

Firstly, it implies intellectual illumination: the kingdom of God, which before stood unrecognized, now becomes clearly visible.

John explains this in terms of the 'anointing' Christians have received which results in their knowing the truth (1 Jn. 2:20). They do not need anyone to teach them (1 Jn. 2:27). Now, in Christ, all believers share in his anointing with the Spirit and have knowledge of the Lord without human mediation, in distinction from old covenant knowledge of God which was mediated through prophets, priests and kings. This is what was in view in the promise of the new covenant (Je. 31:33).

This no more means that the regenerated individual understands everything at the moment of regeneration than that a blind man receiving his sight sees everything immediately and simultaneously. He sees what his eyes are fixed on when sight is given to them, and this is then placed in the wider context. So it is with those who are born from above, and have their spiritual understanding illuminated. This is one reason why the consciousness of individuals at regeneration is bound to differ from one person to another.[5]

Secondly, regeneration involves liberation of the will from its bondage in a nature dominated by sin. Man is incapable of entering the kingdom of God without regeneration. It follows that a central element in regeneration must be the Spirit's empowering of man's will in a kingdom-orientated way. Before regeneration he *will not* come to the light (Jn. 3:5, 20). Now he comes to the light; indeed he will not refuse it.

Thirdly, there is a cleansing aspect to regeneration. This is the most probable meaning of the difficult phrase 'born of water'

(3:5). Various interpretations of this have had currency in the church, ranging from equating it with baptism (implying baptismal regeneration), to the view that the reference here is to natural begetting, as in John 1:12, since water, rain and dew are used variously in ancient thought to refer to male semen, in which case Jesus is simply emphasizing the necessity of being 'twice-born' men and women.

The reference to water is, however, best interpreted in the light of the probable background to this section of Jesus' teaching in the new covenant promise of Ezekiel 36:25–27: 'I will sprinkle clean water on you, and you will be clean; I will cleanse you from all your impurities and from all your idols . . .'. In the rest of the passage, Jesus speaks of only one birth, the birth from above (3:3, 6–7). 'Water and Spirit' probably refers to the two-fold work of the Spirit in regeneration: he simultaneously gives new life and cleanses the heart.[6]

In any event, the cleansing which takes place in regeneration is underlined in Titus 3:5, and perhaps also in 1 Corinthians 6:11: 'You were washed, . . . sanctified, . . . justified in the name of the Lord Jesus Christ.' Here 'washed' and 'sanctified' are tantamount to regeneration. In regeneration desires are renewed and cleansed by what Thomas Chalmers (1780–1847) called 'the expulsive power of a new affection'. The Spirit gives birth to spirit (Jn. 3:6), in the sense of creating an appetite for the new age and its realities. As Ezekiel beautifully expressed it, the Spirit's renewing work makes its recipients 'careful' to do the Lord's will (Ezk. 36:27).

The Spirit's work in regeneration is thus total in the extent of its transforming power. It is the individual as an individual who is regenerated, the whole man. For regeneration is the fulfilment of God's promise to give us a new heart (Ezk. 36:26; *cf.* Je. 31:33), indicating that the Spirit's renewing work is both intensive and extensive: it reaches to the foundation impulses of an individual's life and leaves no part of his or her being untouched.

Regeneration is, consequently, as all-pervasive as depravity. On the basis of such statements as 'the heart is . . . beyond all cure' (Je. 17:9), theologians have spoken of total depravity, meaning not that man is as bad as he could be, but that no part of his being remains untainted by the influence of sin. Regeneration reverses that depravity, and is universal in the sense that, while the regenerate individual is not yet as holy as he or she might be, there is no part of life which remains uninfluenced by this renewing and cleansing work. Indeed, just as total depravity leads to moral and ultimately even to physical disintegration, so total regeneration leads to moral, but also ultimately to physical renewal, in the regeneration of the whole being in the resurrection (Phil. 3:21; 1 Cor. 15:42–44). The new man is put on; he is constantly being renewed by the Spirit (Col. 3:10), and finally will be resurrected and glorified through his power.

Older theologians spoke of this radical change as 'physical'. Although the expression now seems infelicitous, their concern was to emphasize that regeneration is not merely intellectual persuasion; it is a transformation of fallen nature (*physis*). It penetrates deeply. It is the gift of a new heart.[7]

The sovereignty of the Spirit

How does the Spirit effect new birth? His work is both mysterious and sovereign. Jesus compares his activity to the wind, perhaps reflecting the words of Ecclesiastes 11:5: 'As you do not know the path of the wind, or how the body is formed in a mother's womb, so you cannot understand the work of God, the Maker of all things.' We hear the sound the wind makes as it catches objects in its tracks, but we do not know from where it comes or to where it goes. The Spirit's presence is recognized exclusively by its effects. In one sense, therefore, we do not have access to the divine activity in regeneration, only to its immediate accompaniments. We hear 'the sound' the Spirit effects in expressions of faith and repentance. Those formerly unwilling to trust Christ now do so freely and willingly.

At this juncture, the classical Protestant formulations of regeneration rightly refuse to compromise either the integrity of the human person (we are not 'forced' by external pressure) or the necessity of divine monergism (we are 'dead' spiritually and cannot bring ourselves to life by an act of our own will). They thus note that God enlightens men's minds

> . . . spiritually and savingly to understand the things of God; taking away their heart of stone, and giving unto them an heart of flesh; renewing their wills, and by his

almighty power determining them to that which is good; and effectually drawing them to Jesus Christ; *yet so as they come most freely, being made willing by his grace.*[8]

The tension point we encounter here – those who are unwilling being made willing – is, in fact, a sub-set of the larger question of the divine–human engagement, and in many ways parallels the similar mystery of the interplay of the divine and the human in both providence and the inspiration of Scripture. The most common mistake made in attempts to resolve this tension is to seek to divide up the field of activity *between* the Spirit and man (is this a work mostly from the Spirit, but partly from man? or equally from the Spirit and from man?). It is a common assumption that if it is the monergistic work of the Spirit then the will of the human person must be forced. We thus fail to recognize the underlying biblical principle that the Spirit and the individual are both active on the same field – a human life – simultaneously. But the free coming to Christ in faith is dependent on the sovereign drawing of the Spirit. Because the Spirit works in us we are able freely to respond. Sovereign divine activity does not negate the necessity for human activity; rather it grounds it and renders it possible.

Scripture does not view the Spirit's operations on the mental, volitional and affectional powers as independent of the integrity of the individual, as though the regeneration of the individual is an abstract event. Rather, the individual is a thinking–willing–affective creature, a whole person. The Spirit works within the broad context of mind, will and emotions. Consequently, although regeneration is seen by John as a sovereign and monergistic activity, it does not take place in a vacuum, but is effected through the ordinances of God directed to the whole person. There is appeal through the word of the gospel to the mind, the senses are affected by Christian testimony and care, so that faith is constrained. At one level of analysis, the individual changes his or her mind (repentance), and turns to Christ (faith). But that – which he does although he was impotent to do it – he does through the renewing work of the Spirit.

It is already clear, then, that the sovereignty of the Spirit in regeneration is not antithetical to a thoroughgoing emphasis on the role of faith in salvation; for faith is born within the context of the word (Rom. 10:14).

This is underlined in the New Testament by statements which suggest that regeneration itself takes place by means of the word of God (*e.g.* 1 Pet. 1:23; Jas. 1:18; Jn. 15:3, in all of which the word is viewed as instrumental in regeneration). The word of God engages us at the level of our consciousness, evoking a response. It operates at the level of our responsive action.

But how can regeneration take place through the word without this diluting the notion of the Spirit's monergistic, sovereign activity?

Since an emphasis on divine monergism has been a leading characteristic of Augustinian theology, it is not surprising that within this tradition some theologians have been particularly sensitive to this difficulty. The nineteenth-century North American theologian W. G. T. Shedd, for example, argues that what is in view here is the 'gospel dispensation'.[9] Others equate the word with Christ himself, who sovereignly calls into action the seed of new life implanted by the Spirit.

A common resolution is to view regeneration as having a narrower and a broader dimension, a subconscious and a conscious aspect. Thus B. B. Warfield notes:

> At the root of all lies an act seen by God alone, and mediated by nothing, a direct creative act of the Spirit, the new birth. This new birth pushes itself into man's own consciousness through the call of the Word, responded to under the persuasive movements of the Spirit; his [man's] conscious possession of it is thus mediated by the Word.[10]

For the New Testament writers, however, there is no hint of a threat to divine sovereignty in the fact that the word is the instrumental cause of regeneration, while the Spirit is the efficient cause. This is signalled in the New Testament by the use of the preposition *ek* to indicate the divine originating cause (*e.g.* Jn. 3:5; 1 Jn. 3:9; 5:1) and *dia* to express the instrumental cause (*e.g.* Jn. 15:3; 1 Cor. 4:15; 1 Pet. 1:23).

Since the Spirit's work in regeneration involves the transformation of the whole man, including his cognitive and affective powers, the accompanying of the internal illumination of the Spirit by the external revelation of the word (and vice versa) is altogether appropriate. Since faith involves knowledge, it ordinarily emerges in relationship to the teaching of the gospel found in Scripture. Regeneration and the faith to which it gives birth are seen as taking place not by revelationless divine sovereignty, but within the matrix of the preaching of the word and the witness of the people of God (*cf.* Rom. 10:1–15). Their instrumentality in regeneration does not impinge upon the sovereign activity of the Spirit. Word and Spirit belong together.

Individual regeneration is therefore analogous at this point to the final regeneration of all things. Eschatological regeneration and resurrection will take place through the power of the Holy Spirit (Rom. 8:11), as an act of undiluted sovereignty. Yet at the same time it will be effected by the word of God: 'The Lord himself will come down from heaven, *with a loud command* . . . and the dead in Christ will rise . . .' (1 Thes. 4:16). He will say, as he said at the tomb of Lazarus: 'Come out' (Jn. 11:43). But then, as now in regeneration, the instrumental use of the word does not compromise the sovereignty of the Spirit's regenerating actions.

Faith a gift

This is further emphasized in the New Testament by the fact that faith is the fruit of the Spirit's ministry and is seen in the New Testament as a gift of God. Here, again, there is an apparent tension between the Spirit's activity and human response. Paul provides an important perspective for us in this respect by drawing a further analogy between believing and suffering: 'It has been granted to you on behalf of Christ not only to believe on him, but also to suffer for him' (Phil. 1:29). Suffering, like faith, is a grace-gift in Christian experience. But the gift of suffering is not a commodity given to us as a *fait accompli.* We, not God, suffer. Yet this suffering is a gift from him. In a parallel way, faith is not a package placed in our hands. It is the activity of the whole man, directed by the Spirit towards Christ. God does not believe for us, or in us; we believe. Yet, it is only by God's grace that we believe. His gift is simultaneously our act.

The classic text in this connection is Ephesians 2:8: 'It is by grace you have been saved, through faith – and this not from yourselves, it is the gift of God.' There is a well-known exegetical crux here; what is the antecedent of 'this' and, therefore, what exactly constitutes the gift?

To the casual reader, 'faith' reads as the natural antecedent (it is the immediate antecedent). But 'this' (*touto*) is neuter while both of the obvious antecedents are feminine (*charis*, 'grace', and *pistis*, 'faith'); so also is 'salvation' (*sōtēria*), which might be understood as the unwritten antecedent: 'and this [*i.e.* salvation] is not . . .').

It is a long-recognized principle that in languages in which the grammatical gender of a noun may differ from the gender of the thing itself, the gender of a pronoun may agree with the gender of the antecedent itself rather than with the gender of the word which denotes it.[11] In this specific context, since both *pistis* and *charis* are gender-neutral, either might serve as the antecedent.

Three considerations suggest that the antecedent (*i.e.* the thing that is the gift of God), is faith (*pistis*):

(1) It is the immediate antecedent and therefore the most natural one.

(2) It would be an unusual tautology (but admittedly not impossible, as Romans 3:24 and 5:15 indicate) to speak of grace as a gift of God, since *by definition* grace is a gift from God.

(3) It gives a coherent reading of Paul's thought-pattern, which may be paraphrased as follows:

> God made us alive – *by grace* you have been saved (2:5).
> God raised us up – to show his *grace* (2:6–7).
> It is indeed *by grace* you have been saved (2:8)!
> But this *grace* engages rather than ignores our action
>   (salvation is *by faith*, *i.e.* it engages our active response).
> Yet this active *faith* on our part does not prejudice *grace*.
> For even the ability to believe is not ours independently.
> Faith (too) is the gift of God.
> Thus: the salvation which is *by grace* is also *by faith*.
> But, as should now be clear, this salvation,
>   while received by our action (faith),
>   is not thereby 'by works'.
> It engages our activity,
>   but it leaves no room for our boasting (2:9).

Hence:
> salvation is not our work;
> instead, we are God's workmanship (2:10).

Even if we adopt the view that it is 'being saved through faith' that forms the antecedent (the view favoured by Calvin and others), there would still be a hint that faith is a gift of grace. That faith in any case is viewed by Paul as a gift is confirmed in Ephesians 6:23, when he prays for 'faith from God the Father and the Lord Jesus Christ'. There would be little point in praying for what comes from the Father and the Son unless that faith were, in some sense, given by them. Similarly, Peter refers to believers who have '*received* a faith as precious as ours' (2 Pet. 1:1), which seems to refer to the content of faith (*fides quae creditur*) not the act (*fides qua creditur*). Furthermore, in the New Testament, repentance (from which faith is inseparable) is viewed as a gift (Acts 5:31; 11:18; 2 Tim. 2:25); it is no surprise, therefore, if faith is also seen as a gift of grace. Here, then, divine sovereignty is given priority (it is the *sine qua non* of faith) without minimizing the reality and significance of the believer's activity.

Furthermore, the active exercise of faith (it is we, not God, who believe) does not compromise the *grace* of the Spirit's work in the application of salvation. It is of the nature of faith that by it we actively receive Christ and justification in him without contributing to it. After all, faith is trust in another. It is the antithesis of all self-contribution and self-reliance.

Paul hints at this when he says that the promise of salvation is by faith so that it might be by grace, and be guaranteed to believers (Rom. 4:16). Faith engages grace without transforming salvation into human merit.

Warfield expresses this in a pointed way when he says:

> The *saving power* of faith resides thus not in itself, but in the Almighty Saviour on whom it rests. It is never on account of its formal nature as a psychic act that faith is conceived in Scripture to be saving, – as if this frame of mind or attitude of heart were itself a virtue with claims on God for reward . . . It is not faith that saves, but faith in Jesus Christ . . . It is not, strictly speaking, even

faith in Christ that saves, but Christ that saves through faith.[12]

We are saved *by* Christ *through* faith. The saving power of faith does not lie in itself but in the object of its trust. As G. C. Berkouwer writes in another connection: 'Faith does not possess one single constructive and creative moment; it rests only and exclusively in the reality of the promise.'[13] There is a total engagement of the believer, yet at the same time grace is not compromised. The genius of salvation by grace is that it engages man without diluting the graciousness of the salvation received. Otto Weber puts it well: 'Faith, according to the biblical understanding does not consist of man's being set aside, but of his being involved to the uttermost.'[14]

Implications

It should not now surprise us if the evidences of the Spirit's work in regeneration on the one hand, and the actions of faith and repentance on the other, are one and the same and mirror the union with Christ of which he is the bond. By the work of the Spirit we are joined to Christ; we share in the death of the old man and the resurrection of the new. We have died to sin and been raised into new life in Christ (Rom. 6:1ff.); yet, simultaneously, we ourselves crucify the flesh with its lusts, and put off the old man and put on the new (Eph. 4:22–24; Col. 3:9–10; Gal. 5:24). We work out our salvation because, and as, God the Spirit works in us to will and to act according to his good pleasure (Phil. 2:12–13). Thus, those who have the Spirit live according to the Spirit and set their minds on the things of the Spirit; they set their affections on the things above (Rom. 8:5; Col. 3:1–2). A distaste for the old order, and a desire for the new eschatological order, become evident (*cf.* Ezk. 36:25–26).

A similar point is made in 1 John 3:9 and 5:18, in the startling statements that anyone born of the Spirit does not sin (*hamartian ou poiei*). Many commentators and versions understand John to be speaking here of sin as a prevailing habit.[15] But the pointed language he uses (the Christian 'does not do sin') probably refers to the critical and radical deliverance from specific manifestations of the reign of sin which takes place at the point of union with Christ. Instead of remaining captive in concrete ways to the dominance of sin, the Christian becomes righteous precisely in those areas (*cf.* 1 Jn. 2:29; 3:10). Thus, the regenerate Saul seeks the fellowship, not the slaughter, of believers; the new man Zacchaeus gives money away rather than steals it; the transformed Philippian jailer cares for his prisoners rather than mistreats them; the runaway Onesimus, 'useless' in his old life, becomes a faithful servant and is 'useful' to Paul.

Spirit-birth also transforms the Christian's relationship to the present world order. This is expressed variously by the New Testament writers (*e.g.* for Paul we have already been 'crucified' to it, Gal. 6:14). For John, everyone who has been born of God overcomes the world through faith (1 Jn. 5:4). Here 'the world' signifies the world in rebellion against God, under the control of the evil one (1 Jn. 5:19; *cf.* Jn. 12:31; 14:30), in darkness and sin (Jn. 1:5; 12:46). The cravings of sinful man, the lust of the eyes, the boasting of what man has and does – all this is the spirit of the world (1 Jn. 2:16). This is overcome by the one who is born of God. In Pauline terms, in the consecration of faith, the believer's mind is renewed and he does not conform to the world or let it mould him (Rom. 12:1–2), or follow its course (Eph. 2:2).

Central to all of these manifestations of new life is faith which has the new birth as its inaugural context. Everyone who believes in Jesus as the Christ is born of God (1 Jn. 5:1). These are two aspects of one and the same reality, viewed from the perspective of the divine action and the individual's response.

Preparation?

It is clear from the preceding that faith and repentance constitute the phenomenological side of the Spirit's work in regeneration. But how is this brought about? After all, it is difficult to conceive of someone coming to faith in Christ as Saviour and Lord without understanding why a Saviour is necessary in the first place, *i.e.* without a prior sense of personal need for salvation. Without this, the very idea of justification through faith seems incomprehensible. Is there, then, a preparation for justification in which the Holy Spirit is active?

This question brings us back to our earlier discussion of the *ordo salutis* and to the contrast between Roman Catholic and Protestant views of it.

In the context of Augustine's legacy to the church's theology, in which baptism was seen as the *sine qua non* of regeneration and justification was understood as *justum facere*, 'to make just or righteous', medieval theology often emphasized the process of justification.

In this process, 'first justification' was given in baptism, in which guilt and punishment for eternal and actual sin were removed. But the so-called *fomes peccati* (the 'tinder' of sin, which might conflagrate later) remained. For 'final justification', the love of self had to give way to love of God for God's sake. This required the individual to co-operate with God's prevenient grace to do what lay in his powers (*facere quod in se est*, as Gabriel Biel expressed it). Led from the fear of divine justice to the hope of divine mercy, the individual developed a hatred for sin, or contrition.

The problem was, of course, that men were not perfectly contrite. Hence the provision of the sacrament of penance, which bridged the gap between real but inadequate sorrow (*attritio*), and the true contrition (*contritio*) which led to the faith suffused with love (*fides formata caritate*) which brought (second) justification.

Within this system, assurance of salvation was virtually impossible, and to claim to experience it was potentially heretical. Here we see why: certainty of final justification depended on a sufficient contrition, of which no-one could be certain. The whole *ordo* was, in fact, a preparation for a future justification. What had not yet been accomplished could not become the ground for a settled confidence.

The Reformation turned this *ordo salutis* on its head. It distinguished in a biblical way between justification and sanctification, and, following Paul carefully, placed a forensic justification in the foundation of the Christian life, not at its end. It rejected the Roman view of preparation in which penitence prepared the individual for justification.

In doing this, however, the Reformation theologians and their successors did not mean to deny the work of the Spirit prior to actual conversion and justification. They held, in the light of

John 16:8–11, that the bringing of the individual to conviction of sin, righteousness and judgment, which found its initial fulfilment at Pentecost, was a continuing activity of the Spirit in the contemporary world. But conviction is not repentance and faith; it does not further dispose an individual to justification.

Yet does not penitence, or repentance, *precede* and in some sense *prepare* us for faith and justification? Louis Berkhof's widely-used resource book for students appears to take this position: 'There is no doubt that, logically, repentance and the knowledge of sin precede the faith that yields to Christ in trusting love.'[16]

In Scripture, by contrast, faith and repentance are inseparable gifts of the Spirit. The summons accompanying the preaching of the gospel may be phrased as 'Repent and believe' (Mk. 1:15). But, on other occasions, it is simply: 'Repent!' (Mt. 3:2; Acts 2:38; 17:30). At other times, it may be: 'Believe!' (Jn. 3:16; *cf.* Acts 16:30–31). Interestingly, in Acts 17:34 (*cf.* 17:30 above) where the response of repentance was required, the actual reaction of the few converts is described as believing!

It is clear from this that, while denoting different elements in the Spirit's work in bringing about conversion to Christ, both faith and repentance are so essential to it that the one cannot exist apart from the other. As a consequence, the one may be used where both are intended – as though either faith *or* repentance can function in synecdochal fashion for faith *and* repentance. Faith will always be penitent; repentance will always be believing, if it is genuine. There is no regeneration which is not expressed in both faith and repentance.

At the conscious level, however, one may predominate over the other, depending on which object has been a central focus in the events surrounding rebirth. If this is a deep sense of sin, repentance, with its attendant sorrow for sin, may be the dominant influence on the emotions of the individual. Alternatively, the individual may have an overwhelming sense of the grace and graciousness of Christ, in which case faith, with a joyful consciousness of forgiveness and acceptance, may predominate. But neither can properly exist in the absence of the other. Depending on the context of active conversion, the level of consciousness of the one converted may be suffused with a sense of one over the other.

A theological clue to understanding this is found in a fine statement of the Westminster Confession of Faith: faith 'acteth differently upon that which each particular passage thereof [*i.e.* of Scripture] containeth'.[17] The point is that in the varied work of the Spirit the psychological and emotional accompaniments of conversion are correspondingly diverse. But in no case does real conversion take place apart from the presence of both faith and repentance.

The 'conversion' from which sorrow for sin and turning from it are absent, that receives the word only with joy, but knows no other impact from the gospel, is likely to be temporary faith, according to Jesus (*cf.* Mk. 4:16–17). By contrast, the 'conversion' that is only sorrow for sin will eventually feed on itself, and die.

Repentance

What, then, is involved in repentance in this context? Two primary elements:

(1) A recognition of offence against God and the covenant he has made with his people (*cf.* Ps. 51:4, where David's recognition that his sin is against God reflects this covenantal orientation). Isaiah, for example, pictures the people as covenant sons who have rebelled against their Father. The inevitable consequence is that they end up in the 'far country' of exile, individualized in Jesus' parable of the prodigal son (Lk. 15:13), but threatened long ago in the Mosaic covenant (*cf.* Dt. 28:36).

Men are under the covenant judgment of God for their rejection of the obligations of faith and obedience (*cf.* Am. 4:6–11 with Dt. 28:15). Repentance involves a recognition of this; a realization of the significance of being in the 'far country', separated from the Father.

(2) Repentance also involves a turning away from sin in the light of the gracious provisions of God's covenant. Repentance is returning to a spirit of creatureliness before the Creator, in recognition of his mercy to penitent believers (*cf.* Dt. 30:11ff.). Ungodliness is thus rejected and righteousness is embraced.

Such repentance is evoked by the Spirit through a sense of who God is, and therefore by an awareness of the true character of sin. It is a God-centred response; indeed, it is the beginning of true God-centredness. It is a turning away from sin in the turning round to God.

Repentance is as necessary as faith for salvation. Salvation is salvation from sin. It involves more than forgiveness. It includes our sanctification. It must therefore engage those who are saved in the turning away from sin which is involved in repentance. There can be no salvation which allows for an unchanged pattern of continuing in sin (*cf.* Rom. 6:1ff.). But while repentance is as necessary as faith for salvation, it is related to justification in a different way. By faith alone Christ is received and rested on as Saviour. Justification is by faith (alone!), not by repentance. But repentance is as necessary to salvation by faith as the ankle is essential to planting the foot on the ground, or as the beating heart is to the use of the eye for vision. Both are essential, but they are not related to the same act in the same way. Faith is the individual trusting in Christ; repentance is the same individual quitting sin. Neither can exist apart from the other.

We have defined repentance in terms of turning from sin to God in the concrete terms of his covenant relationship with us in Christ. But since that is the activity of self-conscious individuals, it follows that the experience of repentance will vary from individual to individual, just as surely as do their expression and consciousness of sin. God's mercy is not merely a universally applicable medicine for sin; it is prescribed for particular sinfulness and particular guilt. Individual consciousness of repentance, or what we might call the psychology of repentance, is bound to be influenced by this. Here, too, we find the principle which characterizes the ministry of the Spirit: his ways of working are diverse. Herman Bavinck has some wise words in this respect:

> Repentance is, despite its oneness in essence, different in form according to the persons in whom it takes place and the circumstances in which it takes place. The way upon which the children of God walk is one way but they are varying led upon that way, and have varying experiences. What a difference there is in the leading which God gives the several patriarchs; what a difference there is in the conversion of Manasseh, Paul

and Timothy! How unlike are the experiences of a David and a Solomon, a John and a James! And that same difference we encounter also outside of Scripture in the life of the church fathers, of the reformers, and of all the saints. The moment we have eyes to see the richness of the spiritual life, we do away with the practice of judging others according to our puny measure. There are people who know of only one method, and who regard no one as having repented unless he can speak of the same spiritual experiences which they have had or claim to have had. But Scripture is much richer and broader than the narrowness of such confines . . . The true repentance does not consist of what men make of it, but of what God says of it. In the diversity of providences and experiences it consists and must consist of the dying of the old and the rising of the new man.[18]

But within this general framework, there are several elements we can trace that will be common to all incidences of the repentance which is effected in us through the Spirit.

Marks of repentance

In repentance the Spirit produces a new attitude to sin, which will inevitably be accompanied by a sense of shame and sorrow for it (Rom. 6:21; cf. Lk. 15:19). Such an attitude to sin will be as concrete as the sin to which the new attitude is directed. Repentance means returning in a spirit of obedience along the path one has trod in a spirit of disobedience, and is worked out in the specific terms of concrete obedience to the commandments of God (cf. Dt. 30:2). Thus, in the Gospels, the repentance to which the rich young ruler was summoned was to take the concrete form of developing self-denial in the very area he had developed self-indulgence; in the case of Zacchaeus, it meant the returning of what had been taken unjustly (cf. Mk. 10:17–31; Lk. 19:8).

In this sense, Paul describes the repentance which issues from the regenerate heart when he says that the righteous requirements of the law are met in those who walk not according to the flesh, but according to the Spirit (Rom. 8:3–4).

It follows from this that repentance is not limited to the act of the moment, but develops into a permanent lifestyle.

In repentance the Spirit also evokes a changed attitude to oneself. Repentance is dying to the old ways and crucifying one's flesh. Initial repentance is simply the beginning of mortification. It is a deeply radical change. It involves concurring with God's judgment of all reality, including oneself – justifying God in his righteousness and condemning oneself in one's sinfulness. It is taking up the cross and denying oneself – not by ontological self-abnegation, but by the putting off of the old man (Col. 3:9; Eph. 4:22), and by the crucifying of the flesh with its lusts (Gal. 5:24). This too is a permanent change with perpetual implications. It means making no provision for the flesh to fulfil its lusts (Rom. 13:14).

It is worth noting in passing that this has a profound bearing on the issue of the Christian's view of himself or herself. It must always be both simple (we become new men and women in Christ) and yet complex (we are imperfectly renewed). The Christian therefore sees himself or herself as one who has died to sin and been raised to new life. But this mortification and vivification characterize the whole course of his or her life, as we shall later see.

Repentance also has at its root a changed attitude to God brought about through the work of the Spirit. Neither of the first two elements could exist without this. Repentance is rooted in a true view of God. If he should mark iniquities, none could stand; but there is forgiveness with him that he may be feared (Ps. 130:4). Evangelical repentance, the inauguration and continuance of the life of godly fear, is always suffused with the promise and hope of forgiveness. In the theology of Scripture, a sense of sinfulness on its own is never equated with repentance. Thus, the encouragement towards repentance is that 'there is still hope for Israel' (Ezr. 10:2). Peter's genuine repentance after his denial of Christ (which seems to be set in deliberate contrast with Judas' worldly sorrow-repentance and ultimate despair) is produced by his remembering the word of the Lord, which in this case included the promise: 'I will pray for you that your faith fail not, and when you are converted, strengthen the brethren' (Lk. 22:32, lit.; 22:61–62).

The classical pattern of the work of the Spirit in evoking

repentance is found in Psalm 51, which, writes Artur Weiser, does not express:

> . . . the fleeting mood of a depressed conscience, but the clear knowledge of a man who, shocked by that knowledge [*i.e.* of his sinfulness] has become conscious of his responsibility; it is a knowledge which excludes every kind of self-deception, however welcome it might be, and sees things as they really are.[19]

Hence the psalm begins (51:1–6) with a comprehensive analysis of the nature of sin as rebellion (*peša'*, 'transgression'); as distortion ('*āwôn*, 'iniquity'); as failure (*haṭṭā't*, 'sin'); as contrareity ('against you, you only, have I sinned'); as filth that needs to be cleansed ('cleanse me . . . wash me'); as falsehood and lack of authenticity and integrity ('you desire truth [*'met*] in the inner parts'). Repentance also unfolds in a recognition of the danger of sin, as that which places us under the judgment of God (51:4), and in danger of being cast out from him (51:11). It involves the uncovering of the deep-seated intransigence of sin (51:5), since it is rooted in our nature, from the womb.

In the light of this, true repentance inevitably involves a broken spirit (51:17). That is not a highly emotional spirit. It is a spirit in which self-sufficiency and self-defence have been penetrated and broken down.

The same psalm also makes clear that repentance arises not only within the matrix of the Spirit's illumination of our condition, but in the hope of pardon to which he draws us. Appeal is made to the steadfast love of the Lord (51:1); the cry of the penitent is directed to the One who is able to save and who does save (51:14).

Furthermore, the reality of such repentance is evidenced in a new concern for holiness: a new desire for heart-reality and a clean life (51:6–7), for purity and renewal (51:10). Coupled with this is the desire to serve and save others (51:13) which flows from broken pride. Finally, true repentance, because drawn out in the context of grace, leads to, and energizes, worship: 'O LORD, open my lips, and my mouth will declare your praise' (51:15).

David's entire burden is, in one sense, summed up in the plea:

'Do not . . . take your Holy Spirit from me. Restore to me the joy of your salvation' (Ps. 51:11–12). More than official royal anointing is at stake here. David realizes that without the Spirit's ministry there can be neither repentance nor its fruit in the joy of restoration (the verb, significantly, is *šûb*).

The fact that repentance is a gift of the ascended Christ to his people (Acts 5:31) indicates that it comes to us specifically through the ministry of the Spirit. Its nature indicates how manifold and comprehensive his ministry is.

Christ is a 'Prince and Saviour that he might give repentance and forgiveness of sins to Israel' (Acts 5:31). When we ask: 'By what means does God bring us to repentance?', the answer must be that it is by the revelation of himself in his word, illumined by the Spirit. A right view of God as holy and merciful is the only foundation for genuine evangelical repentance. His holiness grounds its necessity; his grace and mercy ground its possibility.

Faith and repentance, as expressions of regeneration, are thus not merely inaugural aspects of the Christian life but characteristics and fruits of the Spirit's ongoing ministry. Indeed, the entire progress of sanctification is but regeneration coming into its own, and faith and repentance becoming more and more the dominant notes of life in the Spirit.

7

THE SPIRIT OF
HOLINESS

The Holy Spirit works in regeneration in order to unite us to Christ through faith. The goal of his activity is transformation into the likeness of Christ (Rom. 8:29). In a word, for the New Testament, sanctification, or holiness, is Christlikeness or, as various theologians throughout the history of the church have described it, 'Christiformity'.[1] Set within the context of justification it is the growth of the seed of regeneration and the outworking of union with Jesus Christ.

Man was made as the image of God and bore his likeness (Gn. 1:26–27). He was called to express it in every aspect of his being. But he fell from that high estate. Salvation, and its outworking in sanctification, consequently have in view the restoration of man as the image of God.

In our sin we have all fallen short of the glory of God (Rom. 3:23). Paul's language here is loaded with the biblical motif of the divine image. In Scripture, image and glory are interrelated ideas. As the image of God, man was created to reflect, express and participate in the glory of God, in miniature, creaturely form. Restoration to this is effected through the Spirit's work of santification, in which he takes those who have distorted God's image in the shame of sin, and transforms them into those who bear that image in glory. This is what it means to become 'partakers of the divine nature' (2 Pet. 1:4, RSV).

Sanctification does not, however, make us become more than human. Rather, men and women become fully and truly what they were created to be; now in principle, hereafter in fullness. This is the perspective of such apostolic statements as 1 Corinthians 15:49: just as we bore the image of the man of dust, we will bear the image of the man from heaven (1 Cor. 15:49; cf. 2 Cor. 3:18; 1 Jn. 3:2).

Holiness in the Old Testament

These considerations should not be lost sight of in the language that Scripture uses for sanctification. The terms for 'sanctify' in Hebrew (qādaš) and Greek (hagiazein) convey the idea of separation. But, already in the Old Testament teaching, this includes undertones of possession for oneself. God separates men and things for his own possession and purpose. More fully, 'to sanctify' means that God repossesses persons and things that have been devoted to other uses, and have been possessed for purposes other than his glory, and takes them into his own possession in order that they may reflect his own glory.

This is the significance for sanctification of the divine covenants in the Old Testament. These bonds which were sealed in blood create or, better, re-create and re-establish the family bond between God and his people. They re-create and restore the fragmented family of God to express the family likeness or image. This is clear especially in the outworking of the covenant in the Exodus. It is the adoption of Israel into God's own family (Rom. 9:4; cf. Hos. 11:1). The original relationship between God and man is restored by grace. Israel is God's son, and is to show forth his praises, bearing increasingly the image of God's glory.

The indicatives and imperatives of the Old Testament covenant relationship are therefore not cold formalities. They have a distinctively familial connotation. They aim at reproducing the family likeness – godliness, or god-likeness – in the people. Just as the heart of the covenantal relationship is 'I will be your God, you will be my people', or 'I am your Father, you are my son', so the heart of sanctification in the Old Testament is an application of this: 'I the Lord [your Father] am holy; therefore you [my children] are to express the family likeness and image – you are to be holy too' (*cf.* Lv. 11:44–45; 19:2; 20:7).

Elements in this revelation of divine holiness and in the format of human holiness were geared to the infancy period of revelation in the Old Testament. Underlying all is the motif of expressing the divine image: being holy as he is holy. Sanctification in the Old Testament involves the first, baby steps of God's adopted son on the road to expressing God's full and final glory. As is true of parental care of very young children, so God's family under the old covenant was governed under the levitical law code by regulations and directives which were specific, comprehensive and often couched in strongly negative terms. Hence, the experience of the period of the Mosaic administration is seen in the light of the new covenant as 'no different from [that of] a slave' (Gal. 4:1). In itself it possessed a glory; but set over against the new, it 'has no glory now in comparison with the surpassing glory' of the covenant at the heart of which lies the work of Christ and the subsequent new ministry of the Spirit (2 Cor. 3:7–18).

In the Old Testament, God's person and character also provide the motive for sanctification: he is holy, therefore his people are to be holy. And God is also the agent of this sanctification: he is the Lord who makes us holy (Ex. 37:13; *cf.* Lv. 20:8; 21:8). The pattern of holiness is always in the form of imperatives of obedience arising out of indicatives of grace. God has redeemed his people from bondage, *therefore* they are to be conformed to his patterns (Ex. 20:1–2). In this connection it is interesting that some Old Testament scholars have held the view that the Decalogue does not merely contain negative commands, but actually gives promise of future conformity to them.

In any event, the ten imperatives were written on tablets of stone and given detailed application for the Mosaic period in the various ethical, civil and ceremonial ordinances in which their principles were applied.

Holiness in the New Testament

The motive, goal and pattern of sanctification in the New Testament have the same basic structure as in the Old, although the content of each is now more fully, or Christocentrically, defined.

The goal is the same: the restoration of the divine image (Eph. 4:24; Col. 3:10). The pattern is the same: the indicatives of God's gracious self-revelation give rise to the imperatives of heart and life conformity to him. But now motive, goal and pattern are more sharply focused, in Jesus Christ. What was revealed in an opaque and fragmentary fashion in the old covenant is made plain in the new. Salvation is in Jesus Christ, who is the *telos* of the covenant; sanctification means being restored to the glory-image of God by being made like Jesus Christ.

In the new covenant, the specific content of the new obedience involves putting off the old and putting on the new man (*cf.* Eph. 4:24; Col. 3:10). The end in view is spelled out in the panoramic statement of Romans 8:29: 'Those God foreknew he also predestined to be conformed to the likeness of his Son, that he might be the firstborn among many brothers.' Christlikeness is the end in view; sanctification is the transformation which produces it. Now 'I am the Lord who sanctifies you' becomes 'I am Jesus who by my Spirit will transform you into my likeness'. 'Be holy, because I am holy' means 'You belong to God's family; Jesus Christ is your Elder Brother; his Spirit dwells in you, enabling you to follow in his footsteps; be like him.' Holiness is Christlikeness. As the Spirit of Christ, the Holy Spirit is the agent of this transformation.

Christ sanctified for us

One programmatic statement in the New Testament summarizes the foundation of sanctification. In his 'high-priestly prayer', Jesus says to his Father: 'For them I sanctify myself, that they too may be truly sanctified' (Jn. 17:19). Under the old covenant the high priest, as representative of the people, underwent a rigorous process of ceremonial sanctification in preparation for his role in the ritual of the Day of Atonement. So too the High Priest who is greater than Aaron must sanctify himself for the true sacrificial ministry of atonement.

Calvin says of Christ that he took both the name and the character of sinners in order to take their place throughout the whole course of his life. By his obedience in life he did what we should have done; by his obedience to the death of the cross he undid the guilt of what we had done in sin. His whole life was sanctified, or devoted to God, to fulfil this ministry.

In the most fundamental sense, the New Testament views Jesus as the author of sanctification, its pioneer (*archēgos*). Perfect humanity, perfect holiness, is first of all expressed in him. Just as he did not die for himself, but to make the effect of his death as propitiation available for us, neither did he live for himself, but to make available to us, by union with him, the sanctification he had accomplished in our humanity. The human holiness that becomes ours through the Spirit has its origin in the holiness wrought out by Christ throughout the course of the incarnation. He has sanctified himself for our sake, so that through union with the Holy One we might be made holy (Heb. 2:10–12), and through participation in the divine nature (*i.e.* his holiness) expressed in our humanity we might escape the corruption of the world caused by evil desires (2 Pet. 1:4).

We have already noted the multi-dimensional nature of union with Christ, rooted not only in the divine ordination but specifically in the Son's union with us in our humanity. Now the relevance of this for sanctification comes to the surface. The nature of sanctification is that it is true God-likeness. But true God-likeness in human form is Christ-likeness. Since Christ-likeness is the full expression of the image of God in man, true sanctification is true humanness.

The only resources for such sanctification are in Christ. Our sanctification is Christ's sanctification of himself in our human-ity progressively applied to and realized in us through the ministry of the Holy Spirit. It is in this sense that Paul says that 'Christ Jesus . . . has become for us wisdom from God – that is, our . . . holiness' (1 Cor. 1:30). In the words of Hebrews, 'Both the one who makes men holy and those who are made holy are of the same family' (*ex henos, i.e.* 'are of one', Heb. 2:11). Sanctification can be ours only by means of the resources of Christ, brought to us through the Holy Spirit as he takes what is Christ's, reveals it to us, and thus conforms us more and more into his likeness, from one degree of glory to another, as we gaze on the glory of the Lord (2 Cor. 3:18).

When we thus see Christ as the author and source and the Spirit as the agent of sanctification, we have a proper foundation for the second element of sanctification.

Participation in Christ

Prior to the incarnation, there was a comparative opaqueness to, and formalizing of, sanctification. To those living in the infancy of special redemptive revelation, it was not always clear why certain elements in the Old Testament lifestyle were marks of sanctification to the Lord. In fact, they were blurred images of Christ, so that only when he came did their real significance appear (he is the 'end of the law' in this sense too, Rom. 10:4). The goal of the law was always the restoration of the image of God. This holiness, established in Christ, is now made ours through participation in Christ by grace and faith.

When the New Testament expounds this, it places special emphasis on union with him in the great pivotal acts of redemption (*e.g.* in Gal. 2:20; Col. 2:6 – 3:17; Rom. 6:1ff.).

No passage is more germane to understanding what is involved in the work of the Spirit in bonding believers to Christ than Romans 6:1ff. Here, in complex detail, Paul describes the heart of sanctification as deliverance from sin and liberty to serve the Lord in righteousness. The former relationship with sin is brought to an end; the Christian is 'freed from sin' (Rom. 6:7, 18).

In Romans 5:12–21 Paul had expounded the riches of Christ's redemptive work by contrast with the sin of Adam. In Adam, all die; in Christ, trespasses are forgiven. Where sin abounded, grace has all the more abounded (Rom. 5:20). The greater the sin, the greater display of grace God has given.

Clearly a false and malicious conclusion might be (indeed, has been) drawn from this. Can we go on sinning on the assumption that our sin will provide a theatre for yet more impressive displays of grace (Rom. 6:1)?

Paul instinctively recoils from such a suggestion of licence: 'By no means!' (Rom. 6:2). The right-thinking Christian's whole being reacts against such a thought, because it cuts across the heart of the gospel; Paul has been explaining that grace reigns *through righteousness* to eternal life (Rom. 5:21). To go on sinning would be to contradict the style of the reign of grace.

To this instinctive recoil, Paul adds an exposition of the significance of the union with Christ into which the Spirit brings us. He explains why Christians do not, indeed cannot, continue in the way of sin: We died to sin. How can we go on living in sin? The idea is self-contradictory.

One of many significant details in Paul's exposition is his use here of a distinctive form of the relative pronoun (*hoitines* [from *hostis*]: *hoitines apethanomen tē hamartia,* 'we who died to sin'). This carries the nuance of belonging to a certain class. It is used in this sense to emphasize a characteristic quality ('we who are those who . . .').[2] We might express the force of Paul's language by translating: 'We *who belong to the category of people who* died to sin.' The idea is that *by definition* believers are those who have died to sin. Since this is so, it is inconceivable, a contradiction of who and what we are, that we would casually go on sinning. To suggest such a thing is to demonstrate that one has not grasped that the grace that brings forgiveness comes to 'reign through righteousness . . . through Jesus Christ our Lord' (Rom. 5:21), that is through union with Christ.

Christian believers have a new and distinct identity because of the bond of union which the Spirit creates between them and Christ. If, by definition, they have died to sin, they cannot go on living in it. Moreover, they have also been raised in Spirit-wrought faith-union with Christ into newness of life (Rom. 6:8, 11). The very idea of continuing in sin, the hallmark of the old life, suggests the impossible – that the Christian can engage in a self-contradiction, denying his new life in Christ.

But by what ministry of the Spirit have believers died to sin and been raised to a new life? And what are the implications? These are the questions Paul raises and answers in what follows. Appropriately, he begins with an appeal to baptism in order to explain the identity of the believer. All who have been baptized have been baptized into Christ's death.

Water-baptism is in Paul's mind here; he uses language similar to Colossians 2:11–12, where water-baptism is undoubtedly in view. But such baptism is, of course, the physical sign of which baptism with the Spirit is the reality. It marks the point at which individuals are publicly identified as belonging to the covenant community, as a Christian. At baptism they receive the name of Christ and are brought under a new authority, baptized out of their own name, as it were, into Christ's name. Here Paul works out in detail what this implies.

If they were baptized into union with Christ, and this is the heart of their new identity, then it follows that they were baptized into Christ's death and resurrection. But, (1) if they were baptized into Christ's death, they share in the significance of that death; and (2) if they were baptized into Christ's resurrection, they share too in what that resurrection means.

The central exegetical question therefore is: What is the significance of Christ's death and resurrection? Paul explains as follows.

Christ's death was a death to sin: 'The death he died, he died to sin' (Rom. 6:10). Death is the wages of sin (Rom. 6:23); Christ paid those wages and submitted to the thraldom of sin on the cross. He came under the dominion of sin, and died to all its claims upon himself. Sin now has no more claim upon Christ our substitute. All its wages have been paid in his death; its claims are exhausted.

If this is the meaning of Christ's death to sin, it follows that it is in this that we participate when by the Spirit we are brought to share in Christ's death to sin. In Christ, in union with him, we have also died to the thraldom of sin. The reign of sin is ended. We are no longer its subjects.

Christ's resurrection in the power of the Spirit was a resurrection into eschatological, pneumatic life (Rom. 1:3–4; 1 Cor. 15:45). The life he now lives, by contrast with the death he died to sin, is a 'life to God' (Rom. 6:10). If we have been united with him, it follows that we have been constituted as Christians, in union with him by the Spirit, to live to God (Rom. 6:4b).

Since both of these things are true of us (and this is what baptism points us to), it is now obvious why Paul recoils from the idea that we can continue in sin that grace may abound. For to do so contradicts the way in which grace has already abounded, namely by the Spirit uniting us to Christ in his death to sin and his resurrection to righteousness. To continue in sin would be to deny our basic identity as Christians. It would be to evacuate our water baptism of all the significance of the Spirit baptism of which it is the emblem.

Paul further explains the implications of this in the most complex statement in his exposition: 'We know that our old self was crucified with him so that the body of sin might be done away with ['rendered powerless', NIV mg.], that we should no longer be slaves to sin – because anyone who has died has been freed from sin' (Rom. 6:6).

Here is the rich tapestry of the Spirit's work; but such crucial expressions as 'old self', 'body of sin', 'rendered powerless' and 'freed from sin' all require more detailed analysis.

Old self (*ho palaios anthrōpos*): In this context, this expression does not refer (as suggested by NIV, 'old self', and by NEB, 'man we once were') merely to what I was in volume one of my biography. Its significance is derived from the background of Romans 5:12–21; it sets the former life in its cosmic, that is its Adamic, context. 'Old self/man' suggests an unwritten contrast with what I am now in Christ, the 'new self/man'. The 'old man' is all that I was in Adam before I was united to Jesus Christ: in the flesh, under the dominion of sin, under the condemnation of the law, and destined for death.

But the old self/man has been crucified with Christ. While that was true representatively at the cross, this 'with Christ' (*syn Christō*) denotes an existentially-realized, Spirit-wrought, union with him which, as we have seen, is multi-dimensional in character. Redemptive-historically this crucifixion took place at Calvary; existentially its significance and implications are realized in us by the Spirit in regeneration, repentance and faith. This latter realization is rooted in the historicity of the former. The believer is no longer identified in terms of the Adamic, but in terms of the Christic. In Paul's terminology, the believer has been 'crucified with Christ'; it is not he, but Christ, who lives; yet he does live – in the life of the new man in Christ – by faith in the Son of God who loved him and gave himself for him (Gal. 2:20).

Body of sin: The direct fruit of the death of the old self/man is that 'the body of sin' is 'rendered powerless'. Some commentators take 'body of sin' to mean 'the mass of sin', sin being viewed as a body or mass, but it is better to take the expression as analogous to the phrase Paul later uses, 'body of death' (Rom. 7:24). There he clearly has the physical body in view. It is, therefore, more likely that, here too, it denotes the actual

147

physical body (to which Paul refers again in 7:11), viewed in one particular aspect of its existence: the body seen as the instrument through which sin exercises its reign, and masters our beings.

Rendered powerless. Because we are new men and women in Christ, our bodies are Christ's by the Spirit (*cf.* 1 Cor. 6:15). They are no longer the property of sin; therefore they are no longer freely available to serve sin's purposes. In this sense the body is rendered powerless as sin's instrument. In the conflict between sin and righteousness, sin can no longer count the believer's body on its side; the body of the believer is now on Christ's side (*cf.* Rom. 6:12–13; 12:1–2). As a consequence, believers are no longer slaves to sin.

Freed from sin. Seen in context, the considerations above help to solve the difficulty caused by the radical statement that follows: 'because anyone who has died has been freed from sin' (Rom. 6:7). In what sense has the Spirit's work in uniting the believer to Christ freed him or her from sin? This is the crucial question for our understanding of sanctification.

Certain interpretations can be rejected immediately, especially those that suggest a quasi-perfectionism. J. B. Phillips, in his otherwise masterful paraphrase of Romans, renders Paul's words, 'A dead man may safely be said to be immune to sin' (probably following what in his day was the standard English commentary on Romans by W. Sanday and A. C. Headlam). But such an interpretation is both exegetically and existentially impossible. Paul clearly did not regard either himself or his fellow Christians as immune to sin. He, like we, could feel its power. He could safely be said *not* to be immune to sin!

Other commentators limit Paul's words to the idea of justification.[3] In fact the phrase he uses, 'freed from sin' (*dedikaiōtai apo tēs hamartias*), might, as an isolated statement, be understood as 'the one who has died is [literally] justified from sin', freed from sin in the sense of being freed from its guilt. But three considerations suggest that Paul's words cannot be limited to a forensic significance here.

(1) In the context, he is explaining why we are no longer *slaves* to sin (Rom. 6:6). He is therefore grounding freedom from sin's thraldom, not merely its guilt, in what he says. Paul's use of *dikaioō* in this context seems therefore to carry the

148

nuance of 'to acquit', *i.e.* 'to set free from obligation'. The Christian is no longer answerable to sin.

(2) Later in the passage, as Paul applies his teaching, he states more directly that the believer is free from sin in the sense of deliverance from bondage to its authority: 'you used to be slaves to sin' (Rom. 6:17) implies that they are so no longer. He adds: 'You have been set free [*eleutherōthentes*] from sin and have become slaves to righteousness' (6:18). Here he uses the standard verb for freedom from captivity or slavery. Since the whole context of Romans 6:16–20 is that of slavery to sin and deliverance from it, not merely the guilt of sin and its pardon, there can be little doubt that Paul is teaching that the believer is delivered from the bondage as well as the penalty of sin.

(3) A further clue here is provided by the fact that, throughout this section of Romans, Paul seems to envisage sin as an alien power and virtually personifies it as 'The Sin' (*hē hamartia*; *cf.* 5:12, 20–21; 6:1–2, 6, 10, 12–13, 17–18, 20, 22–23). His descriptions of its activity serve to emphasize this: sin is portrayed as a king who reigns ('sin reigned in death', 5:21; 'do not let sin reign', 6:12); as a general who employs our bodies as weapons in his warfare ('instruments' or 'weapons' [*hopla*] of wickedness, 6:13); as a master who tyrannizes ('sin shall no longer be your master', 6:14, NEB); and as an employer who pays wages ('the wages of sin is death', 6:23).[4]

Throughout the passage, then, Paul's focus is on the dominion or reign of sin, rather than on the guilt it brings. That reign has been broken for those who have been baptized into Christ, and who through the Spirit have come to share in Christ's death to sin and resurrection to new life.

That does not mean that the inherent nature of sin has changed, even although its rights over the believer have been brought to an end. Nor does it mean that the presence of sin is eradicated. Rather, it means that Christians stand in relation to sin in the same eschatological tension that marks all present life in the Spirit: 'already' its reign has been ended, but 'not yet' has its presence been eliminated.

Failure to grasp this dimension of union with Christ inevitably leads to dramatically wrong conclusions being drawn from the apostolic presupposition that by the Spirit we are freed from sin in Christ. Sometimes this takes the form of an over-realized eschatology and spirituality in which the union with Christ which is ours in the Spirit implies a radical perfectionism, or at the very least a deliverance from the realm of the flesh into the less-troubled realm of the Spirit. But such a view fails to come to grips with the fact that life in the Spirit, in union with Christ, is lived 'between the times'.

Even half a century and more after the event itself, Oscar Cullmann's illustration from the events of the Second World War remains helpful for illuminating the present character of life in the Spirit. In that war, D-Day (the decisive intervention of the Allied Forces' invasion of Europe in 1944) took place a year before the coming of VE-Day (the end of the war in Europe in 1945). In the interim, the battles remained fierce and bloody, even although the decisive act had taken place.

So it is in redemptive history. The D-Day of redemption has taken place in Christ's death, resurrection, ascension and giving of the Spirit. He has acted decisively against the powers of sin, Satan and death which tyrannized his people. Yet the skirmishes with sin (as well as with Satan and death) continue to be severe. They are real and painful. But they take place within a different context from any struggle against sin that marked the old life in Adam from which the Spirit was absent. Now the Christian engages in conflict with sin from the standpoint of deliverance from the prisoner-of-war camp; the decisive victory over the dominion of sin is a present reality in the Spirit; the final victory is assured. But there is still blood-letting, and the whole armour of God must be worn. The Christian is, as Abraham Kuyper underlined, still 'under the treatment of the Spirit'.[5] V-Day is yet to come.

This is confirmed by the fact that Paul follows the series of indicative statements in Romans 6:3–10, in which he describes the new realities of union with Christ, with a series of imperatives in 6:11–14 which draw out the implications for life between the times:

(1) Realize that in Christ the reign of sin is ended and you have died to sin (6:11).

(2) Do not let sin reign existentially, since it has no authority over you actually (6:12).

(3) Do not allow your body to be offered in mercenary service to sin, attracted by the immediate pleasures it offers (6:13).

(4) Deliberately yield yourself to the Lord as one who recognizes his new identity as someone who has 'been brought from death to life'. Put the members of your body in the arsenal of the Lord (6:13).

The demands or duties of grace are co-extensive with the divine work of grace. The pattern of regeneration-faith, in which the Spirit inaugurates us into union with Christ, is continued throughout the whole of life. The imperatives of the gospel operate on the same field as the indicatives. God is sanctifying the whole person, body, soul and spirit (1 Thes. 5:23); the believer must therefore sanctify the whole person, body, soul and spirit. God is working in believers both to will and to do of his good pleasure; believers are, therefore, to work out the significance of their union with Christ in death to sin and life to God, in lives of universal obedience and consecration (cf. Phil. 2:12–13).

Paul's teaching here is the hub of the doctrine of sanctification. It underlines that what it means to have died to sin is not exegeted from our own experience. In this connection John Murray has a telling comment of incisive practical and pastoral significance:

> We are too ready to give heed to what we deem to be the hard, empirical facts of Christian profession, and we have erased the clear line of demarcation which Scripture defines. As a result we have lost our vision of the high calling of God in Christ Jesus. Our ethic has lost its dynamic and we have become conformed to this world. We know not the power of death to sin in the death of Christ, and we are not able to bear the rigour of the liberty of redemptive emancipation. 'We died to sin': the glory of Christ's accomplishment and the guarantee of the Christian ethic are bound up with that doctrine. If we live in sin we have not died to it, and if we have not died to it we are not Christ's. If we died to sin, we no longer live in it, for 'we who are such as have died to sin, how shall we live in it?' (Rom. 6:2).[6]

This same foundation for sanctification is laid by Paul in a different, but no less interesting, context in Colossians 2:6 – 3:17. Here he is combating false teaching on 'life in the Spirit.

151

Reading between the lines, one has the impression that some of the Colossians had not found life in the Spirit to be all they had expected. In particular, they seem to have been taken aback by the continuing influence of sin in their lives. They were therefore fruitful soil for the cultivation of a heretical view of sanctification which promised spiritual fullness. The Colossian heresy, whatever its precise identity, clearly involved a certain mystical asceticism as the pathway to such fullness and perfection (Col. 2:16–23). According to Paul, however, external asceticism can never restrain the indulgence of the flesh (2:23).

What, then, enables believers to deal with sin, to progress in sanctification?

Paul roots his answer in the fact that those who have been baptized into Christ are united to him in such a way that they share in his death, burial, resurrection, ascension and ultimate glorification. This new identity in union with Christ is the groundwork that the Spirit lays for adequately dealing with the continuing presence of sin. On the basis of it, believers are to put off the characteristics of the old man and put on the characteristics of the new, since they have already put on the new man who is being renewed in knowledge in the image of the Creator (Col. 3:10). The fact of union with Christ in his death to sin and new life to God is the foundation for growth in holiness; the knowledge of it provides the motivation.

Imitation of Christ

If the glory of God is the ultimate goal of all things, including our sanctification, conformity to Christ is the immediate goal of that sanctification. We are called to be like him. Our corresponding responsibility is to become like him.

While the notion that the imitation of Christ is the foundation and essence of the Christian life is clearly unbiblical, it would also be deficient to develop a doctrine of sanctification that gave no attention to this New Testament emphasis. For the goal of the Spirit's ministry in sanctification is the reproduction of likeness to Christ, and in this sense to produce the imitation of Christ. It therefore involves following Jesus Christ, taking up the cross and denying self. Indeed, the last two elements are really continuing applications and expositions of the first.

In the context of addressing suffering Christians, Peter notes that Christ had given his disciples an example. The term he uses (*hypogrammos*) refers to the teacher's copper-plate by imitation of which the child learns to write (1 Pet. 2:21).

The imperatives of the gospel are thus to be viewed as the concrete outworking of the imitation of Christ. In the same vein, the life of holy love described in 1 Corinthians 13 is imitation of Christ. The fact of our participation and communion with him through the Spirit makes imitation possible; the exhortations of the New Testament give that imitation concrete form and specific direction.

This is already plain in our Lord's girding himself with the servant's towel (Jn. 13:1ff.). While this was an acted parable of his work, it also served as the teacher's copper-plate: 'Now that I, your Lord and Teacher, have washed your feet, you also should wash one another's feet. I have set you an example [*hypodeigma*; we might say "paradigm"] that you should do as I have done for you . . . Now that you know these things, you will be blessed if you do them' (Jn. 13: 14–15, 17; *cf.* 14:26 for the role of the Spirit in this context).

The principle of imitation is explored in various ways in the rest of the New Testament. Two obvious examples must suffice. Philippians 2:1–11 urges us to grow in Christian unity. The secret of this unity is humility: the mind that we have in union with Christ and in the fellowship of the Spirit is to be the mind-set we exercise with respect to one another, counting each other of greater importance than we count ourselves. Similarly, Romans 15:1–7 urges us to seek the blessing of others, and not to please ourselves. Why not? Paul's answer is one of simple but devastating eloquence. Christ did not please himself (15:3). The implication is so powerful it does not need to be spelled out. Do what Christ did; imitate him because you are his and his Spirit indwells you.

Such progress in life in the Spirit does not, however, take place unopposed or unhindered.

Spirit against flesh

The most fundamental characteristic of the Christian is to be in Christ. Yet believers are not only in Christ; they are in a world marred by the Fall. While they are sanctified in Christ, they are also, for example, in Corinth (1 Cor. 1:2). Furthermore, the new life in the Spirit is lived out in the flesh, in bodily existence that bears marks of a past, subtle, but perpetual addiction to sin. The radical breach with sin as dominion has already taken place; but the final breach with sin in terms of its presence has not yet come. We are not yet made perfect (Phil. 3:12; 1 Jn. 3:8–10). The final crisis of glorification is yet to be.

The Christian lives in a new sphere, in the new aeon. But this new order of existence is lived out in a world still under the dominion of the old. So long as this is true, tension, conflict and struggle are bound to be a leading feature of the status of the believer, and often of his or her subjective consciousness.

There is a dimension to this struggle that involves the world and the devil; but there is a further dimension of it: a conflict between flesh (*sarx*) and S/spirit (*pneuma*).

The terms 'spirit' and 'flesh' are sometimes used in Scripture as wholly anthropological terms, designating the twin dimensions of human existence, physical and spiritual. But already in the Old Testament they stand in contrasting rather than complementary relationship: 'The Egyptians are men and not God; their horses are flesh and not spirit' (Is. 31:3). States Geerhardus Vos, 'According to this statement, "flesh" is the direct opposite of "Spirit" for no other reason than *its* characteristic is inertia, lack of power, such as can only be removed by the Spirit of God.'[7]

In the New Testament this antithesis is further developed: the flesh is unprofitable, only the Spirit profits (Jn. 6:63). Flesh gives birth only to more of the same (Jn. 3:6).

It is now widely recognized that in Paul's writings the antithesis between flesh and S/spirit reflects a supra-individual dimension. The characteristics of life in the flesh include self-absorption, self-reliance and indulgence, dependence on outward ceremony and ritual instead of inner spiritual reality, and clinging to the shadow rather than to the fulfilment in Christ (Gal. 3:3; 5:19–21).

This is, in fact, but the breathing out of an atmosphere of spiritual pollution which has been earlier breathed in. The flesh is an entire world of existence. It stands alongside Adam and the present aeon as a fragmented world order. To be 'in the flesh' is contrasted with being 'in the Spirit' in a way that is clearly parallel to and interconnected with the contrast between being in Adam and being in Christ, belonging to the present evil aeon and belonging to the new eschatological aeon inaugurated by the triumph of Christ and the gift of the Spirit (Rom. 5:12 – 8:27).

Prior to union with Christ, those in Adam are 'in' and live 'according to' the flesh. Now, in Christ, they are 'in the Spirit' and live 'according to the Spirit'. Paul pointedly says that Christian believers are not in the flesh (*en sarki*) but in the Spirit (*en pneumati*) (Rom. 8:9). The antithesis is radical and complete. The idea of a 'sarkic' Christian is an unthinkable contradiction, as Paul underlines (1 Cor. 3:1–3), since to be indwelt by the Spirit is to be 'pneumatic' by definition.

Within his use of flesh–Spirit language, Paul indicates that the situation is yet more complex. Although 'crucified with Christ' (Gal. 2:20), the flesh continues to stand as a threat to life in the Spirit; it 'desires what is contrary to the Spirit' (Gal. 5:17). Hence the injunctions to refuse to allow the mind to linger on the thought of how to gratify the flesh (Rom. 13:14; Gal. 5:16).

Thus, life in the Spirit is not yet lived in the context of the final resurrection order. Rather, life *kata pneuma* is lived in the context of life *kata sarka*. The Christian belongs to the community of the resurrection order, but lives within the context of the present order. Even new life in Christ, lived in the Spirit, has as its context bodily and mental existence which has long been dominated by the flesh.

The conflict or tension which arises can most vividly be portrayed by setting down side by side two statements from Paul:

Galatians 2:20	Romans 7:17ff.
I have been crucified with Christ and I no longer live but	As it is, it is no longer I myself who do it, but it is
Christ lives in me.	*sin living in me . . .*
	I know that nothing good lives in me, that is, in my sinful nature.
	Now if I do what I do not want to do, it is no longer I who do it,

155

but

it is sin living in me

that does it.

Here is the most baffling element of the Christian's present status. The supra-personal flesh–Spirit conflict has a deep echo within the existence of the believer. Christ dwells in the heart through faith (Eph. 3:17). Yet sin also dwells within. True, the situation is not that of two equal powers opposing one another. Grace is reigning through righteousness! We are not 'in' the flesh, but 'in' the Spirit. But for that very reason the tension and conflict are all the more bitter and urgent.

There is a radical and deep-seated conflict-situation in the progress of sanctification that should never be played down. To do so would incline us either to fall into incipient perfectionism (the flesh has no energy in me), or to have an inadequate view of salvation (failing to realize that, by the Spirit, the Lord Jesus Christ indwells us as the hope of glory).

The *locus classicus* of this conflict has traditionally been taken to lie in Paul's teaching in Romans 7:13–25, a passage which has proved to be an exegetical battlefield.

Who is the wretched man?
The view that this passage refers to Paul's Christian life has been held by many of the great figures in the history of theology. Athanasius held it; Augustine changed to it; Calvin expounded it. But weighty names in recent biblical scholarship stand against it, and it has fewer supporters today. A view more akin to that held by the Greek Fathers, and later by Arminius, has tended to dominate New Testament scholarship since the 1930s, following the publication in 1929 of W. G. Kümmel's landmark monograph *Römer 7 und die Bekehrung des Paulus* (*Romans 7 and the Conversion of Paul*). According to this view Paul is not here describing his Christian experience; in a sense he is not describing his own experience at all, at least in the strictly historical sense. Rather, he is viewing himself (in some readings of the text) as a Jew, under the law, but described from the perspective of being a new man in Christ. The 'I' of Romans 7 is, strictly speaking, a rhetorical figure.

Various versions of this 'redemptive-historical' rather than 'autobiographical-existential' approach have been powerfully argued.[8] The key to it is the recognition that here we have a theological description of an individual in the old covenantal era who has not yet discovered the freedom from the law that is given in Christ in the Spirit. Hence, in Romans 7, no reference is made to the ministry of the Spirit, while in chapter 8 references abound.

It would be impossible here to consider this question in full. Furthermore, the agenda historically set for this discussion may well have the effect of diverting us from Paul's actual emphasis on the nature and role of the law. Nevertheless, it is worth noting why the classical interpretation – that this is a description of an aspect of the life of faith – has continued to win supporters.[9]

There is a *prima facie* objection to any exposition of these verses which adopts the view that Paul is here speaking generally or redemptive-historically in such a way that personal and autobiographical elements are absent from his thinking. The sheer intensity of his statements renders such a view improbable psychologically. For Paul would then be describing an 'I' that has had no real existence. Furthermore, the view that the individual under the law (the Old Testament Jew) is being described from the perspective of deliverance from the law means that the statements in Romans 7:14–25 are fictional and rhetorical rather than personal and actual. But the force of the personal in what Paul says (especially in view of the non-autobiographical character of what he has expounded thus far) makes this unlikely.

Furthermore, the continuity of the subject of the passage – the 'I' – in the context of the transition from the past tense (in 7:6–13), to the present tense (used consistently in 7:14–25), is both dramatic and surely significant. It is maintained with such consistency that to interpret the words as having no reference to Paul's present experience seems to be avoiding the obvious, however difficult it may be to untangle some of the exegetical details. Even granted the theoretical possibility that at this point in his letter Paul might engage in a discussion of the pre-Christian condition, the abrupt and consistent change to the present tense militates against the view that he in fact does so.

On the other hand, some version of the classical Augustinian interpretation of this passage is in keeping with the structure of thought in these chapters of Romans. Paul is expounding what it means no longer to be in Adam but to be in Christ. In chapter 6 Paul has argued that the believer is freed from the dominion of sin, but is not yet freed from the presence of sin. Consequently the believer battles against it, in mortal combat. The mighty deliverance of grace sets up a mighty conflict in the Spirit.

The structure in chapter 7 is similar. The believer has died to the law through the body of Christ (7:4). He or she is no longer under its condemnation, but is now 'released from the law' (7:6). Yet the law, as an expression of God's holiness, has not died. Even the best believer is far from perfect according to the standards of the law. So long as he or she is in the flesh, there remains in the believer that which the law condemns and which (viewed in its own light), would make him or her the prisoner of the law. There is therefore not only a struggle with sin involved (6:11–14), but an inevitable sense of frustration in relation to the law, until final deliverance is wrought in the resurrection.

This general perspective is in keeping with a number of further key considerations in specific statements in the passage:

(1) In distinguishing in Romans 7:17 between his true self ('I myself') and the sin that dwells in him, Paul in no sense seeks to absolve himself from responsibility for his sin; yet he distances himself from sin in a way that is surely characteristic of the Christian believer who is 'in Christ' but not yet fully 'like Christ' in obedience to the law's demands.

(2) Paul's recognition (in 7:18) of his corruption in his flesh (*en tē sarki mou*) appears to suggest that there is another perspective from which his life may be viewed (*i.e.* 'in the Spirit'). Again, this dual perspective on life is possible, from the biblical standpoint, only for and of the believer.

(3) Paul speaks of his delight in the law of God (7:22). Although debated, this may be a deliberate echo of the spirit of Psalm 1:2. Paul serves God's law in his mind (7:25). In view of his later remarks about the unconverted mind not being subject to God's law (Rom. 8:7 especially), it is natural to read this as the remark of a man in Christ.

(4) Paul's present recognition that Christ will finally save him from this body of death (7:24) is all of a piece with what has preceded. This is a distinctively Christian confession.

(5) Particularly significant is the final resolution of the position in 7:25b: 'So then, I myself in my mind am a slave to God's law, but in the sinful nature a slave to the law of sin.' Here the duality which is true only of the believer reappears (*autos egō* and *tē de sarki*). The issue is apparently left as an ongoing contradiction. Paul can describe himself from two different perspectives: as to the mind he serves God's law; as to the flesh, he serves sin. This significantly follows the statement in 7:25a about his assurance of deliverance in Christ.

Could this not be an Old Testament believer speaking? Or at least a description of the Old Testament believer from a New Testament standpoint? Perhaps; but to limit Paul's words in this way does not account for either the shift to a consistent use of the present tense or for the clarity of the conviction that Christ brings deliverance.

Paul recognizes that he lives in the context of conflict between two opposite kingdoms. There is more than an apparent contradiction expressed in this view; but it is not between what Paul says in Romans 7 and what he says in chapter 6 or 8. *The contradiction exists within Paul himself,* and surfaces in Romans 6 and 8 as well as in 7. The ultimate cosmic conflict has an overspill in our world, in the clash between this present age and the establishing of the age to come in the church of God. But these two dimensions have their battleground and allies within Paul's own psychosomatic existence. His mind is renewed by the Spirit; he is not in the flesh, but in the Spirit. But he lives in the body (Gal. 2:20) as the body of death. The nature of the flesh as such is unchanged, as is the physical body, even in the man who is not 'in the flesh' in the sense of being dominated by or living according to the flesh. Nevertheless, deliverance from all that hinders complete obedience to God's law is assured. In that light Paul is able to live with whatever tensions his present context creates.

Such a view is not without its difficulties. These include the following: Paul describes himself as being 'sold as a slave under sin' (7:14). He sees himself as a 'prisoner of the law of sin at work' in his 'members' (7:23); he calls himself a 'wretched man' (7:24). He is by nature 'a slave to the law of sin' (7:25). These descriptions are difficult to reconcile with his descriptions elsewhere of life in the Spirit.

Do not such statements indicate that the man in view here cannot be the new covenant believer? This must, surely, be Saul of Tarsus, the unbeliever, or at least Saul before the Spirit comes, even if there are indications – indeed the very details which are taken to point to interpreting the 'I' as a believer – that suggest this is the old covenant man viewed from a new covenant faith perspective.

But these statements simply underline Paul's sense of the inherent contradiction of being one in whom sin continues to dwell when he or she is not under the dominion of the flesh but in the Spirit. For the one who has realized that the synchronous indwelling of the Spirit of Christ and of sin presents an appalling contradiction – not merely a paradox – is bound to express it in terms that verge on, and perhaps even *are*, contradictory.

Paul is not contradicting *himself*, then, when having spoken of freedom from sin in chapter 6 he can still feel himself in chapter 7 to be a prisoner of the law of sin. He is, rather, giving expression to the contradiction that inheres in sharing in the new being in Christ, prior to the time when perfect and final renewal takes place and he is delivered by Jesus Christ from the body of death. Although he has been rescued from the present evil age (Gal. 1:4), he is not yet removed from its sphere of influence.

Nevertheless, these statements should not be thought of as the sum total of the New Testament's perspectives on the Christian life. The apostle is apparently viewing himself from one particular aspect, namely in the light of the holy and spiritual law of God (7:14, 16). In that light, even as a believer, indwelling sin is revealed in all its ugly rebellion against God. Sin remains, and its nature as rebellion and its native enslaving tendencies remain unchanged.

Just as Paul has died to sin yet is not finally delivered from it, so he recognizes that, as one who is in the Spirit, he has died to the condemnation of the law but is not yet made perfect according to its demands.

How can one who has died to sin and is freed from it (6:2, 7, 18, 22) speak about himself as 'sold as a slave under sin' and as a 'wretched man'? Such contradictions in expression underline the fact that the Christian experiences more than a paradox or an antinomy. The believer lives within the context of a real contradiction to which he or she has been introduced by the gift

160

of the Spirit. He or she has been sold as sin's slave; not even redemption obliterates the influences of that bondage – *at least, not yet.* Even when it is being lavishly rebuilt, a ruined castle continues to be marked by past devastations. Rather than tone down the contrast of flesh and Spirit, Paul states it plainly. Only when Christ finally delivers him out of the body of death (7:24) will the contradiction be finally resolved (*cf.* Rom. 8:23).

Paul's cries, therefore, are to be read not so much as cries of despair, of the man without the Spirit, as cries of Christian self-frustration, which will surface in this heightened fashion spasmodically throughout the whole course of his life.

Yet even this view of Romans 7:14–25 should not be taken to suggest that Paul views the Christian as paralysed by sin and the flesh. Rather, it is the Christian's task to put to death the misdeeds of the body (Rom. 8:13ff.; Col. 3:4) in the light of union with Christ and the leading and indwelling of the Spirit of sonship.

Nor is this conflict an equal one. Grace reigns through righteousness *in* us as well as *for* us. Thus, the Westminster Confession's classic statement (despite the infelicity, to our ears, of the expression 'the regenerate part') stresses that:

> Although the remaining corruption, for a time, may much prevail; yet, through the continual supply of strength from the sanctifying Spirit of Christ, the regenerate part doth overcome; and so the saints grow in grace, perfecting holiness in the fear of the Lord.[10]

In summary, then, we may say three things:

(1) The internal aspect of the flesh–Spirit conflict is real; the Christian believer goes through life-long 'withdrawal symptoms' in the development of holiness. Having broken with past addiction to sin creates rather than destroys conflict with it.

(2) Furthermore, this is a permanent reality. But that is not to say that it is continuously or consciously experienced at the same level of acuteness by the believer. Romans 7:14–25 is not the only perspective the believer has on himself or herself, albeit it is an essential perspective.

(3) The resolution of this conflict is not in doubt. In the

present, the believer cries out for deliverance from the body of death, although already possessing the guarantee of that deliverance in the indwelling Spirit. The startling reality of divine sanctification is that it is the presence of the Spirit in our hearts that is the root cause of the establishment of the conflict. It is those who have the firstfruits of the Spirit who groan inwardly as they wait eagerly for the adoption, the redemption of their bodies (Rom. 8:23).

The Spirit *himself* constitutes the firstfruits of final redemption. He is the earnest or deposit and the seal or guarantee of what is yet to be (Eph. 1:13–14; 4:30). In the light of this, the believer no longer lives as a debtor to the flesh to live *kata sarka*; he is not mortgaged to it; rather, his outstanding debt is to the Spirit, to live *kata pneuma*, because he belongs to Jesus Christ and is mortgaged in faith and love to him for all eternity in a debt that can never be repaid (Rom. 8:12).

This is precisely the context of the imperatives of mortification and vivification which constantly emerge from the exposition of the indicatives of redemptive grace and correspond to them. Believers are new men and women in Christ; therefore the old is to be put off and the new is to be put on (Rom. 6:11ff.; Col. 3:5–14) until the adoption for which they long, consummated in the redemption of the body, is accomplished.

Spirit and law

Any assesssment of Paul's teaching in Romans 7 raises the broader question of the relationship of the ministry of the Spirit to the law. This is but an aspect of one of the most fundamental questions in Christian theology: How is the gospel related to the law, the new covenant to the old covenant, Christ to Moses, Pentecost to Sinai?

The events of the Day of Pentecost themselves invite us to consider this question. We have already noticed the antithetical parallelism which appears to operate between Pentecost and Sinai. At Sinai, Moses ascended into the presence of God, and the law of God, written on tablets of stone, was brought down to the people. At Pentecost, Jesus ascended into the presence of God and the Spirit of God was sent down, writing the law on the hearts of the people. Within the context of his explanation of these events, Peter points his hearers to the fulfilment of Joel

2:28–30, with its emphasis on the difference between the Sinaitic administration and the Pentecostal administration. The old, former distinctions under the law are done away with; a new administration has begun through the Spirit.

The Day of Pentecost and the elapse of the Spirit seem to mark the end of the Day of Sinai; and much in the New Testament has the appearance of confirming this premise. John, for example, draws this comparison: whereas the law came through Moses, grace and truth come through Jesus Christ (Jn. 1:17). Certainly, read in an isolated context, this suggests the abrogation of the law.

Paul similarly finds himself specifically accused of teaching the same abrogation (*e.g.* Acts 21:28). Again, many of his statements in a *prima facie* way seem to confirm this: we are justified by faith without the works of the law (Rom. 3:28); we are under grace not under law (Rom. 6:14–15); we are dead to the law and released from it (Rom. 7:4, 6; *cf.* Gal. 2:19); the law of the Spirit has set us free from the law of sin and death (Rom. 8:2). In a word, Christ is the end of the law for righteousness for those who believe (Rom. 10:4). What was glorious in its own day is now, in the Day of the Spirit, seen by comparison to be quite inglorious (2 Cor. 3:10).

However, a closer reading of the New Testament reveals that the relationship between the Spirit and the law is much more complex than this. For one thing, in tandem with this 'abrogatory' strand of teaching stands another emphasis: on continuity. Jesus did not come to destroy but to fulfil the law (Mt. 5:17–20, *cf.* 21–48). In fact, it is love's very nature to fulfil the law (Rom. 13:8–10), which is good and holy and also S/spiritual (Rom. 7:12, 14). It is a hallmark of life in the Spirit that the righteous requirements of the law are fulfilled in those who walk in the Spirit (Rom. 8:3–4).

How is this apparent contradiction to be resolved? Does the coming of the Spirit of Christ end relationships with the law that God gave at Sinai, or not?

The classical resolution of this dilemma is rooted in a formulation of the law which had its *floruit* in the evangelical theology of the seventeenth century. It distinguished three dimensions in the law given through Moses: civil, ceremonial and moral.

In the Mosaic law, these three aspects were tightly and in-extricably interwoven. But the Mosaic law was always intended to be a temporary divine administration of law. As such, it was added to the promise given to Abraham (Gal. 3:17); it was not original to God's covenantal relations with his chosen people. Rather, it served his purposes: (1) in governing a distinct people until the time when the promised Messiah should arise from among them; and (2) in prescribing a way of atonement for those who breached the moral demands of God. Thus, in the Mosaic administration, God's law in its moral requirements (the Decalogue) revealed the need for a Redeemer; in its ceremonial requirements it gave hope of redemption; in its civil regulations it preserved for God the nation from which the Redeemer would arise.

This is the point Paul underlines in his important statement: 'What, then, was the purpose of the [Mosaic administration of the] law? It was *added* [*i.e.* to the promise] because of transgressions until the Seed to whom the promise [*i.e.* in the Abrahamic covenant] referred had come' (Gal. 3:19).

In this context, the Mosaic law basically expounds and applies the perennial law of God for human life in a specific, lengthy, but temporary context. The Decalogue reproduces this in the Mosaic context. This explains why it is possible to draw direct lines from the Decalogue to the opening chapters of the Bible and relate the exhortations in it to the original divine design for human life.[11]

Modern scholarship has shown little patience with this classical three-fold division of the law. But the wholesale rejection of the value of this categorization is premature. It is, of course, important to recognize that from the perspective of the Old Testament the Mosaic law was a seamless robe, and not a patchwork for the Old Testament believer. Yet that is not to say that the Old Testament believer did not recognize its multi-layered character. Some such interpretation is in fact assumed by a number of New Testament emphases. Only given this premise does Jesus' insistence that he fulfils rather than abolishes the law make sense (Mt 5:17–20).

Ephesians 2:14–18 appears to have a similar division of the law in mind. Here Paul speaks of Jesus 'abolishing in his flesh the law with its commandments and regulations'. But, if he can freely refer to the commandment to honour father and mother as valid (as he does in Eph. 6:1), it seems clear that he distinguishes in some sense between the Decalogue (moral law) which he enjoins, and the rest of the Mosaic ordinances. The letter to the Hebrews similarly treats the ceremonial law as in some sense possessing a distinct function over an interim period of time.

Some indication of this multi-layer, or concentric, character of the law is already present in the Old Testament itself. For example, only the Decalogue was proclaimed by God on the mountain; only the Decalogue was inscribed by the divine finger on tablets of stone; only the Decalogue was placed in the Ark of the Covenant. It should, however, be emphasized that *only in the light of the work of Christ* do the threads which held together these aspects of the law come loose and the implicit distinctions become explicit.[12] What was made evident in the giving of the law was that its different dimensions belonged together in the Mosaic administration as foundation principles are related to particular applications.[13] While civil and ceremonial aspects become obsolete, the 'moral' dimension is permanent, and therefore remains applicable in the new covenant era.[14]

More, however, needs to be said. For the status of the law is indeed changed under the new covenant. More than a mere confirmation of the permanent authority of the law is revealed. The hope which was given under the old covenant administration was that it would also be internalized in a new way: in the indicatives of the Spirit's work, God would fulfil the imperatives of the law. Fulfilment, rather than abrogation, is the principle Paul enunciates:

> For what the law was powerless to do in that it was weakened by the sinful nature [*dia tēs sarkos*], God did by sending his own Son in the likeness of sinful man [*en homoiōmati sarkos hamartias*] to be a sin offering. And so he condemned sin in sinful man, in order that the righteous requirements of the law might be fully met in us, who do not live according to the sinful nature [*kata sarka*] but according to the Spirit [*kata pneuma*].
>
> (Rom. 8:3–4)

165

The old covenant indicative 'These commandments . . . are to be upon your hearts' (Dt. 6:6) set before God's people a norm. But, as Jeremiah emphasized, 'Judah's sin is engraved with an iron tool, inscribed with a flint point, *on the tablets of their hearts* and on the horns of their altars . . . *The heart is deceitful* above all things and beyond cure . . .' (Je. 17:1, 9). Sin, not law, was written on the heart, hence the need for the promise of the new covenant. 'This is the covenant that I will make . . . "I will put my law in their minds and write it on their hearts . . . they will all know me . . ."' (Je. 31:33–34). Similar promises are given through Ezekiel: 'I will remove from them their heart of stone and give them a heart of flesh. Then they will follow my decrees and be careful to keep my laws.' Again, this is set within a covenant context: 'They will be my people and I will be their God' – the fundamental Old Testament expression of covenantal relationship (Ezk. 11:19–20; *cf.* 36:25–27).

The anticipation of the new covenant experience viewed from within the old covenant setting is that the new age will bring the fulfilment of what was commanded, namely 'law in the heart'. This is seen as a distinct element in the gift and ministry of the Spirit. Law in the heart and the indwelling of the Spirit are two aspects of the one new covenant reality. This is the key to Paul's somewhat enigmatic statement: 'Do we, then, nullify the law by this faith? Not at all! Rather, we uphold the law' (Rom. 3:31). Law did indeed come by Moses, but the grace and truth to which it pointed came only in Christ and can be effected only by the indwelling of the Spirit. Consequently, the new covenant believer does not receive the moral law in the same way as did the believer under the Mosaic administration; now it is received in Christ who has fulfilled its ordinances and suffered the penalty of its breach in our place, as well as in the power of the Spirit who energizes Christ's people to fulfil it in their own lives. The fruit which the Spirit produces fulfils and exemplifies all that was in view in the negatively-given Decalogue. 'If you are led by the Spirit, you are not under law' (Gal. 5:18; *cf.* Rom. 6:14–15). But in what sense? In the sense that to be under the law is to be in opposition to the law, to have the law 'against' one as a sinner. Yet in Christ this is no longer the case; there is no condemnation for those who are in him; they walk according to the Spirit and display the fruit of the Spirit; 'against such things

166

[*i.e.* the fruit of the Spirit] there is no law' (Gal. 5:23). The ministry of the Spirit produces the *telos* of the law rather than its condemnation. Now the believer who is not under the law is, by the Spirit, 'in-lawed' to Christ (*ennomos Christou*, 1 Cor. 9:21). In being united to Christ by the Spirit the holy law becomes the believer's too.

Kingdom against kingdom

This work of the Spirit in uniting us to Christ brings the Christian life into an eschatological atmosphere. It is lived out in the heavenly realms (Eph. 1:3; 2:6). But these are also the realms of eschatological conflict where the evil day is faced (Eph. 6:12–13). Life in the Spirit is lived in the context of the last days, marked as they are by 'times [*kairoi*] of stress' (2 Tim. 3:1, RSV). The Spirit introduces us to the multi-dimensional conflict which has been inaugurated by Christ's coming. In addition to the war between the flesh and the Spirit, we are brought into a further dimension of conflict.

In the Synoptic Gospels, the inauguration of Jesus into his public ministry marks the beginning of the end, the emergence of the end-time warfare. This is signalled in Matthew's record of the Gadarene demoniacs who, recognizing Jesus as the Son of God, cried out, 'Have you come to torture us *before the appointed time?*' (Mt. 8:29; *cf.* Lk. 8:31). Christ's defeat of Satan in the wilderness temptations is here viewed as an advance incursion of the end-time victory. That is sealed and guaranteed through his death and resurrection (*cf.* Jn. 12:31; Col. 2:15; Heb. 2:14–15; 1 Jn. 3:8; Rev. 12:7–12; Rom. 16:20). But the end is not yet. So long as this is the case, in living 'between the times' the Christian church exists not only within the context of tension between this age and the age to come, and of conflict between the flesh and the Spirit, but also within the war-zone in which the kingdom of God advances against the powers of darkness. The church, as Jesus said, faces the gates of hell.

Abraham Kuyper has finely expressed this:

> If once the curtain were pulled back, and the spiritual world behind it came to view, it would expose to our spiritual vision a struggle so intense, so convulsive, sweeping everything within its range, that the fiercest

battle fought on earth would seem, by comparison, a mere game. Not here, but up there – that is where the real conflict is engaged. Our earthly struggle drones in its backlash.[15]

For this reason we are to put on the whole armour of God so that we may remain standing in Christ.

There is an important parallel here to the end of the dominion of sin. Its *reign* in our bodies has been rendered null and void, albeit its *presence* is not yet finally destroyed. Similarly, Christ has overcome the devil on the cross and disarmed him (Col. 2:15; Eph. 2:2). The conflict of the church and the believer with satanic forces is possible only because we have been set free from his thraldom. It is intensified because of the continuing presence of sin in the believer.

There is, then, an alignment of the flesh–Spirit conflict with the kingdom–Kingdom conflict, for, unlike Christ, Christians are not able to say that when Satan is active, 'He has no hold on me' (Jn. 14:30). There is a point of contact for the kingdom of darkness in the fifth column of indwelling sin. This 'landing ground' lies in our continuing disposition to sin, and is ignored at our peril.

A hint of this perhaps appears already in Romans 7 with its echoes of the opening chapters of Genesis. (In fact Adam's spectre stalks the entire first half of Romans.) In Romans 7:11, the language of Genesis 3:13 (LXX) reappears. In Romans 5:12–21 Paul is in Adam before he is in Christ; but if we are correct in understanding Romans 7:14–25 as a description of Christian experience, then, in a sense, relics of Adam remain in Paul even as a new man in Christ.[16] As we have seen, the one who is indwelt by Christ is still indwelt by sin. Thus, in Romans 7:21: 'When I want to do good, evil [*to kakon*] is right there with me.' Or, could we say, 'the evil one'?

Satan is presented in the New Testament in a broad range of roles of which the Christian must be cognizant, and against which he or she must be well defended: Satan is the hinderer (1 Thes. 2:18); the accuser of the brethren (Rev. 12:10); the devil (*diabolos*), the slanderer (Mt. 4:1ff.; Eph. 6:10ff.; *cf.* 1 Tim. 3:7, 'the devil's trap'; 2 Tim. 2:26). He is the tempter (Mt. 4:3; 1 Thes. 3:5; 1 Cor. 7:5); and the plaintiff or adversary (*antidikos*) who opposes us and who seeks, in Peter's words, to devour us (1 Pet. 5:8).

For this reason, the central imperative of this element of sanctification is: 'Watch and pray so that you will not fall into temptation' (Mk. 14:38). Those who think they stand are to take heed; and those who are concerned for the way others have fallen into temptation must be on their guard, lest in trying to help them they are drawn into the same or similar sin (Gal. 6:1).

The focus of the original temptation was theological: to destroy confidence and trust in God's fatherly benevolence. That motif continues in all Satan's warfare against the elect of God. He knows he cannot destroy their relationship with God, so he endeavours in every way possible to hinder enjoyment of that relationship and pervert it from one of filial communion to one of slavish bondage. It is against this in particular that the whole armour of God is provided as the means of defence. Christ himself wore it (Is. 59:16–17). This is the guarantee of its absolute reliability for us too, as we wear it by drawing on all the resources we have in union with Christ.

The dying and rising of the 'outer person'

The eschatological tensions and conflicts into which the believer is brought through the Spirit create a further dimension to the outworking of union with Christ. Dying to sin and rising to new life in Christ are accompanied by the dying and rising of what Paul calls the outer person (*ho exō hēmōn anthrōpos*, 2 Cor. 4:16), a phenomenon which will be consummated in physical death and resurrection.

Paul hints at this in a programmatic statement: 'I want to know Christ and the power of his resurrection and the fellowship of sharing in his sufferings, becoming like him in his death, and so, somehow, to attain to the resurrection from the dead' (Phil. 3:10–11).

Several unusual features are evident in these words. For one thing, in addition to giving a personal position statement, Paul appears to be speaking against an incipient perfectionism which he sees endangering the stability of the Christians at Philippi (3:12ff.).

A further, arresting feature is the way he mentions knowing the power of Christ's resurrection *before* he refers to sharing the fellowship of his sufferings and being conformed to him in his death, in order to obtain the resurrection. In this chiasmic structure, resurrection–death and death–resurrection, Paul sees that, as one who is united by the Spirit to the risen Christ and who therefore lives in newness of life, he is also united to the crucified Christ and shares in the outworking of Christ's death. There is, therefore, a process, outward as well as inward, in which the pattern of the believer's life is conformed to the basic pattern of Christ's life, namely death and resurrection. It is consummated in the resurrection of the body, when it will be transformed and become like Christ's body of glory (Phil. 3:11, 21).

Calvin refers to this aspect of the Spirit's work in bringing us communion as well as union with Christ as a duplex, or two-fold, mortification (*mortificatio*) and vivification (*vivificatio*). Internally, sanctification involves death to sin, rejection of sin, and consecration to God in new life; externally (since sanctification touches our whole being),[17] it involves the mortification of bearing the cross in all manner of afflictions and persecutions, and ultimately the vivification of the resurrection.[18]

It is in this sense that the Christians in Thessalonica, who experienced great suffering, were a model (*typos*, 1 Thes. 1:7) to other believers. In them the paradigm of union with Christ in his sufferings was clearly displayed for others to see. And this, of course, is God's purpose in two-fold mortification and vivification. He thus conforms his people by his Spirit to the image of his Son (Rom. 8:29). This is the 'good' in view in the way in which the Spirit works things together (Rom. 8:28).[19]

Paul further elucidates the ramifications of this principle in three important passages in 2 Corinthians.

(1) 2 Corinthians 13:4: 'To be sure, he [Christ] was crucified in weakness, yet he lives by God's power. Likewise, we are weak in him, yet by God's power we will live with him to serve you.'

The 'super-apostles' in Corinth despised Paul's 'weakness' ('his bodily presence is weak', 2 Cor. 10:10, AV). They said he was 'unimpressive' (2 Cor. 10:10). Paul responds by indicating that it is in his weakness that he is an analogy of Christ to men. God's power does not necessarily destroy weakness; indeed, his saving power is expressed through the weakness of the cross (*cf.* 1 Cor. 1:25ff.).

Careful attention is required in order to feel the weight of Paul's language here. He does not say: 'We are weak in ourselves, but we are strong in Christ.' That would be true, as he explains elsewhere (2 Cor. 12:10; *cf.* Phil. 4:13). Rather, Paul has a different perspective: bound by the Spirit to Christ crucified and risen, he is weak *in Christ*, as well as powerful in him. His weakness is not only in himself, while (by contrast) he finds strength in Christ through the Spirit. Rather, his weakness is a direct consequence of his union with Christ in his weakness in crucifixion. Paul's weakness is not a motivation for seeking union with Christ in order that he might be strong; it is the direct consequence, implication and outworking of that very union in the Spirit.

This, then, is the way of sanctification, because it is the way of Christiformity, and ultimately the way in which restoration to the divine glory-image is completed.

(2) All that Paul says in 2 Corinthians 13:4 reflects back on his earlier teaching in 2 Corinthians 4:7–12.

Here, again, he is defending his apostleship by describing the character of authentic ministry in Christ. Two features dominate what he says:

(a) There is an unusual use and repetition of the name of Jesus without further title (4:10–11). This draws attention to the humanity which our Lord shared with us.

(b) There is a repeated use of the death-and-life contrast:

> We carry the *death* of Jesus
> to reveal the *life* of Jesus.
> We who are *alive* are being
> given over to *death*
>   His *life* is revealed in our bodies
> that are liable to *death*
>   *Death* works in us;
>   *life* works in you.

Here we come to the heart of Christian experience: by the Spirit we are united to Christ in his death and resurrection. Just as that was the *telos* of Christ's life, and therefore the determining pattern of the whole of it, so it is the *telos* of the Spirit's work in our lives and becomes their determining pattern. Sanctification is the Spirit's outworking into the whole person of a life-through-death in union with Christ.

In terms of sanctification, Paul argues, we are given over to death, external mortification, so that there may be the manifestation of Christ, *i.e.* the manifestation of his life in us. We carry around the dying of Jesus in our very bodies, so that the life of Jesus may also be visible in them. Conformity to the risen Christ is possible only when conformity to the crucified Christ is present.

In terms of the consequences of this, he describes them thus: 'death [*i.e.* the effect of union with Christ in his death] works in us'. The grain of wheat must fall into the ground and die in order to bring forth much fruit (Jn. 12:24); the consequence is that life (the evidence of union with the risen Christ) works in others, for their salvation.

(3) Paul had already spoken graphically of this in 2 Corinthians 1:5. There he says that in union with Christ, as a consequence of the anointing of the Spirit, Christ's sufferings flow over into our lives.

Behind these words may well lie the picture of the high priest in Psalm 133. Aaron was anointed for the service of God; that anointing oil flowed over on to his whole body. Believers, as the body of Christ, participate in the anointing for messianic service of their High Priest. In the same way, Paul says, in fellowship with Christ by the Spirit, an overflow of his sufferings diffuses into our lives. We are not justified by such suffering; our sufferings are not atoning; but they conform us more and more to Christ. Thus, what is lacking in our fellowship in the sufferings of Christ is progressively brought to completion (*cf.* Col. 1:24).

This principle is simply an unpacking of Paul's statement in Romans 8:29. God's purpose is to conform us to the image of his Son; to reproduce the family likeness in us. He does that by employing the pattern he used when his Son sanctified himself for our sake. It was necessary for him to die and rise again, that he might enter into his glory. It is no less necessary for that pattern to be worked out analogously in our lives, that we too, ultimately, may be conformed to the glory-image of God when we finally experience the adoption, the redemption of our bodies and face-to-face knowledge and reflection of the glory of Christ. Hence, according to Peter, Christians rejoice to share the sufferings of Christ so that they may be overjoyed when his glory is revealed. This is the crowning evidence that 'the Spirit of glory and of God rests on them' (1 Pet. 4:13–14).

Union with Christ in his death and resurrection is therefore the ground-plan for the Spirit's work of santification at the most basic level of Christian existence. United with Christ in his death, planted together, or grown together with him in it (Rom. 6:5), believers will likewise share in his resurrection. That is true now, both inwardly and outwardly; one day, in the eschaton, it will be true fully and finally.

8

THE COMMUNION OF
THE SPIRIT

The union with Christ into which the Spirit brings us is the foundation for and prelude to communion with Christ in the Spirit. The believer who is baptized into Christ is baptized into his resurrection as well as into his death, into newness of life as well as into his death to sin. In putting off the ways of the old man, the ways of the new man are put on and life in the Spirit begins.

The whole of the Christian life then, with its deep roots in the love of the Father and its foundation in the grace of Christ, is characterized by what Paul calls the *koinōnia* of the Holy Spirit (2 Cor. 13:14; *cf.* Phil. 2:1). Paul's genitive here (*tou hagiou pneumatos*) poses for us the happy problem of deciding whether the communion is that which the Spirit creates or that in which the Spirit is partner. Strong arguments can be advanced for both, and it is possible that the expression may itself be intended to cover both. It is in communion with the Spirit that we experience the communion which the Spirit creates in the blessings of the gospel in the context of the church of Christ. These are ordinarily inseparable.

This communion of or with the Spirit is, as we have seen, paradigmatically expressed in the life and ministry of Jesus, the man of the Spirit *par excellence*. As such he was filled with the Spirit and walked in the Spirit; Christians are exhorted to enter into a like communion. The New Testament expounds this both in the structure in which it sets the Spirit's ministry, and in the descriptions it attaches to the Spirit's role.

Eschatological structure

Several descriptions of the Spirit's role as fellowship-partner of the Christian possess an inherently eschatological structure; by definition they further underline the already/not-yet nature of all present experience in Christ.

In the old covenant, God was immanent among his people through the Spirit; the consummation of this immanence is found in Christ, the One who is anointed with the Spirit's presence and power; the consequence of his work is the giving of the Spirit to indwell believers.

The indwelling of the Spirit is portrayed in the New Testament as personal in nature: the Spirit *himself* dwells in believers viewed as physical, bodily entities (Rom. 8:11; 1 Cor. 3:16; 6:19). The relationship is more intimate than that of a mere divine influence, but the exact character of the Spirit's indwelling is nowhere explained or explored. In the nature of the case it parallels the mysteries of the divine–human engagement in providence, inspiration and incarnation. The analogy we are offered is that the mutual indwelling of Christ and the believer is shaped according to the pattern of inner-trinitarian relationships. Just as there is a mutual indwelling of Father and Son revealed by the Spirit, so, by the indwelling of the same Spirit, Christ and the believer are united (Jn. 14:20).

The Christian is, in his present mortal body, indwelt by the Spirit (1 Cor. 6:19); in the future his mortal body will be raised and transformed in incorruption, power and glory (1 Cor. 15:42–49). One might even say that the body will be 'Spirit-ized', not in the sense of becoming 'spirit', but by being transformed into a body suited to life in a new world and customized to the dominion of the Spirit. As Vos puts it, 'the Spirit is not only the author of the resurrection-act, but likewise the permanent substratum of the resurrection-life, to which He supplies the inner, basic element and the outer atmosphere.'[1]

A proper emphasis on the *personal* nature of the Spirit may lead us, erroneously, to mutate this impersonal perspective ('outer atmosphere') into a personal one. But to do so would risk the danger of minimizing the multi-faceted nature of the Spirit's work under the guise of maximizing his personal being. These different biblical perspectives must be viewed as complementary, not contradictory. One difference between present and future experience of the Spirit lies in this: now he dwells personally in those who are weak, mortal and shame-touched physical beings; then he will not only dwell in them, but transform their entire physical existence into what, for want of a better term, we must call S/spiritual bodily existence. The nature of his life will suffuse and transform the nature of our lives.

The radical nature of the transformation envisaged here should not be minimized even by a healthy biblical concern to stress the continuity between present existence and the future life. The principle of continuity underlined in the doctrine of the resurrection *of the body* must be safeguarded at all costs, according to Paul (*cf.* 1 Cor. 15:12–19). But continuity must not be maintained to the detriment of discontinuity, for the state of glory greatly surpasses even the state of grace (*cf.* Rom. 8:18–23; 2 Cor. 4:17–18; 1 Jn. 3:1–3). A final, radical work of the Spirit is still to come. Yet the work of the eschatological Spirit is not limited to the future. He invades the present in proleptic fashion by his indwelling.

The character of his sub-eschatological indwelling is expressed by three metaphors which link together his present and his future work, the 'already' and the 'not yet' of Christian experience.

1. Earnest

The Spirit is an *arrabōn* (2 Cor. 1:22; 5:5; Eph. 1:14), a Semitic loan-word for a pledge or down-payment, a guarantee that the final instalment of salvation and glory is assured. In this sense his indwelling is provisional, but belongs to the same order of reality as the consummation.

The movement here is significant. For the Bible, the fullness of the Spirit belongs to the future age, not to the present. Yet it does not fully express the role of the Spirit to say only that we have the Spirit now and will know more of his presence in the future. Rather, what is given to us now is the Spirit who rightly belongs to the future, whose presence indwelling believers implies that future reality has become proleptically present. Vos again expresses this well, albeit in heavily-condensed language:

> The Spirit's proper sphere is the future aeon; from thence he projects Himself into the present, and becomes a prophecy of himself in his eschatological operations.[2]

Paul makes this clear in his statements about the Spirit in Romans 8:9–11 in describing his activity as giving life to mortal bodies. He does this ultimately through the resurrection of the body; but already, before the time, he gives life to bodies of death; then he will bring final deliverance, not from bodily existence but from body-of-death existence (*cf.* Rom. 7:24).

In this capacity the Spirit is the earnest of the final inheritance. His presence as 'life-giving Spirit' in the body of death heightens rather than diminishes the Christian's awareness of the tensions implied in life in the Spirit. Any assumption that the fullness of the Spirit relieves the conflicts of this life misshapes the New Testament teaching. In fact, the presence of the Spirit tends to maximize rather than minimize the sense of contrast between the present and the future, as a second metaphor makes clear.

2. Firstfruits

The Spirit is also the firstfruits of the eschatological consummation: 'we ourselves, who have the firstfruits [*aparchē*] of the Spirit, groan inwardly as we wait eagerly for our adoption as sons, the redemption of our bodies' (Rom. 8:23). The statement is even more remarkable for its cosmic vision than it is for its stirring eloquence. What is now and what is yet to be belong to the same order of reality. Believers are *already* adopted sons of God (*cf.* Rom. 8:12–17). Yet from another point of view they await the adoption as sons in the sense that the resurrection of the body will express and consummate this already experienced reality.

In the Greek Papyri, the term *aparchē* is used of the birth certificate of a free-born citizen,[3] and in view of Paul's statements about children and inheritances it might seem attractive to think of the possession of the Spirit as the guarantee of our legitimacy as children of God.[4] But an agricultural rather than a legal universe of discourse is more likely here. In Paul's Jewish world, the firstfruits were both the beginning of the harvest and the pledge of its coming fullness. This the Feast of Pentecost celebrated. As such, *aparchē* serves well as a description of the Spirit's new covenant presence. To have the Spirit is to have not only the guarantee of the final redemption, but to possess already that which (or better, the One who) is definitive of that final condition, namely the Spirit of Christ.

Nor should this be thought of purely in the objective terms of a new status. Earlier in Romans Paul had spoken of the Christian's rejoicing in the hope of sharing in the glory of God (Rom. 5:2). 'Hope' here, as elsewhere, is not a vague and sentimental wish, but confidence in a still-future reality. Such hope will not prove disappointing, Paul argues, because God has already 'poured out his love into our hearts by the Holy Spirit, whom he has given us' (Rom. 5:5). Heaven is 'a world of . . . love' (Jonathan Edwards).[5] Already the Spirit enables believers to experience an overflow, as it were, from that world. Although only the firstfruits of what is yet to be more fully experienced, viewed in itself it is an *outpouring* of divine love, as the use of the verb *ekcheō* in Romans 5:5 indicates (*cf.* its use in connection with the Spirit in Acts 2:17, 18, 33). We experience the richness of the love of God in the Spirit now, as well as then.

This being inundated with a sense of the divine love has been a hallmark of Christian experience in many different traditions throughout the ages. But it should not be understood to refer to a generalized, mystically interpreted, divine love, for Paul specifies here and elsewhere its character: it is historically manifested in and conditioned by Christ's death and defined in terms of it. The proof and measure of this love is that Christ died for sinners while they were still ungodly and weak (Rom. 5:5–8; *cf.* 1 Jn. 4:9–10). The love of Christ has a constraining force on the believer as the result of the interpretation of the cross as vicarious (2 Cor. 5:14).

This too is an aspect of the Spirit's general ministry in bringing glory to Christ. Within this redemptive-historical framework the sense of God's love suffuses the Christian's consciousness and leads him or her to say: 'the Son of God . . . loved me and gave himself for me' (Gal. 2:20). In the light of this, Christians are 'filled with an inexpressible and glorious joy' which is the Spirit's fruit (1 Pet. 1:8; Gal. 5:22; *cf.* 1 Thes. 1:6; Rom. 14:17). The present experience of Christ by the Spirit is a foretaste of the future fullness. Even in suffering and persecution Christians may enjoy this foretaste because the Spirit rests on them in his dual capacity as 'the Spirit of grace and glory' (*cf.* 1 Pet. 1:8; 4:13–14). Truly, 'The men of grace have found glory begun below' (Isaac Watts).

3. Seal

Christians are not to grieve the Spirit by whom they were sealed for the day of redemption (Eph. 4:30). Paul includes being 'marked in him with a seal [*sphragis*], the promised Holy Spirit' among the many spiritual blessings which are ours in Christ (Eph. 1:13; *cf.* 2 Cor. 1:22).

Sealing may indicate a variety of things: it secures and may also authenticate an object with a view to some future occasion (for Paul, 'for the day of redemption').

In the history of theology, considerable discussion has centred on the nature and timing of this sealing. Already, in the post-apostolic period, the idea of the seal of the Spirit was coalesced with baptism, and there have always been advocates of the view that baptism itself is in view.[6]

The usage of the New Testament, however, implies that it is the Spirit himself who is the seal of the believer, just as the sealing of Christ (Jn. 6:27) is best understood not as his water baptism as such, but as the coming on him of the Spirit at his baptism. In the New Testament, conversion and baptism were ordinarily two aspects of the same event chronologically as well as theologically; but while thus joined they are also clearly distinguished – the thing signified is never reduced to the sign, nor inseparable from it. The role of faith, born of the Spirit, is always seen as the vital link between the two (*cf.* Gal. 3:2–3).[7]

A later and most interesting discussion on the seal of the Spirit arose within the context of the experimental theology of the English Puritan movement. Here, in the wake of fore-runners such as William Perkins, Richard Sibbes (1577–1635), the 'Sweet Dropper', was a notable exponent of a view which would exercise considerable influence on the evangelical tradition.[8]

Sibbes thought about the seal of the Spirit on the analogy of the seals with which he was familiar: these might, for example, bear the image of the monarch and reproduce his or her likeness. For him, therefore, the function of the seal of the Spirit was to stamp afresh on our lives the image of Jesus Christ.

In addressing the further question of the nature of the genitive (does the seal *of* the Spirit denote the seal which the Spirit effects, or is the Spirit himself the seal?), Sibbes argued that, since this sealing is wrought by the Spirit, the Spirit cannot himself be the seal. Rather, the sealing must be some effect of the presence of the Spirit in the believer. In particular Sibbes interpreted it as his confirming work, which takes place *after* the first exercise of faith. 'As faith honours God, so God honours faith with a super-added seal and confirmation.' Sibbes recog-nized that this is of an eschatological nature, producing 'spiritual ravishings which are the very beginning of heaven', so that the Christian 'is in heaven before his time'. This involves a secret assurance that the believer is Christ's; it is 'a sweet kiss given to the soul'.[9]

Two observations are appropriate here. The first is that this kind of description of spiritual experience is by no means limited to the distinctives of Puritanism. Such experiences, albeit described in different nomenclature, are widely attested within the Christian tradition.

But, secondly, such experiences are not self-interpreting; they are generally interpreted and located within a prior grid of biblical exegesis. Having had such experiences after first coming to living faith, Sibbes and others, like Thomas Goodwin, located them theologically in the light of the older tradition of translating Ephesians 1:13: 'in whom [*i.e.* Christ] also after that ye believed (*pisteusantes*), ye were sealed with that holy Spirit of promise' (Eph. 1:13, AV; *cf.* Acts 19:2).

The translators in the days of James I (James VI of Scotland) limited the significance of the aorist participle here (*pisteusantes*) to the past. But the action denoted by the aorist participle may precede, coincide with, or follow the action of the main verb. Here, in Ephesians 1, the seal of the Spirit acts as a 'deposit guaranteeing our inheritance'. The twin facts of the Spirit's presence in every believer, and the assumption that the blessings delineated in Ephesians 1 belong to *all* those who are in Christ, support the view that the sealing and the believing are two aspects of one and the same initiation event.

Paul's use of the seal metaphor later in Ephesians 4:30 confirms this. He counsels Christians generally not to grieve the Holy Spirit with whom they were sealed for the day of redemption. The sealing of the Spirit can hardly be an experience or event subsequent to conversion when it is assumed to belong to all Christians – a point even more heavily underlined if Ephesians is viewed as a circular letter.

It would be equally wrong, however, to think of the seal of the Spirit as an indwelling presence which had no counterpart in the subjective consciousness of the believer. As we have already seen in connection with the presence of the Spirit as *arrabōn* and *aparchē*, if the Spirit is given as *sphragis*, we should anticipate a corresponding effect on the consciousness of the one who receives the seal. Sibbes and others were right, therefore, to note that the Spirit brings assurance of the inheritance which is being kept for Christians and for which they are being guarded by God through faith (*cf.* 1 Pet. 1:4–9). Thus even those contemporaries of Sibbes who hesitated to follow his exegesis of Ephesians 1:13 recognized the validity of the experiences which he described, but tended to regard them as the fruit of the Spirit's indwelling rather than as an additional work of the Spirit.[10]

Spirit of sonship

Of all the descriptions given to the Spirit in the New Testament, the richest is probably 'Spirit of sonship'. Although it is used only once, it is with some insight that John Calvin lists this as the first title of the Spirit,[11] corresponding to what must be seen as the highest of the privileges of redemption, namely sonship.

The theme is eloquently explored by Paul in Romans 8:12–21:

> Therefore, brothers, we have an obligation – but it is not to the sinful nature, to live according to it. For if you live according to the sinful nature, you will die; but if by the Spirit you put to death the misdeeds of the body, you will live, because those who are led by the Spirit of God are sons of God. For you did not receive a spirit that makes you a slave again to fear, but you received the Spirit of sonship. And by him we cry, '*Abba*, Father.' The Spirit himself testifies with our spirit that we are God's children. Now if we are children, then we are heirs – heirs of God and co-heirs with Christ, if indeed we share in his sufferings in order that we may also share in his glory.

Paul's eloquent exposition works through the multi-faceted implications of adoptive sonship; first in terms of the obligations it places on those who are led by the Spirit as God's sons. The 'leading of the Spirit' in view here does not refer to mystical elements in divine guidance, but to the moral character of Christian behaviour: God's sons are to exhibit the family trait of holiness, and this implies putting sin to death through the power of the indwelling Spirit (Rom. 8:13).

The Spirit whom believers have received is not a spirit of bondage, but the 'Spirit of sonship'. The evidence of this is that in the Spirit 'we cry "*Abba*, Father"', the implication being that the Christian participates in a communion with God first experienced by Jesus himself, hence the echo of Jesus' own prayer-language in the prayer life of the church (Gal. 4:6; *cf.* Mk. 14:36).

This astonishing use of child-language ('Father') is so remarkable that it has sometimes obscured the force of Paul's teaching; for the verb he uses, 'cry' (*krazein*), is powerfully onomatopoeic and indicates the presence of intense feeling. It is used in the Septuagint of loud cries and intense emotion (Jb. 35:12; Ps. 3:5, LXX) and similarly in the New Testament of the screaming of the Gerasene demoniac (Mk. 5:5), the shrieks of the spirit who possessed the epileptic boy (Mk. 9:26), the cries of blind Bartimaeus (Mk. 10:47–48) and the cry of Jesus on the cross (Mt. 27:50). The atmosphere here is not tranquillity but crisis.

The connection between this and what follows ('The Spirit himself testifies with our spirit that we are God's children') is unstated and undisputed. It is best to take these words as epexegetical of the antecedent statement. At the very least this crying '*Abba,* Father' is illustrative of, perhaps even definitive of, the Spirit's bearing witness with our spirits that we are God's children and therefore heirs together with Christ.

The logic is clear: through the Spirit we enter into the sense of sonship which Jesus experienced in the context of our humanity; we therefore have experiential evidence of our adoption. Knowing this we also come to realize the implications of our new status: we are children of God, brethren of Christ (*cf.* Rom. 8:29) and therefore heirs together with him (8:17). All this set in the quasi-legal context of the dual testimony of the believer's spirit and the Holy Spirit which (according to Old Testament law) establishes the truth in the mouth of two witnesses (Dt. 19:15). But even more striking than the logical implications is the experiential phenomenon: it is in the *cry* that God's children utter that the Spirit bears witness.

Paul's verb *(symmartyreō)* may mean either 'bear witness with' or 'bear witness to'. C. E. B. Cranfield rejects any idea of the Spirit's joint witness ('witness with') on the grounds that any witness of our own spirits to our sonship to God is quite irrelevant: 'But what standing does our spirit have in *this* matter?' (*i.e.* of confirming our sonship to God) he asks.[12] The question is an appropriate one, but Cranfield's answer ('Of itself it surely has no right at all to testify to our being sons of God') displays over-sensitivity of a Barthian character in its fear of ascribing anything in the way of witness-ability to the human spirit.

The fact is that the Christian's own spirit does display an awareness of sonship, as the rest of the New Testament makes clear (*e.g.* 1 Jn. 3:1ff.), amazing though this is. The problem is that this awareness is often weakened, and God's children may even find themselves doubting their gracious status and privileges. What Paul is saying, however, is that even in the darkest hour there is a co-operative and affirmative testimony given by the Spirit. It is found in the very fact that, although he may be broken and bruised, tossed about with fears and doubts, the child of God nevertheless in his need cries out, 'Father!' as instinctively as a child who has fallen and been hurt calls out in similar language, 'Daddy, help me!' Assurance of sonship is not reserved for the highly sanctified Christian; it is the birthright of even the weakest and most oppressed believer. This is its glory.

This interpretation is confirmed not only by Paul's use of several *syn* compounds in this general context (heirs together with, suffering together with, being glorified together with, Rom. 8:17), but also by the way he phrases his statements in the earlier parallel passage in Galatians 4:1–7. There it is the Spirit, not the believer, who is said to call out '*Abba*, Father' (Gal. 4:6), whereas in Romans 8:16 it is the believer who calls out. These two statements are best harmonized by recognizing that the cry '*Abba*, Father' is seen by Paul as expressing the co-ordinated witness of the believer and the Spirit. There is one cry, but that cry has two sources: the consciousness of the believer and the ministry of the Spirit. Thus the Spirit bears witness along with our own spirits that we are God's children in the cry which comes from our lips, '*Abba*, Father'. Just as no-one can say 'Jesus is Lord' except by the Spirit (1 Cor. 12:3), in a similar way no-one can say '*Abba*, Father' except by the same Spirit. B. B. Warfield expresses this well when he describes the Spirit's witness thus: 'Distinct in source, it is yet delivered confluently with the testimony of our own consciousness.'[13]

Here, too, the description of the Spirit's ministry underscores its sub-eschatological character. The cry which expresses his joint testimony is set in the context of both creation and the Christian groaning in anticipation of the 'glorious liberty of the children of God'; it is the cry of one who already knows the reality of adoptive sonship, but who longs for its consummation in 'the adoption, the redemption of our bodies' which is yet to be (Rom. 8:23). Only then will be fulfilled the eschatological covenant promise which already has its inception: 'I will be his God and he will be my son' (Rev. 21:7). The cry '*Abba*, Father' is thus the most basic instinct of those who, by the Spirit, have been reborn into the family of God and have come to share in the divine nature.

The expression 'communion of the Holy Spirit', if understood to include communion *with* him, further implies a bond of fellowship within a context of mutual knowledge. Here we come to a significant hiatus in discussions of the Spirit. It is commonplace to discuss the question of his divine personhood, his work in the application of redemption and in the fruit he produces, or the nature of his gifts and their role in the contemporary church; but communion with him in a developing knowledge of him is much less frequently explored.

It might be thought that this hiatus has solid biblical foundations. After all, the Spirit does not draw attention to himself; he has even been referred to as the 'shy' member of the Trinity. His task is to glorify Christ, not to speak of or draw attention to himself (*cf.* Jn. 16:13–15). But to draw the conclusion from this that we should not focus our attention on the Spirit at all, or grow in personal knowledge of him, is a mistake. The fact that within the economy of the divine activity he does not draw attention to himself but to the Son and the Father is actually a reason for us to seek to know him better, to experience communion with him more intimately, not the reverse. He is to be glorified together with the Father and the Son.

The revelation of the Spirit's identity and the enhancement of communion with him are key themes in the discourse in John 13 – 16. Since 'the primary object of the death of Christ was the communication of the Holy Spirit',[14] it was incumbent on Jesus to explain to his followers why and how it was to their advantage that he was leaving them in order for the Spirit to come to them (Jn. 16:7). He does this by teaching them to think of the Spirit as the Paraclete.

The Paraclete

Jesus promised to send the disciples another paraclete (*allos paraklētos*, Jn. 14:16). In this context, as we have seen, this indicates that the Spirit is a paraclete of the same kind as Jesus himself. He is 'another, like Christ'.

As the One who has accompanied Jesus throughout his ministry, the Spirit will come to the disciples in that specific capacity. He has been 'with' them, in Christ; now he will be 'in' them as the Spirit of Christ (Jn. 14:17).

The distinction in view here is not between his presence with and his dwelling in the disciples as such, but between the ministry of the Spirit in Christ (*i.e.* 'with you' in this sense) and his subsequent ministry as the Spirit of Christ in the disciples ('in you'). By this new mode of indwelling, Christ's ministry will be continued and advanced. As Raymond E. Brown notes: 'Virtually everything that has been said about the Paraclete has been said elsewhere in the Gospel about Jesus.'[15] Both come into the world; both are sent by the Father. Jesus is the Truth, the Paraclete is the Spirit of truth; Jesus is the Holy One of God, the Spirit is the Holy Spirit. Jesus is the teacher, as is the Paraclete. Jesus bears witness, and the Paraclete is a witness. The world does not recognize Jesus, nor does it recognize the Paraclete.

Most remarkable of all, Jesus goes to the Father in order to prepare a dwelling-place (*monē*, Jn. 14:2) for the disciples, while the Paraclete comes from the Father in order to prepare a dwelling-place (*monē*, Jn. 14:23) for the Father and the Son. That the only two occurrences of *monē* in the New Testament should be in such close juxtaposition is a strong pointer to the parallel which is being underlined here. As Paraclete (1 Jn. 2:1), Christ makes a home for his people in the presence of the Father; as Paraclete, the Spirit makes a home for the Father and the Son in the believer, who becomes individually as well as ecclesiastically 'a dwelling in which God lives by his Spirit' (Eph. 2:22). The Spirit is the divine 'home-maker', unknown and unrecognized by the world (Jn. 14:17b), but effecting new life, growth, nourishment and change within the family circle.

The teacher

As the Paraclete who is like Christ, the Spirit fulfils the function of teacher. Doubtless this has a special redemptive-historical significance for the disciples, since the Spirit's teaching ministry to them is related to the giving of Scripture (Jn. 14:26; 16:13). But there is also a broader dimension. For when the Spirit comes he also brings illumination to Christ's disciples. By the Spirit they will be taught inwardly the nature of their relationship to Christ as well as Christ's relationship to the Father: 'On that day you will realise that I am in my Father, and you are in me, and I am in you' (Jn. 14:20).

'That day' in this context looks forward not only to Christ's resurrection but also to the gift of the Spirit at Pentecost. Herein lay strong encouragement for the first disciples. They feared that they would know less of Christ and that their wonted intimacy would come to an end when he departed from them.

Now he taught them that in fact they would know him better and understand more about him and their relationship with him. On 'that day' they would recognize: 'I am in my Father, and you are in me, and I am in you.'

No language can define, far less exhaust, the meaning of these relationships. The Spirit would help the disciples to grasp the intimacy of the Son's indwelling by and of the Father – what earlier theologians called *circumincessio* or *perichoresis*, the mutual indwelling of one another by the persons of the Trinity, the 'dancing around' of each other in which the mutual harmony and love among the persons of the Trinity find expression. The Spirit thus effects the realization that the Son dwells in the bosom of, and face to face with, the Father (Jn. 1:1, 18). In this way he displays the glory of the Son.

Even more than this is taught by the Spirit. From him the disciples learn that they are 'in' Christ and Christ also dwells in them. Rather than 'losing' him, they will 'gain' him in a more intimate way. In keeping with this, union with Christ becomes virtually the central theme of the rest of the New Testament.

Spirit of intercession

As Paraclete, the Spirit is also the Spirit of intercession. Although the Spirit is given in response to prayer (especially in Lukan theology, *e.g.* Lk. 11:13), his ministry in prayer is mentioned infrequently. Yet it is possible to piece together a brief composite picture of his work in terms of the broader theology of the New Testament.

Prayer is an expression of worship and adoration as well as of personal need. No-one can call Jesus 'Lord', or God 'Father' except by the Spirit (1 Cor. 12:3; Gal. 4:6). Like Jesus, it is in the Spirit that Christians are able to rejoice in the works of God (Lk. 10:21).

To 'pray in the Holy Spirit' (Eph. 6:18; Jude 20), therefore, is not ecstatic in the sense of unintelligent. Rather, it is the analogy in the life of prayer to what walking in the Spirit is in the whole Christian life: conformity to the word which God has spoken. Praying in the Spirit is prayer which conforms to the will and purpose of the Spirit. This is what Tertullian, and Calvin following him, called legitimate prayer: committing oneself to holding on to the promises of God until they take effect.[16]

At another level, prayer is an expression of weakness and need. We pray because we recognize our powerlessness; we make requests to God because we cannot meet them ourselves. But Paul indicates the necessity of the Spirit's ministry in an even more profound weakness than this:

> The Spirit helps us in our weakness. We do not know what we ought to pray, but the Spirit himself intercedes for us with groans that words cannot express. And he who searches our hearts knows the mind of the Spirit, because the Spirit intercedes for the saints in accordance with God's will.
>
> (Rom. 8:26–27)

Here the believer is portrayed as subject to such weakness that coherent petition is impossible. Prayer becomes but a groan. But this groan is an indication of the presence and ministry of the Spirit. While taken by Chrysostom to refer to speaking in tongues, and more recently by Ernst Käsemann to refer to some kind of ecstatic utterance in the congregation, the element of heart-frustration and inexpressible emotion in what Paul says points us in another direction: incoherence. This is a portrayal of the absolute and total weakness of the believer, a weakness too weak to express his or her need coherently.

The grace of the Spirit's ministry is that even when Christians are too weak to formulate prayer, he effects the Father's determination to gather his children into his arms and engage them in his purposes. On such occasions, the inexpressible groans of intercession are akin to the grunts or groans of those whose cerebral abilities have been impaired, yet which are marvellously interpreted by their loved ones.

A simple theme thus emerges as we review what communion with the Spirit means: the blessings he brings provide grace for those who are in need. It is in weakness that God reveals his power through the Spirit (2 Cor. 12:9; cf. 1 Cor. 1:25b, 27b). In this, supremely, the Spirit is another Paraclete, like Christ.

9

THE SPIRIT &
THE BODY

Exploring the ministry of the Spirit is, in some respects, like climbing a high mountain. From the perspective of the climber, a lower peak is ascended only to reveal that the summit is still to be ascended. In an analogous fashion, individual regeneration involves a radical personal transformation; but to see only this would be to miss the full scale of the Spirit's operation and to be satisfied with the view from the lower slopes. For personal regeneration is but one aspect of a new creation which is still to be consummated. As we have noticed, since it is rooted in the resurrection of Christ, it is inseparable from, and must be seen in the light of, a broader, corporate work of renewal in which the Spirit of Christ is engaged throughout history.

Christ's programme is summarized in the words: 'I will build my church; and the gates of hell shall not prevail against it' (Mt. 16:18, AV). In the midst of the eschatological conflict (indexed by the verb *katischuō*, 'prevail'), Christ is calling not merely individuals to himself but an *ekklēsia*, an entire assembly.

This corporate character of Christ's work is expressed to varying degrees in some of the analogies used by the New Testament to describe Jesus' followers. They are sheep in a flock, branches of a vine, friends of a bridegroom, stones in a temple, the new Israel. Hence the exhortations of the New Testament, while intended to be taken to heart individually, are generally expressed in the plural to the whole church. The Spirit does not isolate individuals but creates a new community.

In Pauline theology, no analogy is more central than the one which he alone employs: the church is the body of Christ into which we are brought by the ministry of the Spirit:

> The body is a unit, though it is made up of many parts; and though all its parts are many, they form one body. So it is with Christ. For we were all baptised by [*en*] one Spirit into one body – whether Jews or Greeks, slave or free – and we were all given the one Spirit to drink (1 Cor. 12:12–13).

Here, entrance into the body of Christ, constituted as it is of many parts, is effected by Spirit baptism. Two questions immediately arise: (1) What does Paul mean when he speaks about the church as the 'body' of Christ in which the social and cultural barriers between people are broken down? (2) How is the Spirit involved in baptism into this body?

The body of Christ

The first of these questions has called forth a small mountain of discussion in efforts to trace the origin of Paul's use of the analogy of the body in the hope of clarifying the meaning he attaches to it. To a certain extent that endeavour may well be a false chase; textual meaning cannot be derived merely from the origin of or inspiration for a term. At best, the analysis of the various ways in which the concept of the body might have arisen in Paul's world of thought will provide us with a range of possibilities.

The literature of the Roman empire provides us with precursors of the concept of the human body being used as an analogy for a group of people bound together in important

192

respects. The best-known of these is the fable of Menenius Agrippa (*c.* 494 BC), which Livy records in his *History of Rome.* Menenius Agrippa appeals to the plebs to refrain from revolt by way of a fable in which the various parts of a body, envious of the stomach, refuse to feed it – with the result that the entire body wastes away.[1]

Others have appealed to Paul's sacramental theology, and to the participation of Christians in the one broken loaf which is simultaneously the emblem of the body of Christ and of the unity of his people. More recently appeal has been made to a local Corinthian phenomenon: archaeological excavations of the Corinthian Asclepion have unearthed terracotta representations of various parts of the human anatomy, presumed to represent parts of the body healed by the son of Apollo, Asclepius, the god of healing in the Greek pantheon.[2] But, in view of Paul's use of the analogy elsewhere, this connection seems quite unlikely.

The simplest, and perhaps the best, explanation of the origin of the metaphor is that the idea of a community as a 'body' was 'in the air'. Paul employs it in his own distinctive way and for his own purposes. In particular, the 'body' he describes is unique because it is Christ's. He is its head and ruler. Just as he is head over the cosmos (Eph. 1:22) and directs it according to his providential purposes, so he is head over the church (Col. 1:18) and directs it according to the principles of his kingdom. Here 'head' (*kephalē*) carries a relational, not an anatomical, connotation. Christ is the Lord and ruler of both *kosmos* and *ekklēsia.* Individuals are brought into the church which is the body of Christ, that is the fellowship of those who, because united to Christ by grace and faith, are bonded inextricably together in the one bundle of life; they belong to one another because they belong to Christ their Lord or head.[3]

Baptism with the Spirit

What, then, is the nature of the Spirit's activity in baptism into this body?

Baptism and the Spirit are related together on seven occasions in the New Testament. Six of these clearly refer to Pentecost, and do so in virtually identical language with respect to the role of the Spirit:

Matthew 3:11	*en pneumati hagiō*
Mark 1:8	*en pneumati hagiō*
Luke 3:16	*en pneumati hagiō*
John 1:33	*en pneumati hagiō*
Acts 1:5	*en pneumati . . . hagiō*
Acts 11:16	*en pneumati hagiō*

In each of these cases, Christ himself is the baptizer. The Spirit is the medium. The seventh reference is:

1 Corinthians 12:13 *en pneumati.*

What is the force of the preposition *en* in this statement? Does it indicate that the Spirit is the agent ('by the Spirit'), or the medium ('with/in the Spirit') of this baptism? The answer may in turn shed some light on the further questions: When did this baptism take place? What does it involve?

While *en* may be translated as 'by', 'with' or 'in', the conclusion that Paul sees the Spirit as the medium ('with/in the Spirit') and not the agent ('by the Spirit') is irresistible. For one thing, the language of Spirit-baptism remains essentially unchanged wherever we encounter it, and thus the New Testament consistently sees Christ, not the Spirit, as the Baptizer: 'he will baptize . . .'.

In 1 Corinthians 12:13, Paul's point is that the body is one because all of its members share in the one Spirit whom they have received simultaneously with their incorporation into Christ's body. These are two aspects of one and the same reality. Consequently, it should be clear that Paul refers neither to a work of which the Spirit is the author, nor to a post-conversion experience of the Spirit, but to the initial reception of the Spirit, the river of living water of whom believers may drink and never thirst again (*cf.* Jn. 4:13–14; 7:37–39).

All Christians are thus baptized into one body by Christ; the Spirit is the medium of that baptism. But life in this body is governed by the means Christ establishes for his people's development and growth: in particular by the ordinances of baptism, the Lord's Supper and ministry.

Baptism

The administration of water baptism is a sign of inauguration. That was true of Jewish proselyte baptism, although there has been much discussion about whether or not it antedates that of the Gospels.[4] It was certainly true of John's baptism, which marked the inauguration of genuine repentance in response to the coming of the kingdom. Jesus' baptism at the hands of John in turn marked his public entrance into the messianic age and into the ministry which would reach its centre-point in the baptism of the cross (*cf.* Lk. 12:50).

Baptism with the Spirit inaugurates us into the life of union with Christ. Baptism with water marks this outwardly: 'Repent and be baptised, every one of you, in the name of Jesus Christ for the forgiveness of your sins. And you will receive the gift of the Holy Spirit' (Acts 2:38). Here repentance, water baptism, the forgiveness of sins and the gift of the Spirit are seen as correlative aspects of the one reality of entrance into Christ, and thus into (the fellowship of) the name of the Father, the Son and the Holy Spirit (Mt. 28:19).

From time to time in the history of the church the question has been posed: In view of the S/spiritual and internal character of the new covenant in Christ, are such external rites consistent with its newness? Does this not demean the fullness of the ministry of the Spirit? Thus, in the full flood of the 'inner light' teaching of the seventeenth century, Robert Barclay comments: 'This baptism is a pure spiritual thing . . . of which the baptism of John was a figure, which was commanded for a time, and not to continue for ever.'[5]

By way of contrast, however, the early church continued the practice of water baptism in the spirit of Matthew 28:18–20, and distinguished carefully between water and Spirit baptism (Acts 10:47; *cf.* 11:16). Here, Barclay and those who shared his perspective failed to recognize the theological structures which undergird the external and physical rite of baptism. Both baptism and the Lord's Supper function in exactly the same way as the signs (words) used in the verbal expressions of the gospel; in and through them Christ is made known. Indeed, rather than becoming obsolete in the age which is dominated by the Spirit of Christ, baptism and the Lord's Supper further illustrate the way in which the gospel is fitted to our human as well as our sinful condition. Hence the Great Commission implies that baptism is to be administered so long as disciples of Christ are made and he himself continues to be present with the church (Mt. 28:18–20).

The Spirit of God acts as the inward bond of all God's covenant relationships with his people. Each covenant into which he has entered with them has been confirmed by a specific sign sealing the promise enshrined in the covenant word. The rainbow in the case of the Noahic covenant, and circumcision in the case of the Abrahamic covenant, are obvious illustrations (Gn. 9:8–17; 17:1–4). These symbolize the covenant promise and act as physical signs which confirm it to faith. While the language of 'sign and seal' is used exclusively of circum-cision (Rom. 4:11), it well describes the *modus operandi* of all covenant signs. Thus, for example, Noah could gaze at the covenant sign after a storm and be assured that God was remembering his covenant promise (Gn. 9:12–17). In addition to the promise itself, the sign acted as a physical and visible confirmation (seal) of it.

According to John's own testimony, the central function of his baptism, in distinction from its existential and personal significance for those who received it, was to provide the historical context in which the Messiah would be unveiled: 'the reason I came baptising with water was that he might be revealed to Israel' (Jn. 1:31). This much-overlooked statement, taken with the testimony given to Jesus at his baptism (Mk. 1:11) and his own view of the cross as the fulfilment of all that his baptism meant (Lk. 12:50; Mk. 10:38–39), underlines that even in the case of Jesus water baptism served to point to its inner meaning (sign) and to confirm this to him as he received it (seal). His baptism was attended by the word of the Father to explain its significance, and by the Spirit of the Father coming to equip him to bring what was signified to full realization in his true and final baptism on the cross, as the forging of a new covenant in his blood, at the heart of which new covenant stood the gift of the Spirit (Ezk. 36:26–27).

The two events in the Old Testament which are viewed by the New Testament as 'baptisms', or at least as analogous to baptism, both have the form of water-ordeals through which the elect of

196

God passed to deliverance while others fell under a curse. This was true both of Noah and his family (1 Pet. 3:18–21), and of Moses and the Israelites (1 Cor. 10:2).[6]

Jesus' true baptism on the cross also has the character of a water-ordeal. Psalm 69 is a description of just such a water-ordeal:

> Save me, O God,
>   for the waters have come up to my neck.
> I sink in the miry depths,
>   where there is no foothold.
> I have come into the deep waters;
>   the floods engulf me.
>
> (Ps. 69:1–2)

This psalm is regarded in the New Testament as messianic in character, and its words are placed on the lips of Jesus (Ps. 69:9 in Jn. 2:17 and Rom. 15:3; 69:4 in Jn. 15:25; 69:25 in Acts 1:20; 69:22–23 in Rom. 11:9–10). On the cross, the great ordeal symbolized by his water baptism takes place in reality. The sign administered in the Jordan is fulfilled in the overwhelming force of the storm of divine wrath which breaks over his head on the cross. He experiences a sorrow and desolation which, of itself, almost kills him (Mk. 14:33–34). Here, the symbolism of his circumcision (Lk. 2:21) and of his baptism coalesce (*cf.* Col. 2:11–15). Christ is 'cut off from the land of the living' (Is. 53:8). He is oppressed (Is. 53:7–8) as the 'iniquity of us all' is placed on his shoulders (Is. 53:5–6, 8, 10).

By this means, forgiveness and salvation are brought to us through the Spirit. Christ underwent the covenant curse so that the blessing given to Abraham might be fulfilled in the gift of the Spirit to those who believe (Gal. 3:13–14).

New covenant baptism is baptism into the name of Jesus, *i.e.* it signifies and seals the substance of faith-union with Christ to that very faith which unites us to him. From it, therefore, faith draws all that is signified and sealed by water baptism. In this way, the Spirit draws our eyes to the inner meaning of the baptism of Jesus on the cross for us.

The work of the Spirit in generating and activating faith is, therefore, the *tertium quid* between the sign and the reality it signifies. This is implied in the New Testament teaching; it is assumed in all of the New Testament's formal statements on baptism.

Paul's teaching in Romans 6 is a prime example of this principle. All who have been baptized into Christ Jesus are encouraged to think of themselves as baptized into his death, buried with him, and raised into newness of life in his resurrection power.

Naturally, interpreters tend to signal their ecclesiastical affiliations here in assuming either a quasi (or actual) sacramentalism or, by way of reaction, insisting that what Paul has in view is not water baptism but Spirit baptism. *Tertium non datur*; there is no third option allowed. But it would be to miss the thrust of the New Testament's general teaching to imagine that the rite by itself, apart from faith, effects what it signifies. A *tertium quid* is assumed; there is a third possibility: the ministry of the Holy Spirit in uniting us to Christ. As a result, through baptism, the Spirit illumines to faith the meaning of union with Christ and its significance to us ('On that day you will realise that . . . you are in me, and I am in you', Jn. 14:20). Thus, there is a direct parallel between his ministry in relationship to the word and his ministry in relationship to the sacrament. Both are objective signs; in both cases the Spirit unfolds and applies their meaning, and he effects in believers the reality to which they point.

Baptism is often viewed as though it were primarily a mirror of our spiritual experience of conversion, and as though its core significance were testimony to our faith in Christ. It is thus interpreted as a sign of our response to the gospel in conversion. But this is not the New Testament's perspective, and it minimizes the illuminating ministry of the Spirit in relation to baptism, not to mention the corresponding minimizing of the blessing of baptism, since all the individual tends to see in it is the reflection of his or her own faith-commitment.

Rather, baptism is first and foremost a sign and seal of grace, of divine activity in Christ, and of the riches of his provision for us. It is not faith that is signified or sealed. It is Christ. He is the one whose grace we see in the water of baptism. Faith is therefore not sealed directly by baptism. Rather, Christ's gospel is sealed by the sign to which, as to the promise in the word, faith

198

responds. Thus, the gospel is confirmed to us by the Spirit working with the sign interpreted by the word, and by that confirmation faith itself is strengthened and assured.

Thus in baptism, just as in and through Scripture, the Spirit bears witness to Christ, takes from what belongs to him and shows him to his people, clothed in the garments of his messianic ministry. The word never returns in failure but fulfils its function, either in transforming or in hardening (Is. 55:11; Mk. 4:10–12). Similarly, the sacraments of the gospel will, in keeping with our response to the ministry of the Spirit in displaying the grace of Christ, either transform in grace or harden under judgment. Paul explicitly hints at this when he warns the Corinthians that, in coming to the Lord's Supper in a careless spirit, they do not leave unchanged. In fact, they eat and drink judgment (1 Cor. 11:27–30). It is just as possible to transgress against the Spirit in reacting to the emblems of the gospel as it is in rejecting the word of the gospel.

Martin Luther, recognizing this principle, would say to himself when hard-pressed with temptation, 'I am a baptised man'; thus recalling the grace and resources of Christ which the Spirit illumines through baptism, he responded with a confession of faith. In this way, baptism realizes what it signifies, just as God's word accomplishes that for which he sends it.

An understanding of the way in which the Spirit uses baptism (as well as the Supper) preserves us from the twin errors common in sacramental theology: (1) the error of so subjectivizing the symbolism of the rite that our use of it throws us back upon our own actions, decisions and experiences, and thus distorts the function of faith, which is to turn away from the resources and actions of the believer to the grace that is his or hers in Jesus Christ; and (2) so objectifying the effectiveness of the blessing of the symbol that we identify the reception of the sign with the reception of what it signifies, and give no place to the faith which finds Christ himself unveiled in the sign, or to the ongoing ministry of the Spirit. The efficacy of baptism and the Lord's Supper can no more be separated from the ministry of the Spirit than from the efficacy of the reading and hearing of the Scriptures.

199

The Lord's Supper

Baptism and the Lord's Supper have important features in common: both are covenant signs and seals; both point us to Jesus Christ and his saving grace. Nevertheless, each serves its own specific function and has a distinctive focus. Baptism is inaugural and is received only once as a sign of union with Christ. The Lord's Supper, on the other hand, is a sign of ongoing communion with Christ and is to be received frequently.

To what does the Spirit bear special witness in the Lord's Supper?

The heart of the Supper is the broken bread and outpoured wine, which serve as symbols of Christ's broken body and shed blood. The reception of them is a means of communion with Christ as the one whose body was broken and whose blood was shed for us: 'Is not the cup of thanksgiving for which we give thanks a participation [*koinōnia*] in the blood of Christ? And is not the bread that we break a participation in the body of Christ?' (1 Cor. 10:16).

This, too, like baptism's symbolism, must be understood in covenantal terms. The eating of the passover lamb (of which the Supper is the fulfilment, 1 Cor. 5:7–8) implied fellowship in the blessing of the lamb's death, in protection from the curse of God's judgment expressed in the work of the angel of death (*cf.* Ex. 12). It meant to be bound together with the covenantally redeemed and blessed people of God.

The same is true of the Supper. It seals the new covenant in Christ's blood. Like the passover lamb, Christ has, in death, borne the judgment curse of God in order to share with us the blessings of the presence of God.

In the upper room, Jesus gave his disciples the new covenant cup of fellowship with God. Later, in the garden of Gethsemane, he received from the hand of his Father the cup of judgment and covenant curse. His appeal, 'If it is possible, may this cup be taken from me' (Mt. 26:39), alludes to the cup of divine judgment of which the Old Testament prophets had spoken (Ps. 75:8; Is. 51:17, 22; Je. 25:15, 17; Ezk. 23:31–33; Hab. 2:16 – the passages make for harrowing reading). In drinking the cup, Jesus came under the divinely appointed curse of the covenant, dying in darkness (Mt. 27:45; *cf.* Gn. 15:12) and in hunger, nakedness, poverty and thirst (*cf.* Dt. 28:45–48). He was overwhelmed by the experience of being the cursed one hung on a tree (Gal. 3:13). He felt himself forsaken by God, smitten by him and afflicted (Is. 53:4–6, 10; Mt. 27:46).

Later, after his resurrection, he showed his hands and his feet to his disciples (Lk. 24:37). It is with the crucified Christ now risen that they had fellowship. He was recognized in the breaking of the bread.

Thus the fundamental dynamic of God's covenant is operative: God takes the judgment curse to his own heart; those who believe receive instead the covenant blessing through faith, which is, in essence, communion with Christ, crucified, risen and exalted.

It should be clear now why the role of the Spirit is so vital in the Supper. Only by understanding his work can we avoid falling into the mistakes which have dogged both Catholic (*ex opere operato*) and evangelical (memorialist) misunderstandings of the Supper. It is not by the church's administration, or merely by the activity of our memories, but through the Spirit that we enjoy communion with Christ, crucified, risen, and now exalted. For Christ is not localized in the bread and wine (the Catholic view), nor is he absent from the Supper as though our highest activity were remembering him (the memorialist view). Rather, he is known through the elements, *by the Spirit.* There is a genuine *communion* with Christ in the Supper. Just as in the preaching of the Word he is present not in the Bible (locally), or by believing, but by the ministry of the Spirit, so he is also present, in the Supper, not *in* the bread and wine, but by the power of the Spirit. The body and blood of Christ are not enclosed in the elements, since he is at the right hand of the Father (Acts 3:21); but by the power of the Spirit we are brought into his presence and he stands among us.

In this context it is hard to resist the thought that it is to the ministry of the Spirit in the Supper that John points us when he records Jesus' words to the church at Laodicea: 'Behold, I stand at the door, and knock: if any man hear my voice, and open the door, I will come in to him, and will sup with him, and he with me' (Rev. 3:20, AV). Does this point us to what John believed the church might enjoy with him when it was 'in the Spirit on the Lord's day' (Rev. 1:10)?

Throughout history, the church's theologians have struggled to sustain this perspective. Isidore of Seville (560–636), for example, appears to have emphasized that the Holy Spirit makes the body of Christ present to believers, so binding himself to the body of Christ that he mediates the *virtus* or power of the Supper to those who receive it in faith. Ratramnus of Corbie (died 868), in his celebrated controversy over the presence of Christ at the Lord's Supper with Paschasius Radbertus (died 865; sometimes thought of as *the* theologian of transubstantiation), similarly sought to preserve the understanding of Christ's real presence as his presence by the Spirit.

Probably no theologian has struggled more to express this mystery than John Calvin. And yet, even in his strongest expressions of the meaning of the Supper, an admission of mystery remains:

> Even though it seems unbelievable that Christ's flesh, separated from us by such great distance, penetrates to us, so that it becomes our food, let us remember how far the secret power of the Holy Spirit towers above all our senses, and how foolish it is to measure his immeasurableness by our measure. What, then, our mind does not comprehend, let faith conceive: that the Spirit truly unites things separated in space.
>
> Now, that sacred partaking of his flesh and blood, by which Christ pours his life into us, as if it penetrated into our bones and marrow, he also testifies and seals in the Supper – not by presenting a vain and empty sign, but by manifesting there the effectiveness of his Spirit to fulfil what he promises. And truly he offers and shows the reality there signified to all who sit at that spiritual banquet, although it is received with benefit by believers alone, who accept such great generosity with true faith and gratefulness of heart.[7]

Such thinking (his so-called 'virtualism', because of his emphasis on the *virtus* of Christ's ascended humanity) permeates Calvin's eucharistic teaching. Christ comes to his people in the very body in which he was incarnate, crucified, buried, resurrected, ascended and is now glorified. Life is thus 'infused into us from the substance of his flesh'.[8]

Calvin's language has evoked radically different reactions even within the tradition which traces its lineage to him. Last century, theologians such as Charles Hodge and R. L. Dabney, doughty defenders of Calvin's theology in the Northern and Southern States of America, and William Cunningham, the gifted Scottish theologian, all reacted to such teaching negatively, questioning it as either seriously mistaken or simply incomprehensible. Elsewhere, by contrast, it has been greeted as virtually Calvin's deepest sacramental insight.[9]

There is no doubt that Calvin's language is much more realistic than evangelical teaching on the Lord's Supper has been accustomed to be; and, consequently, his exposition is read as being excessively material. But, then, the same could surely be said of the language of John 6:51–58 and, for that matter, of 1 Corinthians 10:16; we must be careful lest parity of reasoning would imply that discomfort with Calvin's language masks a discomfort with the language of Scripture itself. Calvin himself insisted that not everyone who holds to a *real* eating and drinking of Christ holds to a *carnal* eating and drinking.

What has often been overlooked in this context is the role and the power Calvin attributes to the Holy Spirit. Fundamental to his thinking about the Supper is the outworking of the correlation between Christ ascending and the Spirit descending. The Spirit descends in order to raise us up into fellowship with Christ (*cf.* Col. 3:1–4). Similarly, in the Supper, the Spirit comes to 'close the gap' as it were between Christ in heaven and the believer on earth, and to give communion with the exalted Saviour.

But the question Calvin is further asking is: With what Christ does the believer commune at the table? His answer is: Christ clothed in the humanity in which he suffered, died, was buried, rose, and in which he has now ascended in glory. There is no other Christ than the enfleshed Word (*Logos ensarkos*). There is no other way of grace than through union and communion with him as *ensarkos*. In the Supper, then, we commune with the person of Christ in the mystery of the hypostatic union; we do so *S/spiritually*, *i.e.* through the power of the Spirit.

Calvin need not be interpreted as saying more than this. We

ourselves should not say less, otherwise we either deny the reality of the *koinōnia* of which the New Testament speaks (1 Cor. 10:16), or, just as seriously, we find ourselves denying the continuing reality of the humanity of the glorified Christ. The difficulty here lies not so much with what Calvin says in his teaching on the Supper, as in the way that much Christological thinking does not take adequate account of the fact that there is no other Christ. It does not take the truth of the bodily resurrection and ascension of Christ with full seriousness. Once this is grasped, Calvin's eucharistic theology becomes less puzzling, albeit the truth it represents (as the Reformer himself concedes) remains mysterious. But the mystery is no greater than in other aspects of the Spirit's work.

What, then, is the role of the Spirit in the Supper?

It can be well described in the words of John 16:14. The Spirit will take from what is Christ's and 'make it known' to his disciples. He does this fundamentally through apostolic revelation, so that nothing is revealed in the Supper that is not already made known in the Scriptures. But in the Supper there is (1) visual representation, and (2) simple and specific focus on the broken flesh and outpoured blood of Christ. This takes us to the heart of the matter, and indeed to the centre of the Spirit's ministry: to illumine the person and work of Christ. No new revelation is given; no other Christ is made known. But, as Robert Bruce (1554–1631) well said, while we do not get a different or a better Christ in the Supper from the Christ we get in the Word, we may well get the same Christ better as the Spirit ministers by the testimony of the physical emblems being joined to the Word.[10]

Christian writers in the past, doubtless influenced by an allegorical interpretation of the Song of Solomon, have employed the language of courtship, love and marriage to describe the relationship between Christ and his people. They have spoken of the 'kiss' of Christ. This is the secret ministry of the Spirit. Just as the physical emblem or action of a kiss communicates (as well as symbolizes) love, so the physical emblems which point to a crucified and risen Saviour are employed by the Spirit working in the heart to communicate to Christ's people the love he has for them. As a confirmation of grace to faith, the Supper is used in the hands of the Spirit to minister peace, joy, love and assurance. Here there can be 'inexpressible and glorious joy' (1 Pet. 1:8), a Spirit-given foretaste of the fullness of the presence of Christ which the believer anticipates as he proclaims Christ's death 'until he comes'. Then the regenerating work of the Spirit will be consummated (1 Cor. 11:26). Then, when the Spirit says 'Come!' (Rev. 22:17), the full reality expressed by the symbols will be present, and they will become, like the temple building, redundant (Rev. 21:22).

10

GIFTS FOR
MINISTRY

The ascended Christ continues to express his love to his people by means of the sacraments. They mark entrance into and continuance in the fellowship in the one body of which Christ is the head; in these gifts, expression is given to the unity which exists within the diversity of the people of God (1 Cor. 10:17; Eph. 4:1–7).

The New Testament, however, also emphasizes that the ascended Christ strengthens the unity of the diverse members of his body by gifts of another kind which are also given through the Spirit.

The correlation between the ascension of Christ and the descent of the Spirit signals that the gift and gifts of the Spirit serve as the external manifestation of the triumph and enthronement of Christ. Paul underlines this by the way in which he cites Psalm 68:18 in Ephesians 4:7–8: 'When he ascended on high, he led captives in his train and gave gifts to men.' The outpouring of these gifts of the Spirit marks the

downfall of Christ's enemies and the beginning of the building
of the church (Mt. 16:18). As in the case of the building of the
tabernacle (Ex. 31:3), so in the case of the building of the new
temple of God, gifts of the Spirit are given to equip the people of
God and to enable them to set on display the glory of God, the
fullness of Christ, in the temple of God (Eph. 4:12, 16). Christ
thus adorns his bride, his body.

In our own time, these 'action gifts' (spiritual gifts) have
become as much an arena of debate and disagreement as the
'sign gifts' (the sacraments) were in earlier church history.

Two things may be said here by way of preliminary comment
on this vexed area of discussion.

(1) Central to the exercise of any gift of the Spirit is the
ministry of the word given to God's people. There is no
comprehensive list of the gifts of the Spirit in any one passage of
the New Testament. But in the lists which do exist (Rom. 12:3–8;
1 Cor. 12:7–11, 28–30; Eph. 4:11; 1 Pet. 4:10–11), it is clear
enough (see table below) that the ministry of God's revelatory
word is central to the use of all other gifts; it stabilizes and
nourishes them; they give expression to that word in various ways.

1 Cor. 12:8–11	1 Cor. 12:28	Rom. 12:6–8	Eph. 4:11	1 Pet. 4:11
wisdom-word	apostles	prophecy	apostles	speaking
knowledge-word	prophets	service	prophets	serving
faith	teachers	teaching	evangelists	
healing gifts	miracle-workers	exhorting	pastors/	
miracle-working	healing	giving	teachers	
prophecy	helps	leadership		
distinguishing spirits	administration	mercy-ministry		
speaking in tongues	tongues			
interpreting tongues				

While an eclectic grouping of these various gifts is difficult,
and perhaps even the attempt is wrong-headed, a basic structure is clearly present: the revelatory word through apostle and
prophet is foundational (Eph. 2:20), while all else is informed
by and flows from this. Thus, whether God's revelatory
word comes immediately through apostle or prophet, or
mediately through the exposition of the Scriptures (cf. 1 Tim.
4:13; 2 Tim. 3:16 – 4:5), it exercises the dominant role in the
life of the church and occupies a canonical status. The Spirit
who gives the word uses it to equip the people of God to employ

the specific gifts they have individually received (Eph. 4:11–16).

This general perspective is of great practical significance for the life of the church; to lose sight of it would be to lose the balance of Scripture.

(2) The second point to note is the emphasis which the New Testament places on the role of love in the exercise of spiritual gifts (implicit in Rom. 12:3–8, more explicit in 1 Pet. 4:10–11, and the governing principle in 1 Cor. 13:1ff. as well as in Eph. 4:16): *i.e.* the body upbuilds itself when its gifts are exercised in love. Thus the *fruit* of the Spirit ('love . . .', Gal. 5:22) should be distinguished from the *gifts* of the Spirit, but ought never to be absent in their exercise. For without love, and the humility which accompanies it (Rom. 12:3; 1 Cor. 4:7), the purpose of the gifts of the Spirit is thwarted (1 Cor. 13:1–3). They are given through the Spirit of Christ to equip believers to serve one another in the body of Christ and thus to set on display the unity of the church in the context of its diversity, and vice versa. For this, love is essential.

Fundamental to this perspective are two principles: (a) Spiritual gifts reflect more about the grace of the Giver than they reveal about the gracious condition of the recipient. In the New Testament it is regarded as a serious possibility that an individual may experience and exercise spiritual powers yet lack grace and salvation (*e.g.* Mt. 7:22). The author of Hebrews refers to the possibility of experiencing the powers of the age to come without possessing the 'things that accompany salvation' (Heb. 6:5, 9). (b) Gifts are given to enable their recipients to minister to others. Implied in their possession is the two-fold principle of dependency on Christ and service for others, since the gifts of the Spirit are given essentially to the individual for the edification of others rather than for himself or herself.

To ignore these considerations as guiding principles in the exercise of spiritual gifts is a recipe for spiritual and possibly also moral disaster in the church.

Certainty about the precise nature of all of the gifts which the New Testament mentions may not be possible. Greater clarity is attainable in the case of the gifts related to those whose task was the ministry of the word of divine revelation – apostle, prophet, evangelist, pastor and teacher – although even here debate continues to take place.

Apostles, in this context, are those who were directly

appointed by Christ and gifted with the Spirit to bear witness to his resurrection (Jn. 15:26–27; 20:1–3; 1 Cor. 9:1–2). Others in the New Testament designated 'apostles' seem to have been messengers of the churches rather than eye-witnesses of the risen Christ (Acts 14:14 may use the word in this sense).

Prophets also exercised a foundational ministry. The church is 'built on the foundation of the apostles and prophets, with Christ Jesus himself as the chief cornerstone' (Eph. 2:20). 'Prophets' here have usually been seen as a separate group within the earliest churches, who received the gift of speaking the divine word of revelation as contemporaries of the apostles. It has, however, been argued that Paul's statement is an hendiadys: 'the apostles who are prophets'.

This latter view has been defended in detail by Wayne Grudem in his influential study *The Gift of Prophecy in the New Testament and Today*.[1] As we shall see, this serves his thesis that there are two different 'levels' of prophecy in the New Testament, so that we can speak of 'non-revelatory' prophecy which continues in the church today without threatening the finality and sufficiency of Scripture. But in the light of the distinction that Paul makes between prophets and apostles (Eph. 4:11; *cf.* 1 Cor. 12:28), it is doubtful whether this is the most natural reading of the text. In the lists of gifts which appear to follow a hierarchical ordering, the role of the prophet stands closer to that of the apostle than does the role of the evangelist, even though the latter appears to have functioned as a kind of apostolic plenipotentiary.[2] This seems to underline the revelatory character of a prophet's ministry.

'Pastors and teachers', sometimes viewed as two distinct roles, has recently generally been read as an hendiadys, describing the work of one individual in terms of a dual function. Whether these various titles are also alluded to under the ideas of the serving, teaching and leadership that are in view in Romans 12:7–8 may be questioned. Doubtless the gifts involved in fulfilling these ministries spread beyond those who were recognized in the church in a quasi official way.

The gift of healings (the plural form in 1 Cor. 12:9, 30 is striking) is, presumably, to be identified with the direct healings of the apostles described in the Acts of the Apostles (*e.g.* Acts 3:6–8; 5:16; 8:6–7; 14:9; 28:9). More difficult is dogmatic certainty about such ideas as the *logos* ('message', NIV) of wisdom and knowledge. Perhaps the most natural interpretation is to think of the former as practical insight into the ways of God, and the latter as insight into the revelation of God in Christ, although one needs to remember that earlier in 1 Corinthians Paul has called Christ the wisdom of God, so that a hard and fast distinction may not exist here.

What is noteworthy, however, in view of the way the later church would develop a narrow and centralized concept of ministry, is the relatively subtle distinctions between some of these gifts exercised presumably by different people: wisdom is distinguished from knowledge, teaching is distinguished from exhortation. Body-wide giftedness was anticipated, and room for its exercise taken for granted. Manifestations of the Spirit for the common good (1 Cor. 12:7) in word-ministries were widespread among the people of God. Ministry in the New Testament is always, in the most fundamental sense, charismatic.

The New Testament nowhere analyses the precise nature of these spiritual gifts, or their relationship to an individual's natural abilities and dispositions. That relationship is, inevitably, complex. But we may surely assume from the wholly divine and wholly human character of the way in which the Spirit gave Scripture that he does not totally bypass the specific character-istics of our humanity in distributing these other gifts.

The most pressing difficulty of analysis arises when we consider the nature of speaking in tongues and prophecy. This is due to a paradoxical combination of circumstances: on the one hand, the apparent decline of these gifts in the period following the end of the apostolic era and, on the other hand, the dramatic surge in claims of their restoration or continuation in the past century or so. Attempts have been made to demonstrate their continuation or recurrence in the history of the church, but the spasmodic character of the evidence simply underlines their absence from mainstream Christian experience.

The revival or restoration of these phenomena, claimed today, while statistically overwhelming, creates additional com-plexity in assessing the identification claimed between the New Testament and the contemporary phenomena, and also the differing interpretations of their significance. Contemporary restorationists, seeking an explanation for this, tend to conclude *either* that most Christians between the second and the twentieth centuries did not exercise faith in an appropriate way, *or* that the reappearance of these gifts presages the dawning of the final days. The weakness of the former view is that it is scarcely consistent with the often-repeated testimony that, for example, the experience of speaking in tongues comes unbidden and in a sovereign fashion. (Why did it not come sovereignly throughout the ages?) The weakness of the latter is the distinctive eschatology to which it is bound.

Two issues must therefore be explored: (1) the nature of these phenomena in the New Testament period, and (2) the question of continuation or cessation.

Tongues

Speaking in tongues as an effect of the Spirit's coming is explicitly mentioned in four contexts in the New Testament: on the Day of Pentecost (Acts 2:4, 11), at the house of Cornelius (Acts 10:46), by the 'disciples' at Ephesus who had received only the baptism of John (Acts 19:6), and in the context of the church at Corinth (1 Cor. 12, 14 *passim*).

The nature of speaking in tongues has been frequently discussed, and cannot here be explored at length.[3] Fascinating, if somewhat perplexing, questions arise in this connection. Why is this, in distinction from other gifts, exclusively found in the New Testament and not in the Old (unlike prophecy, miracles, healings and other gifts)? Why is there clear reference to the phenomenon in only one New Testament letter? Is the phenomenon identical in every instance?

This last question is of some importance. It has been argued that the real miracle at Pentecost was one of hearing (Acts 2:6, 8, 11), and that the 'tongues' were in fact a form of ecstatic utterance rather than an identifiable language. But this is an unnatural reading of Acts 2:1–13, which records a speaking in other tongues as well as a hearing in the 'native language' and 'tongues' of those present on the Day of Pentecost.

It is difficult to resist the conclusion that the tongues spoken in the household of Cornelius and by the 'disciples' at Ephesus were identical in character to those at Pentecost. But what of the tongues to which Paul refers in 1 Corinthians? Here exegetes are not agreed. Certainly *glōssa* (*cf.* Acts 2:4; 1 Cor. 12 – 14) ordinarily refers to an actual language; and, furthermore, Paul recognizes that speaking in tongues requires interpretation or translation since it communicates a coherent message. Categorically different gifts of the Spirit do not seem to be in view.

The difference between Pentecost and Corinth lies in the fact that those who heard tongues in Jerusalem already possessed the key for their interpretation: they understood the foreign languages since they were their native tongues (Acts 2:11); no translation was required. By contrast, in Corinth it was necessary for an interpreter to speak. But there is no reason for thinking that there was any essential difference between the nature of the tongues spoken in the two contexts.

But were these tongues identifiable *human* languages? Here, too, we find division of opinion. It has been claimed that 'tongues' refers to the language of angels, in view of Paul's intriguing reference to 'the tongues of men *and of angels*' (1 Cor. 13:1). Angelic language is mentioned in the apocryphal *Testament of Job* in 48:3, where Hemera, one of Job's daughters, speaks in an angelic dialect. It is possible, however, that 'tongues of angels' (like a number of expressions in 1 Corinthians) expresses a Corinthian claim, rather than apostolic understanding. That would fit well with elements in the false teaching current at Corinth (the over-realized eschatology which led some to hold that the resurrection had already taken place and that therefore believers were already like the angels in heaven). But the idea that tongues represent the language of angels is not consistent with the use Paul makes of Isaiah 28:11–12 in 1 Corinthians 14:21. Here he explains that part of the inner significance of uninterpreted tongues is the way they can act as 'a sign, not for believers but for unbelievers' (1 Cor. 14:22). For Paul, tongues serve partly as the sign of God's judgment on his covenant people. What marks the reversal of Babel and indicates the universality of the new covenant also signals judgment on the covenant people for the rejection of Christ. Babylon reversed is, in another sense, Jerusalem judged ('their loss means riches for the Gentiles', Rom. 11:12). The use of languages other than the common covenant tongue is a sign of divine hostility. Angelic speech would scarcely be appropriate as a rejection sign! In keeping with Paul's application of Isaiah,

213

then, it is more consistent to see the tongues in Corinth as foreign languages requiring translation and interpretation. As at Pentecost, when interpreted, such speaking in tongues was equivalent to prophecy (Acts 2:17–18; 1 Cor. 14:5).[4] The phenomena, if not actually identical, are certainly functionally equivalent in the church.

Prophecy

In the Old Testament the prophet (*nābî'*) was the mouthpiece of God, and the instrument of divine revelation. That revelation came, of course, in various forms and was delivered in a variety of ways (Heb. 1:1; Acts 2:17). Common to all modes, however, was the notion that the words of the Lord became the words of the prophets: his words in their mouths and on their lips (Dt. 18:18–19; *cf.* Je. 1:9). Thus, to prefix one's statements with the sacred claim 'This is what the Sovereign Lord says' was to profess to be a vehicle of divine revelation.

Prophecy in the New Testament has been similarly understood. But with the widespread conviction which arose within the church that the Scriptures constituted a unique and completed repository of divine revelation, it became common to interpret many New Testament references to 'prophecy' as tantamount to preaching, thus allowing those passages to have a direct significance for the ordering of contemporary church life. Thus William Perkins' late-sixteenth-century work *The Art of Prophesying* is a handbook for young students and ministers to teach them the art of expository preaching. More recent studies have explored the possibility that prophecy should be understood as immediate, unpremeditated insight into the meaning of Scripture.

Recently a number of writers have suggested that in the New Testament we encounter two levels of prophetic ministry: (1) that associated with the apostles and characterized by an implicit claim to infallibility, and (2) a second level of prophecy which lays claim to divinely-given insight, but not necessarily to infallibility of utterance. This view has been especially, but not exclusively, argued for by Wayne Grudem in several publications.[5]

Grudem notes that in the Hellenistic world the semantic

214

range of the term 'prophet' was very wide indeed, and he argues that we should recognize a similar range in the New Testament. While a distinction was made in Hellenistic religion between the different 'levels' of prophecy involved in inspiration and interpretation,[6] however, the controlling background to the New Testament's thinking is not Hellenistic but Hebraic prophecy, with its implicit, and at times explicit, claim to divine inspiration, not least when it reflected on future events.

Grudem holds that in the new covenant era the role of inspired prophets is continued in the work of apostles, and that this latter title is used to avoid confusion with the 'prophets' of the contemporary religious culture. Thus, in Ephesians 2:20, the 'apostles and prophets' on whom the church is built is a hendiadys for 'the apostolic prophets'. But this is hardly persuasive reasoning. While it is true that there are important analogies between the roles of Old Testament prophets and New Testament apostles, if the church had been sensitive to the possibility of a misunderstanding of the term 'prophet', it would make no sense to use it at all, and certainly not of the apostles.

In his earlier work Grudem spoke of two different *kinds* of prophecy; in the later work he clarifies his intention by speaking of two different *levels of authority*. He then seeks to demonstrate that the first of these involves a claim to infallibility; the second does not. The first is therefore non-continuing; the second may continue.

Grudem underlines several indications in the Acts of the Apostles which he believes support his thesis. The following are (in my view) his most important arguments:

(1) In Agabus' prophecy about the coming famine (Acts 11:28), Luke's language ('through the Spirit') expresses a 'rather loose relationship between the Holy Spirit and the prophet, since it allows room for a large degree of personal influence by the human person himself'. Grudem here argues on the analogy of Romans 8:37 and 1 Timothy 1:14.[7]

This, however, is an unhelpful argument. Grudem's own doctrine of Scripture requires that the ministry of the Spirit which effects the inerrancy of the prophetic Scriptures also ordinarily leaves room for the full expression of the personal characteristics and activity of the human author. But, as he recognizes, this does not reduce its authority to a lower level or weaken its infallible character.

Recorded New Testament prophecy inevitably has the same underlying form, as the words of Agabus make clear: 'The Holy Spirit says' (Acts 21:11). The inadequacy of Grudem's thesis at this point is seen by the fact that it places him in the paradoxical situation of implying that, when Agabus spoke under the general influence of the Spirit ('through the Spirit', Acts 11:28), he more accurately prophesied the future than when he spoke (less accurately, in Grudem's view) of Paul's destiny as what 'the Holy Spirit says' (Acts 21:11)!

The case of Agabus may not be essential to this thesis,[8] but it *de facto* plays a major role in the demonstration of it since it is claimed as an explicit New Testament illustration of fallible prophecy which is not false prophecy. The problem with the thesis is that, if this is the case, the line between fallible and false becomes dangerously thin. We may well ask: How fallible is false? For if we follow the two-level prophecy hypothesis in this particular instance, Agabus was doubly in error: (a) His prophecy errs in detail – and, in Grudem's view, in details which lie at the heart of the prophecy. (b) In addition, Agabus does not seem to be aware of the very distinction that Grudem regards as widespread in the New Testament era – the distinction between first- and second-level prophecy. Otherwise, instead of saying 'The Holy Spirit says' (Acts 21:11), he should have said something like: 'It looks to me as though the Spirit is perhaps indicating that something like this may well happen to Paul if he goes to Jerusalem; but I could be wrong, especially on the details.' Luke's record certainly gives no indication that Grudem's hypothesis was the working assumption of either Agabus or Paul.

(2) Grudem holds that his view is established by the prophesying of the 'disciples' at Ephesus. Their prophecy is 'certainly different from the divinely authoritative speech of Paul and the other apostles'.[9] But this confuses significance with inspiration. What these Ephesian believers 'prophesied' must, in Grudem's view, have been relatively incidental by comparison with the weighty statements of the apostles. True, but irrelevant. For the relatively incidental and insignificant is not by definition less accurate or less divinely inspired than the weightier and

more significant. Doubtless, the statements 'All have sinned and fall short of the glory of God, and are justified freely by his grace through the redemption that came by Christ Jesus. God presented him as a sacrifice of atonement, through faith in his blood' (Rom. 3:23–25) are of almost infinitely greater moment than the message 'Greet Herodion, my relative' (Rom. 16:11). But Grudem himself would not thereby hold that the former possesses an inspiration or authority which is 'certainly different' from the latter. Nor, presumably, was Paul any more active in framing the wording of the latter than that of the former.

(3) According to this hypothesis, Acts records prophecies which Paul disobeys. This he would not have done if he regarded them as carrying infallible divine authority. Implicitly, then, Paul recognized different 'levels' of prophetic utterance. In Acts 21:4, Luke says of the disciples at Tyre that 'Through the Spirit they urged Paul not to go on to Jerusalem'. While prophecy is not explicitly mentioned here, the parallel with Acts 11:28 ('Agabus stood up and through the Spirit predicted that a severe famine would spread over the entire Roman world') is evident. Unless we wish to accuse Paul of rejecting the clear directive of God, we must attribute a secondary status to such prophecy.

Grudem himself, however, interprets this event in a way which seems to defeat his own pleading for a second authority-level in such prophecy:

> Suppose that some of the Christians at Tyre had some kind of 'revelation' or indication from God about the suffering which Paul would face at Jerusalem. Then it would have been very natural for them to couple their subsequent *prophecy* (their report of this revelation) with their own (erroneous) *interpretation*, and thus to warn Paul not to go.
>
> *In short, this passage indicates a type of prophecy which was not thought to possess absolute divine authority in its actual words: the prophets at Tyre were not speaking 'words of the Lord'.*[10] (Italics mine.)

The explanation given in the first paragraph here is adequate in itself. It does not require the conclusion drawn in the second (italicized) paragraph. Paul recognized the difference between the revelation given in the Spirit and the interpretation placed on it by these Christians (a distinction recognized in Grudem's terms 'prophecy' and 'interpretation'); clearly he accepted the former as divinely-given prophecy but rejected the latter as contrary to God's already revealed purpose for his life ('Compelled by the Spirit, I am going to Jerusalem, not knowing what will happen to me there. I only know that in every city the Holy Spirit warns me that prison and hardships are facing me', Acts 20:22–23).

Such an interpretation is all the more likely in view of the heightened repetition of the scene at Caesarea. Now it is not merely the disciples at Tyre who speak of Paul's danger; it is no less than Agabus, the man whose earlier prophecy proved both accurate and highly significant for the actions of the church (*cf.* Acts 11:28–30). In this instance the entire apostolic band pleads tearfully with Paul to avoid Jerusalem (note the characteristic Lukan 'we' in Acts 21:12). The psychological pressure was enormous (Acts 21:13); but Paul resisted it. He realized that a prophecy of the events which would take place if he went to Jerusalem was not itself an indication that he should not go. There is no need to resort to the thesis that two levels of prophecy are in view, especially when neither the New Testament in general nor Agabus in particular refers to or shows a consciousness of such a distinction. What is in view is a distinction between a divinely-revealed prophecy and an erroneous conclusion drawn from it. Paul is not refusing divine prophecy, but a mistaken response to it; mistaken because he knows that his destiny is to suffer for the sake of the gospel; mistaken even if prefaced by 'We are saying this through the Spirit'.

(4) Grudem appeals to Acts 21:10–11: '[Agabus] took Paul's belt, tied his own hands and feet with it and said, "The Holy Spirit says, 'In this way the Jews of Jerusalem will bind the owner of this belt and will hand him over to the Gentiles.' " ' Grudem calls this a 'a prophecy with two small mistakes',[11] since (a) the Jews did not bind Paul, and (b) the Jews were not the ones who delivered Paul to the Gentiles. In fact, it was the Romans who bound him (Acts 21:33; *cf.* 22:29) and, rather than being delivered by the Jews to them, Paul had to be rescued from the Jews by the Romans (Acts 22:24).

Several questions arise here. One is whether such an interpretation is reading a general statement as though it were intended to give specific details. Grudem in fact holds that these 'details' are the essential elements in this particular prophecy. But the implications of this greatly reduce the credibility of Agabus. For if we are to assume that the early church shared Grudem's view of two-level prophecy, Agabus either did not understand it, or he seriously over-reached himself; for he claims to speak as the mouthpiece of the Spirit. It is hard to see how mistakes in essentials can be regarded as 'small'! The once accurate prophet, whose prophecy deeply affected apostolic behaviour, is now muddle-headed and misleading, if not actually false.

It will hardly do to suggest, as Grudem does, by means of appeal to the Apostolic Fathers Ignatius and Barnabas, that when Agabus says 'This is what the Holy Spirit says' (Acts 21:11), this is the equivalent of 'This is generally (or approximately) what the Holy Spirit is saying to us'.[12] For Agabus does not seem to have understood that equation, nor, judging by the manner of his reporting, did Luke. Furthermore, the passages in Ignatius and Barnabas to which appeal is made provide no foundation for such an argument.[13]

Moreover, Paul's own retrospective account of the events in Acts 28:17–20 seems to be expressed by Luke as a deliberate echo of Agabus' prophecy. A comparison is illuminating:

Agabus (Acts 21:11)		**Paul** (Acts 28:17)
The Jews of Jerusalem	→	In Jerusalem
will		I was
bind		arrested [bound]
[*dēsousin*, from *deō*]	→	[*desmios*, from *deō*]
and will hand him over		and handed over
[*paradōsousin*	→	[*paredothēn*
from *paradidōmi*]		from *paradidōmi*]
to the Gentiles.	→	to the Romans.

Grudem complains[14] that the NIV translation of *desmios ex Ierosolymōn paredothēn eis tas cheiras tōn Rōmaiōn* is misleading. The translation should have clarified that Paul was delivered into the hands of the Romans as a prisoner *from* [*ex*] *Jerusalem*, not made a prisoner *in Jerusalem*. Paul is speaking about being taken from Jerusalem as a prisoner and delivered into the hands of the Romans, not about being seized in Jerusalem and there handed over to the Romans.

This may be so. But the repetition of Agabus' language in Paul's statements suggests that the apostle himself saw the (more general?) statements of Agabus fulfilled in the actual events. In addition, it is significant that the language of both passages echoes Paul's own words in Acts 20:20–23 (where the passive of *deō* and the noun *desmos* are also used). It might equally be complained that the NIV translates *desmios* as 'arrested' rather than 'bound', thus obscuring the possibility that Paul is referring to what the Jews did when they seized him and dragged him from the temple. It is quite possible that the Jews themselves bound him in order to do this (perhaps with Paul's own belt!). In any event, Grudem's reading of Agabus' prophecy is neither the good nor the necessary consequence of the text. Rather than seeing Agabus as committing 'two small mistakes',[15] Luke's language presents his record in order to enable the reader of Acts to sense that Paul realized a lengthy series of prophecies was being fulfilled. Agabus' version of the widespread prophecy about Paul's future came, after all, in the unusual form of an acted parable. Inevitably the fulfilment may contain details which are not present in the prophecy but are consistent with it. Rather than confirming Grudem's thesis that the prophecy of Agabus contains basic errors, Paul's testimony assumes its accuracy. We have no reason to believe that Agabus' prophecy failed. Luke gives no indication that Paul thought it had done so.

While the argument for two levels of prophecy proves unconvincing, part of Grudem's agenda here is the laudable one of promoting Christian unity and fellowship. His thesis appears to hold out a *via media* which might bridge the gulf between the charismatic and the cessationist views of prophecy and of spiritual experiences in general. If it were recognized by advocates of both views that the form which continuing prophecy takes today belongs to a completely different authority-level from the revelatory prophetic ministry of the apostles, the tendency to create polarization, or antagonism, in discussion and debate would be minimized. Some differences would be seen to be more semantic than real. Cessationists, like charismatics, may have unusual mental experiences: what one cessationist has called 'feelings, impressions, convictions, urges, inhibitions, impulses, burdens, resolutions'.[16] If they recognized that this is virtually identical to what is intended by 'prophecy [lower level]', and if continuationists made more modest claims for 'prophecy', then mutual understanding and greater harmony could be attained. Continuationists would avoid such implicitly infallibilist expressions as 'This is what the Lord says', so that there would be no question of their prophecies appearing to rival the authority of Scripture; cessationists and continuationists would then be able to recognize that they share similar experiences of spiritual illumination even if they describe or categorize them differently. Mutual agreement would be within reach.

Cessationist and restorationist, charismatic and non-charismatic, do, surely, share much in spiritual experience. But the flaw in Grudem's thesis is the assumption that the two-level hypothesis is present in the New Testament. Furthermore, there arises the more fundamental question of whether or not the New Testament leads us to expect the continuation of prophecy and similar gifts.

A case for continuation?

The facts would appear to be as follows. In the apostolic age, signs and wonders attended the witness of the early church. Healings, prophecies, speaking in tongues, exorcisms and other unusual phenomena are mentioned in the Acts of the Apostles. Indeed, they are mentioned precisely because they are 'unusual' even by the standards of the experience of New Testament Christians.

Sometime relatively shortly after this period these phenomena gradually began to disappear from the mainstream life of the church. Claims about their continuation or restoration appear from time to time from the second century onwards.

Interpreting this is by no means easy, for several reasons. For one thing, it is difficult to assess the relationship between the church's development of stronger structures and episcopal hierarchy and the place accorded to the extraordinary. Did increased formalism (even in a non-pejorative sense) destroy spirituality and faith?

On the other hand, many appeals to the continuation in the church of the phenomena described in Acts appear to lack a controlling principle. What, for example, are we to make of the extraordinary third-century Bishop of Neo-Caesarea, Gregory Thaumaturgus, to whom Gregory of Nyssa and Basil of Caesarea attributed remarkable powers: not only exorcism and healing, but even causing stones to levitate at his command, and drying up a lake to settle a conflict over its ownership between two brothers? Are we, with Cardinal Newman,[17] to regard these as perfectly credible and simply a continuation of the phenomena of the New Testament? Are we to see a core of historical facts here encrusted by legend (since in Gregory's case the events were recorded a century after his death)? Or are these records to be treated sceptically? Is such reserve a sign that we have betrayed supernaturalism to the rationalism of the Enlightenment?[18]

Such miraculous attestation has frequently been claimed in the Catholic tradition, and indeed is a common element in the process of the canonization of a saint. There is, of course, a certain consistency in this, since Rome also holds that revelation continues beyond Scripture.

During the past century, experiences of the gifts of prophecy, speaking in tongues, healing and other 'extraordinary' phenomena such as 'slaying in the Spirit' have been widely claimed by many individuals and whole groups from both Roman Catholic and Protestant traditions. It is estimated that there are now perhaps in the region of three hundred and fifty million people (rapidly increasing) who would identify themselves within this pentecostalist/charismatic grouping. A vast number of professing Christians, therefore, not only believe that these particular gifts of the Spirit continue in (or have been restored to) the church, but also believe that their own experiences confirm this. Many speak in tongues, or prophesy, some have supernatural powers of knowledge, while yet others heal or 'slay'; others laugh and run, bark like dogs or roar like lions; and all in the power of the Spirit.

The case for continuation rests on four basic considerations.

(1) The 'brute fact' of contemporary experience. (Can so many millions of Christians be wrong, or misguided?)

(2) The New Testament nowhere states that any of the gifts of the Spirit would be withdrawn; therefore they continue.

(3) The cessationist view would imply that there are two distinct, or at least distinguishable, dispensations in the new age which Jesus inaugurated through his death, resurrection and the gift of the Spirit, namely the apostolic age and the post-apostolic age. But the New Testament knows only one age, namely the age inaugurated by the eschatological Spirit. It may therefore be assumed that these gifts were intended for the church throughout the new age and are characteristic of it.

(4) In recognizing that prophecy will eventually cease, Paul indicates that this will take place only when 'perfection comes' (1 Cor. 13:10). Then the imperfect will disappear. In view here is the eschaton. Implied, therefore, is the view that prophecy (and presumably other gifts) will continue until the return of Christ.

In the light of these considerations, the cessationist position, which once prevailed without serious rival as the accepted orthodoxy in the Reformation churches, is today widely regarded as reactionary and, indeed, as potentially quenching the Spirit. Continuationism or restorationism now bids well to become normative evangelical orthodoxy. Nevertheless, the restorationist position continues to face serious difficulties which it has never been able to overcome.

A case for cessation?

The cessationist position may be briefly outlined as follows.

(1) Restorationism provides no generally convincing *theological* explanation for the disappearance of certain gifts during the greater part of the church's existence. To attribute this to lack of faith is surely inadequate (if not spiritual and theological hubris) in view of the quality of faith possessed by many Christians of former eras, not to mention the principle (much underlined in other contexts by 'continuationists') that the Spirit distributes his gifts freely and sovereignly.

In this context, it has become commonplace to dismiss the classical twentieth-century 'defence' of cessationism, B. B. Warfield's Smyth Lectures, published in 1918 as *Counterfeit*

Miracles, on the grounds that Warfield cannot appeal to a single text of Scripture to prove his view. This is inadequate for two reasons. In the first place, Warfield's lectures were intended to be largely historical; his central purpose was not to deal with the issue exegetically. Doubtless, therefore, cessationists should have been a little slower to appeal to Warfield as though his intention was to provide a thorough-going biblico-theological case; but, by the same token, standard criticism of his work misses its real point.

In the second place, however, a certain sleight of hand is involved in this argument. It is a logical fallacy to hold that the proof of the negative on its own ('no text in the New Testament teaches cessation') establishes an alternative positive ('the New Testament teaches continuationism').

(2) This last point is of considerable significance, for the restorationist or continuationist view tends to assume that the unusual and miraculous are biblically normal and normative and therefore naturally continue. In fact, in the Scriptures themselves, extraordinary gifts appear to be limited to a few brief periods in biblical history, in which they serve as confirmatory signs of new revelation and its ambassadors, and as a means of establishing and defending the kingdom of God in epochally significant ways. Without this perspective, some biblical miracles would be trivial and almost on the level of magic tricks. Only within this kingdom context does a floating axe head (2 Ki. 6:1–5) or a coin in the mouth of a fish (Mt. 17:27) make coherent sense.

Outbreaks of the miraculous sign-gifts in the Old Testament were, generally speaking, limited to those periods of redemptive history in which a new stage of covenantal revelation was reached and during which the kingdom of God required special defence against the danger of annihilation by the powers of darkness: the days of the Exodus, the entry into the promised land, and the establishment of the people there; the time of Elijah and Elisha and the establishing of the prophetic ministry; and the days of the Exile. Of course God continued to work powerfully at other times, sometimes in remarkable ways. But these sign-deeds were never normative. Nor does the Old Testament suggest they should have continued unabated even throughout the redemptive-historical epoch they inaugurated.

Where are the miracles of Jeremiah, Obadiah, Malachi, Amos and the other prophets? In Scripture itself, it is clear that in the nature of the case these special signs functioned temporarily in a confirmatory way, defending and establishing the kingdom, within the context of a new epoch of God's revealed purposes.

Consistent with this pattern, the work of Christ and the apostles was confirmed by 'signs and wonders'. 'Jesus of Nazareth was a man accredited by God to you by miracles, wonders and signs, which God did among you through him' (Acts 2:22). Similarly, Paul and Barnabas spoke 'boldly for the Lord, who confirmed the message of his grace by enabling them to do miraculous signs and wonders' (Acts 14:3). Christ accomplished much through Paul, 'in leading the Gentiles [note the significance of the new advance beyond Judaism] to obey God by what I have said and done – by the power of signs and miracles, through the power of the Holy Spirit . . . It has always been my ambition to preach the gospel where Christ was not known, so that I would not be building on someone else's foundation [again the new advance is significant]' (Rom. 15:18–20).

Consistent with this is the way in which these unusual phenomena serve as confirmatory signs (albeit by no means the only ones) of genuine apostolic ministry. For Paul they are among 'the things that mark an apostle – signs, wonders and miracles' (2 Cor. 12:12). A similar perspective is suggested by the author of Hebrews: 'This salvation, which was first announced by the Lord, was confirmed to us by those who heard him [i.e. the apostles]. God also testified to it by signs, wonders and various miracles, and gifts of the Holy Spirit distributed according to his will' (Heb. 2:3–4). Here, again, apostolic ministry and special confirmations of it are inextricably linked together. The specific significance attributed to these phenomena is related to that which is most characteristic of apostolic ministry in its foundational aspect.

It is a frequently-used counter-argument that, while these gifts were exercised by the apostles, experience of them was by no means limited to them; for example, the work of both Stephen (Acts 6:8) and Philip (Acts 8:6) was attended by miraculous signs.

Stephen and Philip, however, appear to have acted as

apostolic delegates, *i.e.* as what the New Testament describes as 'evangelists' (Philip is later specifically thus designated, Acts 21:8). Indeed, it may be that this is a better categorization for them and their companions in ministry in Acts 6:1–7 than to think of them as the first 'deacons', even if distinct diaconal ministry may be traced back to this incident. The point being made is not that *only* apostles exercised these gifts, but that these gifts served a distinct function as confirmatory evidences of the apostolic gospel and ministry in the churches and therefore established the reliability of the new revelation then being given.

Since this is recorded in the New Testament as an epexegetical clue to the meaning of these phenomena, it would be illegitimate to interpret them apart from this matrix. Apostles exercised a foundational ministry which was given appropriate attestation. As a result, manifestations of the Spirit which served as confirmations of new revelation appeared in the churches. The primary function of these gifts itself suggests their impermanence. Given the historical setting, it would be as misguided to expect the cessation of these confirmatory signs to be synchronized with the death of the last apostle, as it would be to assume that the acceptance of the canon of Scripture would be dated at the hour in which the last book of the New Testament was first read. In the nature of the case, such cessation would be as gradual as the gathering and establishing of the canon. In this sense the gradual cessation of these gifts follows the pattern which their inner significance suggests.

Paul's statement that 'when perfection comes, the imperfect disappears' (1 Cor. 13:10) has sometimes been understood by cessationists to refer to the completion of the canon of Scripture, and with it the cessation of the special gifts of which prophecy, tongues and revelatory knowledge are representative (1 Cor. 13:8). Then we will see 'face to face' and not 'a poor reflection' (1 Cor. 13:12; the background here is Nu. 12:8; the reference is to Moses' intimate, face-to-face, non-enigmatic communion with God). Even Moses' knowledge of God was enigmatic by comparison with what was then coming in the new covenant revelation (2 Cor. 3:12–13). Hence, it is argued, this 'perfection' or 'completion' (*i.e.* of the new revelation) will be accompanied by the cessation of prophecy and the stilling of tongues ('the imperfect', 1 Cor. 13:10).

The majority of modern scholars have rejected all forms of this interpretation on the grounds that, for Paul, 'the perfect' is an eschatological, not a canonical, concept. Paul's contrast, '*Now* I know in part; *then* I shall know fully, even as I am fully known [*sc.* by God]' (1 Cor. 13:12), can refer only to the beatific vision. Some argue further that, since it stands in parallel to the earlier statement 'when perfection comes, the imperfect disappears' (1 Cor. 13:10), the cessation of tongues and prophecy must be coincident with the end of the age. This necessarily implies their continuation until the end of the age.

While this is not the only passage to which appeal is made,[19] if this exegesis is correct then the issue of what Scripture teaches is a settled one. Two responses may be made.

First, it is still arguable, although less popular among modern exegetes, that by 'perfection' Paul refers not to the heavenly vision, but to an interim yet comprehensive (complete) knowledge of God made available by the totality of apostolic teaching. Otherwise not only tongues and prophecy but also the apostolic writings (and therefore the New Testament) are characterized as imperfect.

We might paraphrase 1 Corinthians 13:8–12 in the following way:

> Love will never come to an end, since God himself is love; but special gifts like prophecy and speaking in tongues and the word of knowledge will, since they are only temporary ways in which the God of love makes himself known to us. At the moment the knowledge of God we receive from prophecy, tongues and words of knowledge gives us only fragmentary knowledge of God. When we have the whole picture these gifts will give way – 'when perfection enters, imperfection creeps away'; 'the grown man puts away his baby toys', as they say.
>
> Tongues, words of knowledge, prophecies – they are all like looking into the mirrors for which you Corinthians are so famous! But even a mirror with 'Made in Corinth' on it is a poor substitute for seeing (and therefore knowing) yourself as clearly as some-one else can see and know you![20] But in the future,

when we have the complete knowledge God has planned for us, we will not need to depend on these imperfect mirrors of tongues, words of knowledge and prophecy. Then we will know God completely, not merely in a fragmentary way – just as others know us.

Such a paraphrase has the merit of questioning the ease with which 'perfection' and 'know fully, even as I am fully known' have been equated with the parousia and 'being known by God', and indicates that, however the exegetical questions are to be settled, less triumphalism is surely required. With faith and hope, love continues, while prophecies, tongues and words of knowledge are partial and will cease because they function temporarily; *when* is stated only in the most general way; indeed, 'when perfection comes, the imperfect disappears' may be little more than an appeal to a general proverbial saying. (Is it significant that precisely here one finds several continuationists appealing to Calvin's quasi proverbial saying that when the sun rises all lesser lights are extinguished?)

Secondly, exegetes who adopt opposing views on the broader question of cessation have held that this passage states no more than the general point that these gifts will cease at some future point; exactly when is not in view. D. A. Carson, a moderate continuationist, notes that these words would not 'necessarily mean that a charismatic gift could not have been withdrawn earlier than the parousia';[21] while Richard B. Gaffin, Jr., a cessationist, in holding that the horizon in view in the expression 'perfection' is the return of Christ, argues that it is 'gratuitous' to argue from this passage that the gifts mentioned continue until the parousia. Such a view

> . . . reads Paul too explicitly in terms of the issues raised in the present-day controversy over spiritual gifts . . . Paul is not oriented here to the distinction between the apostolic, foundational present and the period beyond. Rather he has in view the entire period until Christ's return, without regard to whether or not discontinuities may intervene during the course of this period, in the interests of emphasizing the enduring quality of faith, hope, and especially love (vv. 8, 13).[22]

If the New Testament does not make a specific pronouncement, the function of these gifts will determine their longevity.

The continuationist-restorationist view does not take sufficient account of the fact that the New Testament itself divides the last days into apostolic and post-apostolic dimensions or periods. There is a foundation-laying period, marked by the ministry of the apostles and prophets, and there is a post-foundational, post-apostolic period in view (as Eph. 2:20 implies). It should not surprise us that phenomena occur in the former period which are not designed to continue beyond it, any more than the miracles of Moses, Elijah or Elisha continued to be performed by their gifted successors.

It is often forgotten that the issue of miraculous attestations of the gospel is not peculiar to the contemporary church, nor is the cessationist position either an invention of Warfield or merely a reaction to twentieth-century developments. It was a major and critical element in the debates which emerged in the sixteenth century, during the time of the Protestant Reformation. One of the most stringent criticisms of the Reformation movement by the Roman Catholic Church was that it had no miraculous attestation! Part of Rome's argument for the authenticity of its doctrine lay in an appeal to the attestation of it by the miraculous. Calvin's response to this, in his famous Letter to Francis I which prefaces his *Institutes*, was essentially redemptive-historical in nature: the new covenant was attested by the outpourings of the miraculous. That is adequate testimony. We have no novel message; we need no novel outpouring of the miraculous.[23]

(4) In terms of the individual gifts which in the Augustinian tradition were viewed as belonging to the apostolic age, the restorationist view of glossolalia in particular faces further difficulties.

We have argued that the tongues-speaking in both Acts and 1 Corinthians is most naturally read as the speaking of foreign languages. But contemporary glossolalia is not normally identified with the speaking of foreign languages.

Further, outside of 1 Corinthians there is no record of either the occurrence or regulation of this phenomenon. Appeal to the way in which the Spirit 'intercedes for us with groans that words cannot express' (Rom. 8:26) as an example of speaking in tongues is, surely, wide of the mark; groans are not glossolalia; what cannot be expressed cannot be identified with languages which can be spoken.

Of course, arguments from silence are slippery; but this broader silence, especially in the Pastoral Letters, which were clearly written to regulate post-apostolic church life, does seem to be eloquent of a shift in orientation which had already taken place from the immediacy of tongues and their interpretation to the teaching of the apostolic tradition (cf. 1 Tim. 1:10–11; 3:9; 4:6; 6:3; 2 Tim. 1:13; 2:15; 3:10 – 4:5; Tit. 1:9; 2:1). It is particularly noteworthy that the Pastoral Letters do not anticipate the necessity of regulating the exercise of such gifts as prophecy and speaking in tongues.

In the New Testament, translated tongues are treated as the equivalent of prophecy (an identification embryonically present in the reference to prophesying in Acts 2:14–18 as an explanation of the tongues of Pentecost). Unless there is translation or interpretation, prophecy is clearly superior to tongues. But if there is interpretation, then 'revelation or knowledge or prophecy' is shared (1 Cor. 14:6). When interpreted, therefore, tongues-speaking is the functional equivalent of prophecy[24] and is revelatory in nature.

Christian theology has generally differentiated between revelation and illumination. The conceptual distinction is a biblical one (Ps. 119:18; 2 Tim. 2:7), although the same terminology ('revelation') may be used of both. Revelation is given in a special sense to Paul and the apostles (Eph. 3:5); yet he prays that the Ephesians will have a Spirit of revelation to know God better (Eph. 1:17; cf. Mt. 16:17). The common terminology denotes not a single concept but either of two related ideas which have certain analogous characteristics. Revelation is used by Paul to refer to both the giving of the truth and the illumination of its meaning. But these are clearly distinct phenomena. A categorical distinction exists between the lasting authority which attaches to apostolic revelation and the subjective 'revelation' or illumination which comes to all the people of God through the Spirit. Systematic theologians have wisely marked this by a semantic distinction between 'revelation' and 'illumination', even though it remains perfectly legitimate for us to pray for the 'Spirit of . . . revelation, so that you may know him better' (Eph. 1:17).

Despite disclaimers,[25] the issue at stake here is the sufficiency of Scripture for the directing of the church and the individual. God's revelation has always been sufficient for each stage of redemptive revelation. The climax of redemption in Christ was accompanied by a correspondingly sufficient revelation in the Scriptures, so that the principle of scriptural sufficiency which Paul describes (2 Tim. 3:16–17), while rooted in the Old Testament, now includes both Testaments. But while the New Testament was being written, the guiding principle, or canon, of the early church was multiplex: the Old Testament, the apostolic directives, prophecies, and those parts of the New Testament already written. Now this multiplex canon, or rule of faith and life, gives way to a single canon: the Scriptures of the Old and New Testaments. They now contain 'everything we need God to tell us for salvation, for trusting him perfectly, and for obeying him perfectly'.[26]

The logical implication of the sufficiency of Scripture is that no additional revelation is needed by the church or the individual. What is needed is illumination. Hence, the Reformation doctrine of *sola Scriptura* over against the Roman Catholic Church's doctrine that both Scripture and tradition constitute divine revelation.[27] This view of *sola Scriptura* found classical expression in the Westminster divines' statement:

> The whole counsel of God, concerning all things necessary for his own glory, man's salvation, faith, and life, is either expressly set down in scripture, or by good and necessary consequence may be deduced from scripture: unto which nothing at any time is to be added, whether by new revelations of the Spirit, or traditions of men . . .[28]

This brings us directly to the 'storm centre' of current debate. New revelation, be it in the form of tradition or the golden tablets of Joseph Smith, principially undermines the sufficiency of Scripture, and becomes *de facto* the dominant factor, at least at certain points, in the canon by which the individual lives. Is it not, therefore, special pleading on the part of evangelicals to claim that prophecies *received by them* function in an altogether different way? While it is denied that additions are being made to the canon of Scripture, it is nevertheless implied that an actual addition is being made to the canon of living. Otherwise, the illumination of Scripture and the wisdom to apply it would be sufficient.

It is not adequate in this context to suggest (as Grudem and others do) that those who exercise second-level prophecy should avoid prefacing their 'prophecies' with such statements as 'Thus says the Lord'. After all, Agabus, in the biblical 'example' of second-level prophecy, prefaces his words with 'The Holy Spirit says' (Acts 21:11). This is the common language of prophecy. In terms of origin, authority and reliability it belongs to exactly the universe of discourse which Acts else-where uses of the divine inspiration and the plenary authority of Scripture (Acts 4:25; *cf.* 1:16; 28:25).

There is, however, an opposite danger, although it may not be equal in magnitude. It is possible for cessationists to reject genuine *illumination* precisely because it is (falsely in their view) presented in terms of the formula of *revelation*. Unfortunately, even the second-level prophecy thesis exposes itself to such a reaction. Expressing illumination as though it were revelation does not commend legitimate biblical insights.

Grudem himself suggests that the expression 'Thus says the Lord' should be 'dropped', and appears to agree with Timothy Pain that wording such as 'I think the Lord is suggesting something like . . .' would be more appropriate.[29] It is right to suggest that this former language leads to a confusion of 'second-level prophecy' with canonical prophecy. But surely we need to go further; for *no level of prophecy in Scripture is introduced by 'I think the Lord is suggesting something like this'*. To speak thus is not to speak prophecy at all. The recognition that *this is not prophecy in any biblical sense* would solve the difficulty without any danger of the quenching of the Spirit which restorationists so fear.

The stakes are heightened in this debate not only by the doctrinal issue of the sufficiency of Scripture but by the apparent brute facts of personal experience. It may be helpful therefore to distinguish between a denial of the reality of an experience and a difference in interpreting it. Here the long-recognized principle that there is an analogy in the Spirit's work in revelation and his work in illumination may help. Thus, for example, the seventeenth-century theologian John Owen, a cessationist, argues that while some special gifts in the New Testament era are no longer given to the church, some continuing gifts have much in common with them:

> But although all these gifts and operations *ceased* in some respect, some of them absolutely, and some of them as to the immediate manner of communication and degree of excellency; yet so far as the edification of the church was concerned in them, something that is *analogous* unto them was and is continued.[30]

There are, for example, important analogies between the ministry of the apostle and the ministry of the preacher. Illumination of the mind took place in the authoring of the New Testament revelation, but it also takes place in the process of studying biblical teaching: Scripture, the Spirit and the workings of the human mind are involved in both contexts. The existence of the analogy should not, however, mislead us into a confusion of the vocabulary or the concepts.

The problem here is, indeed, partly one of categorization. Theologians have long struggled with how to distinguish between revelation and illumination, and have often majored on the exposition of the former category. On the one hand, neo-orthodoxy has tended to coalesce and even confuse revelation and illumination so that revelation is not actual until there is illumination. On the other hand, the charismatic danger is to confuse illumination with revelation in such a way that the difference between the apostolic revelation and our understanding of and response to it is in danger of collapsing *de facto*. If God's special revelation continues in an extra-biblical manner, it is a psychological probability that it will come to exercise a canonical function. It is curious that evangelicals, who have so often assumed that this is a fatal flaw in the Roman Catholic doctrine of continuing extra-biblical revelation (in tradition), do not recognize the parallel within Protestantism.

The Spirit must not be quenched, or prophecy despised (1 Thes. 5:19–20). All Spirit-given illumination and insight must be received and welcomed for what it is. To categorize it as prophecy, however, is at best to confuse the completed with the ongoing work of the Spirit, and at worst to divert the people of God from the sufficiency of Scripture.

What, then, of tongues-speaking? Can the cessationist view really withstand the evidence of the experience of millions of contemporary Christians? Yet there is widespread basic disagreement about what actually constitutes the phenomenon of tongues-speaking. Is it language (heavenly or earthly)? Is it free vocalization? Is it identical with the experiences in the Acts of the Apostles? Are there two kinds of tongues in Scripture? And are both kinds in exercise today? These questions underline the difficulty of accepting contemporary claims at their face value, particularly when they differ from or contradict one another. With due respect, it will hardly do to say, with Gordon Fee, that it is 'probably somewhat irrelevant' whether contemporary and Corinthian tongues speaking are identical, so long as there is an analogous relationship between them (i.e. a kind of functional equivalence).[31]

If, as we have argued, there is only one kind of tongues-speaking in Scripture, and this is a God-given ability to speak foreign languages ordinarily unknown to the speaker, then, quite apart from theological arguments, much that is claimed as 'biblical' tongues cannot be identified with the New Testament phenomenon. At best it is free vocalization, whether deliberately practised or spontaneously evoked.

Such activities, as is widely recognized, induce a sense of psychological well-being. It would not be altogether surprising if this produces in Christians a euphoria which, because interpreted through a Christ-centred grid, is different from the experience of free vocalization in a non-Christian context. It need not be regarded as demonic (albeit in some contexts it may even be an expression of the demonic); it ought not to be regarded as any more spiritual than speaking English, and in many ways, less so.[32] And even free vocalization, if its significance is misinterpreted, may lead to more sinister repercussions.

No right-thinking Christian would deny that God continues to be active in the world, to do wonderful things for his people, and especially to answer their prayers in keeping with his promises. It is still appropriate for the sick not only to consult a doctor but to 'call the elders of the church to pray over him and anoint him with oil in the name of the Lord'. The promise

234

remains that 'the prayer offered in faith will make the sick person well; the Lord will raise him up' (Jas. 5:14–15). People continue to be healed by God – through, above and even against means.[33] Indeed, writes John Owen, 'It is not unlikely but that God might on some occasions, for a longer season, put forth his power in some miraculous operations.'[34] It would, however, be a mistake to draw the conclusion from this that such events are normative or that in these events *individuals* are receiving again the coronation gifts of Pentecost. It is misguided to think that we ought to try to categorize every element of contemporary experience in this way. To attempt to do so would be tantamount to assuming that we are able systematically to analyse and categorize all of the events and experiences which constitute the providences of God.

An explanation?

How, then, can we explain the phenomena to which so many testify? The question is legitimate, if by no means an easy one; it poses certain difficulties for both continuationists and cessationists. The difficulty for the continuationist view is to account for the difference between the twentieth century and all previous ages of church history. On the other hand, how can we explain the experience of three hundred and fifty million people, most of whom claim to speak in tongues, many of whom claim to prophesy, while others claim to heal?

Unlike other theological differences (*e.g.* over the relationship between the body of Christ and the bread of the Lord's Supper), these are observable and measurable phenomena. The facts seem to speak for themselves. Yet this is precisely the heart of the problem: the phenomenon is indeed an experienced reality, but it is not a self-interpreting reality. This applies equally to tongues and prophecy, words of wisdom and knowledge, and to the working of miracles and healing by human hands. An important, but largely unrecognized, element of interpretation is involved in continuationism.

We have noted this above with respect to tongues. In the case of prophecy, it would be more consistent with its revelatory nature (and therefore its existentially canonical function) for continuationists to recognize that their insights into God's word and their sense of God's purpose are not actually prophecy at all, but illumination, fallible insight and contemporary application of biblical truth.

Moreover, what of the recurrence of the New Testament gift of healing? This, surely, is a 'brute fact'. Here it is necessary to tread with great care. God continues to answer the prayers of his people for healing (Jas. 5:14–15). The conviction that certain gifts exercised by individuals in the New Testament were not meant to continue in the church permanently should not be taken to imply that God no longer works in glorious supernatural ways on behalf of his people. Even if one were to grant what is sometimes too readily assumed – that healing is much more frequent among continuationists than among cessationists – the reason may not lie in the interpretive grid adopted but in the faith which seeks (and may even anticipate) the intervention of God.

The only help we are given in the New Testament to exegete 'gifts of healing' (1 Cor. 12:9, 30) portrays this gift in terms to which contemporary claims bear little resemblance. Massive numbers of healings are effected; congenital defects are healed; those crippled from birth are immediately able to walk; there is no record of failure, either partial or total, no suggestion of relapse and, presumably, we are to imagine none. This is a different order of reality from the contemporary. God is still Yahweh who heals (Gn. 15:26); but he has no new revelation to give which is attested by 'gifts of healing' given to individuals. The only new revelation we are to anticipate will come at the final apocalypse of Christ. Then, unprecedented and final healing will take place on the grandest of all scales.

The same principle holds good more broadly with respect to the 'experience' of baptism with the Holy Spirit, which has often been closely linked to continuationism. Denial of divine experience is not necessary; only the interpretation of it. What has been mistaken for a post-conversion baptism with the Spirit may well be a new filling of the Spirit, a new fullness of assurance and joy, a new boldness in giving expression to faith in Christ. These are not tasted experientially once and for all in the first filling of the Spirit which takes place in regeneration, conversion and Spirit baptism.

If this is so, misinterpretation on a large scale seems to have taken place in the twentieth century. In so far as that is true, a reinterpretation which anchors experience in more biblical categories will not only produce a broader theological harmony on the doctrine of the Holy Spirit; it will also marry experience to truth in such a way that greater stability and richer fruit of the Spirit will be created in the life and character of the church of Jesus Christ. This, after all, is the goal which all the gifts of the Spirit are given to serve (*cf.* Eph. 4:7–16).

The Spirit and preaching

A central place is given in the New Testament's lists of gifts to the teaching and preaching of the word of God. This was already true in the apostolic age, as the ministry of the apostles makes clear.

Paul's ministry in Ephesus exhibits this focus with great clarity. It was marked by the confirmatory signs of apostolic ministry even beyond the normal: 'God did *extraordinary* miracles . . .' (Acts 19:11). Yet the centre-piece of Paul's work took place in the lecture hall of Tyrannus, where for two years he daily taught the disciples. His own commentary on that period of his life is illuminating: he taught the Ephesians; he preached the king-dom and proclaimed the whole counsel of God (Acts 20:20; 25; 27). In fact one textual tradition suggests that he did this during the daily siesta period, for several hours, perhaps as many as five, each day.

In the light of this, Paul's instructions to Timothy, who was later ministering in Ephesus, take on special significance. His focus of attention is on the central role of biblical teaching and preaching in the post-apostolic period. Timothy is not only to give attention to reading (1 Tim. 4:13), but to devote himself to handling the word of God properly (2 Tim. 2:15). He is to preach in a way that will make it clear how Scripture is 'useful for teaching, rebuking, correcting and training in righteousness'. As he thus preaches the word, he is to 'correct, rebuke and encourage – with great patience and careful instruction' (3:16 – 4:2; the chapter division is misleading here).

In this connection, Paul regards the word of God as 'the sword of the Spirit' (Eph. 6:17), by which he means not only that it has been forged by the Spirit (inspiration), but also that it is employed by the Spirit with powerful effect (*cf.* Heb. 4:12–13). Through it the Spirit honours Christ and brings conviction of sin (Jn. 16:8–11) as he did through the preaching of Peter on the Day of Pentecost. While the tongues-proclamation impressed some of those who heard it, it was Peter's preaching from the Scriptures, not the tongues-speaking, which effected the conversion of three thousand people.

Elsewhere Paul indicates what lies at the heart of such effective communication. It is not human rhetoric, wisdom or oratory but power – the hallmark of the Spirit (*cf.* Acts 1:8). His preaching to the Corinthians was 'not with wise and persuasive words, but with a demonstration of the Spirit's power' (1 Cor. 2:4). His preaching to the Thessalonians was of a similar character: 'our gospel came to you not simply with words, but also with power, with the Holy Spirit and with deep conviction . . . you welcomed the message with the joy given by the Holy Spirit' (1 Thes. 1:5–6).

Several things characterized such preaching. The first was Paul's evident focus on the person and work of Christ (1 Cor. 1:23; 2:2), and particularly on Christ crucified as the power and wisdom of God. The second was the way in which it fitted within the grid of the Spirit-given function of the Scriptures (teaching, rebuking, correcting and healing, and training in righteousness, *cf.* 2 Tim. 3:16 – 4:2). The third was the context in which it was set in the life of the preacher. Here our earlier discussion of union with Christ is relevant, for Paul's powerful preaching seems to have been frequently a correlate of his experience of trial and stress. He was 'in weakness and fear, and . . . much trembling' in Corinth (1 Cor. 2:3). It was in the wake of suffering and insult in Philippi that he preached with much fruitfulness in Thessalonica (1 Thes. 2:2). In Christ he was weak, yet he lived with Christ to serve in his ministry (2 Cor. 13:5).

The hallmark of the preaching which the Spirit effects is 'boldness' (*parrhēsia* = *pan* + *rhēsis*, Acts 4:13, 29, 31; Phil. 1:20; *cf.* 2 Cor. 7:2). As in the Old Testament, when the Spirit fills the servant of God he 'clothes himself' with that person, and aspects of the Spirit's authority are illustrated in the courageous declaration of the word of God. This boldness appears to involve exactly what it denotes: there is freedom of speech. We catch occasional glimpses of this in the Acts of the Apostles. What was said of the early New England preacher Thomas Hooker becomes a visible reality: when he preached, those who heard him felt that he could have picked up a king and put him in his pocket! There is a sense of harmony between the message which is being proclaimed and the way the Spirit clothes himself with the messenger. Here Gordon Fee's cutting words surely hit the mark:

> The polished oratory sometimes heard in . . . pulpits, where the sermon itself seems to be the goal of what is said, makes one wonder whether the text has been heard at all. Paul's own point needs a fresh hearing . . . The danger always lies in letting the form and content get in the way of what should be the single concern: the gospel proclaimed through human weakness but accompanied by the powerful work of the Spirit so that lives are changed through a divine–human encounter. That is hard to teach in a course in homiletics, but it still stands as the true need in genuinely Christian preaching.[35]

Preaching God's word is the central gift of the Spirit given by Christ to the church. By it the church is built up into Christ (Eph. 4:7–16). Will it prove to be one of the enigmas of contemporary church life, when viewed from some future age, that a demise of the quality of and confidence in the exposition of Scripture, and a fascination with the immediacy of tongues, interpretations, prophecy and miracles, were coincidental?

11

THE COSMIC
SPIRIT

The church has spoken throughout the ages of the *Spiritus creator*, the creator Spirit. The New Testament shows, in a variety of different ways, that his work in the life, ministry, death and resurrection of Christ is to be seen as the inauguration of a new creation through the second man and last Adam; he is *Spiritus recreator*. What has already been accomplished in Christ by the Spirit is now reduplicated in the new humanity by the same Spirit.

The Spirit who hovered over the waters on the first day of creation also hovered over the virgin Mary in the conception of the head of the new creation, Jesus. Now, in the present day (which also constitutes 'the last days'), the same Spirit hovers over men and women to bring new birth to them 'from above'.

The question arises here, in pneumatology no less than in Christology: What is the relationship between the created order of things and the redeemed order? In Christology it is commonplace to speak about a cosmic Christ. The Creator is also the

Redeemer; in him all things will be reconciled (Col. 1:19–20). The present cosmos finds its ultimate meaning in the future cosmos, since its destiny is wrapped up with the future of the sons of God (Rom. 8:20–21).

What, then, of the Spirit? If he is the creator Spirit, can we also speak of him as the cosmic Spirit, so that God's purposes for the world as such, not merely for individuals, or indeed for the church, will be brought to consummation through his ministry? This has become a commonplace emphasis in modern theology, often expressed in a very distinctive post-Enlightenment fashion. The major epistemological impact of the Enlightenment on theology lay in the rejection of the transcendent as knowable. It was not disclosed through the immanent. This shift manifested itself in many different ways. In terms of the doctrine of the Holy Spirit, it emerged in a loss of confidence in the orthodox trinitarian formula in which the Spirit was seen as the third person of a God who can be known, and as one who serves as the executive of the Father and the Son. 'Spirit' came to be thought of in immanent but non-personal terms. A kind of unitarian immanence theology was the result: the Spirit is God identifying himself with the world. The panentheism characteristic of later process theology is one expression of this: in God as Spirit we live and move and have our being. He is not far from any of us; his experience and ours are inextricably linked and mutually interdependent.

Universalisms

Universalism of various kinds is characteristic of such theology. Although not confined to liberal Protestantism, it is characteristic of this perspective to see the Spirit of God as at work in a unifying fashion in all peoples and religions. Christianity may be the apex, but it is not antithetically related to other religions: the same S/spirit may be traced in all major 'faiths' and even in none. The recognition of the cosmic presence and activity of the Spirit thus rendered obsolete the old radical displacement missionary theory (that Christ must replace all other rival deities). Such exclusivism is contrary to the Spirit, mistaken, intolerant, colonialist and patronizing. Claiming the Spirit's empowering, the church misrepresented the Spirit's significance. In the wake of this theology, the churches' Boards of World Mission have become Boards of World Mission *and Unity*. We are one in Christ, and there is one Spirit *who transcends man's response to revelation*.

Stanley J. Samartha gives expression to this approach (which has come to characterize much of the work of the World Council of Churches) when he writes: 'Wherever the fruits of the Spirit are to be found . . . whether in the lives of Christians or neighbours of other faiths, is not the Spirit of God present?'[1]

This is widely interpreted not only as a recognition of the general benevolence of God and his sustaining of cosmic order and guarding the creation from its tendency to chaos, but also of his redemptive grace. Particularly among Roman Catholic theologians this has come to be expressed in terms of the doctrine of the so-called 'anonymous Christian'. By this doctrine, a way is sought of maintaining the long-standing Catholic principle *extra Ecclesiam nulla salus est*[2] ('outside the Church there is no salvation'), while yet allowing for widespread salvation (if not necessarily totally universal, in the Origenist sense of *apokatastasis*).

Karl Rahner, with whom the idea of the anonymous Christian is so often associated, gives expression to a major driving force behind this approach when he suggests that the Christian cannot accept that 'the overwhelming mass of his brothers . . . are unquestionably and in principle excluded . . . and condemned to eternal meaninglessness'.[3]

He appeals to the theological principles of the Noahic covenant which, he holds, is sealed in Christ for all, and the Pauline conviction that God is the Saviour of all, especially of those who believe (1 Tim. 2:4). He thus grounds the conviction that, in Christ, it is in what takes place in the heart by the Spirit, *not* in the cognitive understanding of theological propositions about Christ, that salvation is to be found. In Rahner's thought, man's being is itself 'ordered to the unsurpassably Absolute'. Man therefore accepts revelation whenever he truly accepts himself; in doing so he accepts Christ, who is God's revelation.

Rahner has, inevitably, been criticized from within Roman Catholicism, from both sides: by Hans Urs von Balthasar for relativizing the uniqueness of the actual revelation of Christ in the gospel; and, on the other hand, by Hans Küng for denigrating non-Christian religions by his emphasis on the Christ-revelation! But the Catholic principle to which Rahner gives expression has proved highly attractive to many, as the Second Vatican Council made clear in its *Decree on Ecumenism* in *The Constitution of the Church.* Expressions of this vary, but within Roman Catholic Augustinianism, with its emphasis on the idea of love, it has become commonplace to state that since the fruit of the Spirit is love, wherever love is manifested there the Spirit of God is at work.[4] In an unexpected way, here the religion of 'the man in the street' and the sophisticated pneumatology of modern theologians seem curiously to merge.

When we consider this emphasis on the cosmic and universal ministry of the Spirit in the light of the explicit statements of the New Testament, we immediately encounter a surprising datum. The New Testament places the Spirit and the world in an antithetical, not a conciliatory, relationship. The world cannot see or know the Spirit (Jn. 14:17); the Spirit convicts the world (Jn. 16:8–11); the spirit of the world and the Spirit of God stand over against each other (1 Cor. 2:12–14; 1 Jn. 4:3).

This principle, characteristic of older conservative theology, was stated with great vigour by W. H. Griffith Thomas in his Stone Lectures at Princeton in 1913:

> Although most modern writers on the subject of the Holy Spirit speak of the Spirit as related to the world of mankind, nothing is more striking than the simple fact that not a single passage can be discovered in the New Testament which refers to the direct action of the Spirit on the world . . . even those who favour the view of the Holy Spirit's action on the world fail to adduce definite New Testament evidence for it.[5]

Thomas argues that we cannot attribute 'all the strivings of conscience in the heathen world'[6] to the Holy Spirit. This he attributes to the Logos rather than to the Spirit. This is a questionable division of labour, but there is interesting corroboration of his general perspective in Gordon Fee's *God's Empowering Presence.*[7] In the course of a massive exegetical study of almost one thousand pages on Paul's teaching on the Holy Spirit, no mention is made of the relationship between the Spirit and the cosmos.

What are we to make of this? If the Old Testament can speak of the pagan Cyrus as anointed by God to fulfil his will (Is. 45:1), should it not follow that the Spirit of God will be even more broadly and generously at work in the epoch in which he has been poured out on all flesh? After all, do not the seven spirits who are sent out into all the earth (Rev. 1:4; 5:6–7) serve as symbols for the one Spirit of God who upholds all things as the immanent executive of the being of God? And if it is true, even granting Mosaic authorship, that Genesis 1:2 was written in the light of, and on the other side of, the Spirit's work in the Exodus (cf. Is. 63:9–14), should we not expect that the Spirit who is the executive of the new exodus in Christ (cf. Lk. 9:31) should also be thought of as the cosmic Spirit, active in and through all, and the one who brings all into communion with God?

The wisest theological approach, here as elsewhere, is always to move outwards from concrete biblical statements to settled principles, only then extrapolating to broader generalizations. Any other procedure lacks controls, and loses the ability to exercise discrimination with respect to identifying the work of the Spirit, which, as we have seen, never ceases to be mysterious.

An interesting example of this problematic appears in a statement by the Dutch theologian Hendrikus Berkhof. He argues that:

> The French Revolution, with its ideals of liberty, equality, and fraternity, had far more to do with Jesus Christ than had those who resisted it in the name of Christ. After the French Revolution we witnessed the *emancipation* of the slaves, the women, the laborers, the colored races. Since the Second World War this revolutionary movement goes in an accelerated speed over the whole world. The liberating and transforming power of the Spirit of Jesus Christ is at work every-where where men are free from the tyranny of nature, state, color, caste, class, sex, poverty, disease, and ignorance. Eugene Rosenstock speaks in this context even of a biological change in man's nature. I prefer to

speak of a pneumatological change. The age-old
structures of man's life with their dehumanizing
effects are replaced by the transforming powers of the
Spirit.[8]

Berkhof goes on to speak of this work of the Spirit as a part of
the conforming of humanity to its head, Jesus Christ.

The questions arise: Does the Spirit work in this way without
reference to the revelation of Christ and his work, and the
evoking of living faith? By what canon of judgment are we able
to detect the work of the Spirit in the world, approve it and join
ourselves to it? How do we know what is the Spirit of God and
what is the spirit of this age? If it is true that the Spirit is engaged
in activity which appears to be resisted by professing Christians
(as Berkhof suggests was true at the time of the French
Revolution), then an answer to this question is all the more
urgent for the church.

In this connection a common hermeneutical principle is
often employed, which involves identification and universaliz-
ability: what is stated to be true of a particular individual in
Scripture is assumed to be true of the whole of humanity *mutatis
mutandis*. To illustrate: from the fact that the Spirit endowed
Bezalel with gifts of design and craftsmanship (Ex. 31:1–15), it is
assumed that all artistic gifts, however used, are general
endowments of the Spirit. What objection then could there be
to Nancy Sinatra's claim in her biography of her father, *Frank
Sinatra: An American Legend*, that 'in some very profound way the
Holy Spirit moves and abides in him' – even in singing 'I did it
my way'?[9] The problem arises when such gifts, attributed to the
Spirit, have a tendency to be conflated with the marks of the
covenant bond of salvation. This assumes too much. It is
appropriate to believe, with Calvin and many others, that all
truth is God's truth, even when it is found in the mouth of the
ungodly, and that all good gifts come to us from above (Jas.
1:17). Yet it is quite another thing to assume that this is an
evidence of the Spirit's saving or transforming presence.

Again, it is one thing to argue on the basis of Romans 8:28 that
the Spirit is working in everything. But what Paul affirms is
restrictive: God works for the good of those who love God and
have been called according to his purpose, which he immediately

describes in the soteriological terms of justification and glorification. He is not there making a general statement that can be applied universally.

Nevertheless, according to Scripture we are made as God's image, and in some sense remain so even in our fallen condition. What Elihu says in the book of Job is a universal principle: 'It is the [S]pirit in a man, the breath of the Almighty, that gives him understanding' (Jb. 32:8). Job himself confirms the accuracy of this: 'The Spirit of God has made me; the breath of the Almighty gives me life' (Jb. 33:4).

Rich, varied and remarkable capacities and abilities are therefore present in the human race, because the Spirit continues his work as the executive of God in relation to the created order. He is the minister of the kindness of God to the just and the unjust alike (Mt. 5:45). But these are exhibitions of God's restraining mercy while his Spirit contends with man (Gn. 6:3). Without this the world would either destroy itself or be destroyed. The mercy is real, but it is not arbitrary. It is set within limits and has a view to repentance (Rom. 2:4; 2 Pet. 3:3–9). It is within this context alone that this general ministry of the Spirit should be assessed. All the more so because it is clear in the New Testament that even the exercise of 'spiritual gifts' should never be identified with the Spirit's work in saving grace. It is possible for the former to be present where the latter is, sadly, absent.

In view of this, it is wiser to say with Calvin:

> We ought not to forget those most excellent benefits of the divine Spirit, which he distributes to whomever he wills, for the common good of mankind. The under-standing and knowledge of Bezalel and Oholiab, needed to construct the Tabernacle, had to be instilled in them by the Spirit of God (Ex. 31:2–11; 35:30–35). It is no wonder, then, that the knowledge of all that is most excellent in human life is said to be commu-nicated to us through the Spirit of God. Nor is there reason for anyone to ask, What have the impious, who are utterly estranged from God, to do with his Spirit? We ought to understand the statement that the Spirit of God dwells only in believers (Rom. 8:9) as referring to the Spirit of sanctification through whom we are

consecrated as temples to God (1 Cor. 3:16). None-theless he fills, moves, and quickens all things by the power of the same Spirit, and does so according to the character that he bestowed upon each kind by the law of creation. But if the Lord has willed that we be helped in physics, dialectic, mathematics, and other like disciplines, by the work and ministry of the ungodly, let us use this assistance . . . But lest anyone think a man truly blessed when he is credited with possessing great power to comprehend truth under the elements of this world (*cf.* Col. 2:8), we should at once add that all this capacity to understand, with all the understanding that follows upon it, is an unstable and transitory thing in God's sight, when a solid foundation does not underlie it.[10]

Calvin distinguishes not only between the general and special gifts of the Spirit (unusual abilities falling into the latter category) but also between both of these and the saving activities of the Spirit, which are quite different from either general or special gifts. In attributing all good to the Spirit's activity, we must be careful to underline that the Spirit dwells in believers only. Not all divine activity is saving activity.

This indwelling is not only a limiting concept, however; it has limited implications for the present. The biblical hope points us to a future period when the redemptive activity of the Spirit will be unlimited.

Cosmic and eschatological Spirit

Joel prophesied that the Spirit would be poured out on all flesh before the great and terrible day of the Lord came. The early church understood the Day of Pentecost to be the fulfilment of this prophetic word. But the Old Testament anticipated wider-ranging effects of the Spirit's ministry when, as Isaiah declared:

> . . . the Spirit is poured upon us from on high,
> and the desert becomes a fertile field,
> and the fertile field seems like a forest.
> Justice will dwell in the desert

and righteousness live in the fertile field.
The fruit of righteousness will be peace;
  the effect of righteousness will be quietness and
    confidence for ever.

(Is. 32:15–17)

(*Cf.* Is. 44:3; 65:17–25; 66:22–23; Ezk. 36:27; 2 Pet. 3:13; Rev. 21:1–4).

These promises are not finally fulfilled in the event of Pentecost. In view here is a renewal of the face of the whole earth to an extent hitherto not seen (*cf.* Ps. 104:30). The vision refers to the regeneration of all things. How are we to understand this, and how is the Spirit related to it?

The answer to that question is found in the relationship between protology and eschatology, between the first Adam and the last Adam.

The first Adam was created as the image of God. The knowledge of God and communion with him in righteousness and holiness were the hallmarks of his life (Eph. 4:10; Col. 3:24). Yet he was created for a condition or state beyond his present one; otherwise, the testing conditions which he underwent in the context of Eden served no purpose. His protological condition was intended to be the harbinger of an eschatological condition which, in the event, remained unrevealed because unattained. Although unspecified, many indications are given to suggest that this final condition was one of *glory*. Not least of these is Paul's statement that, when man sinned, he refused to glorify God as God and exchanged the glory of God for images of created beings lesser than himself (Rom. 1:21–22). 'All have sinned and fall short of the glory of God' (Rom. 3:23). The mark we were created to reach, but have missed, was glory. We have sinned and failed to attain that destiny.

Against this background, the task of the Spirit may be stated simply: to bring us to glory, to create glory within us, and to glorify us together with Christ. The startling significance of this might be plainer if we expressed it thus: the Spirit is given to glorify us; not just to 'add' glory as a crown to what we are, but actually to transform the very constitution of our being so that we become glorious.

In the New Testament, this glorification is seen to begin

249

already in the present order, in believers. Through the Spirit they are already being changed from glory to glory, as they gaze on/reflect the face of the Lord (2 Cor. 3:17–18). But the consummation of this glorification awaits the eschaton and the Spirit's ministry in the resurrection. Here, too, the pattern of his working is: as in Christ, so in believers and, by implication, in the universe.

The Spirit accomplishes this first in Christ. He is related to Adam, the first man, as antitype to type: 'Adam . . . was a pattern [*typos*] of the one to come' (Rom. 5:14). The man of the dust of the earth is the type of the man from heaven (1 Cor. 15:48). These are the first and the second men. In the first Adam comes condemnation, death and shame; through the last Adam comes obedience, righteousness, justification, life and glory. The Spirit is life because of righteousness (Rom. 8:10).

There is no true man between Adam and Christ the second man; there is no need of a further Adam after Christ, because there is no need of a further Adam-function being fulfilled after Christ the last Adam. He is the first, indeed the only, man to pass through the period of testing unscathed. He was comprehensively obedient. As a consequence, he is the first man to enter into the intended eschatological destiny of the protological world, the first to be glorified in our humanity by its resurrection and transformation (Jn. 17:1, 5, 24; *cf.* 7:39; 11:4; 12:16, 23; 13:31; Acts 3:13). In the glorification of his humanity as *archēgos* lie the pattern, the resources and the cause for our glorification.

The Spirit and the last Adam

How, then, is the work of the Spirit related to the resurrection of Christ, of those who belong to Christ, and ultimately of the cosmos?

We have already seen that the resurrection of Christ is his redemption. In it he was justified by the Spirit (1 Tim. 3:16). This justification, however, is coterminous with his sanctificatory deliverance from sin. In Christ the forensic and the transformationist are one (Rom. 6:7). More, justification, sanctification and glorification are one; declaratory, transformatory and consummatory coalesce in this resurrection.

Although at times Paul attributes Christ's resurrection to the

Spirit in a somewhat circumlocutory way, there is no doubt that he does so:[11] 'through the Spirit of holiness [he] was declared with power to be the Son of God, by his resurrection from the dead' (Rom. 1:4; cf. 1 Tim. 3:16). Even when Paul ascribes the resurrection to the activity of the Father, it is clear that he sees a close connection between the Father and the Spirit as his executive in the world (Rom. 8:11). Indeed, the remarkable statement that Christ was raised from the dead *by the glory* of the Father (Rom. 6:4) may be a periphrastic allusion to the dynamic operation of the Spirit. The effect was to transform Christ's body into a body of glory which forms the prototype for the resurrection body of all believers. This latter is effected 'by the power that enables him to bring everything under his control' (Phil. 3:21) – again, an implicit, if circumlocutory, reference to the ongoing work of the Holy Spirit. The implication appears to be that if this transformation takes place in resurrection by the Spirit, it was first thus in the case of Christ. The final harvest has as its harbinger Christ the firstfruits (1 Cor. 15:20). The image and the image-bearers are one in Spirit to the end, so that when Christ appears in glory image-bearers are one with him in that glory (Col. 3:4). We are raised in Christ, with Christ, by Christ, to be like Christ.

The complex exposition of this in 1 Corinthians 15 may be summarized as follows: Adam is the type of Christ; he is the first man, while Christ is the second man. As Adam is the first of one race (the old humanity), so Christ is the first of a new race (the new humanity). Adam is the first representative man (Rom. 5:12–21), Christ is not merely the *second,* but the *last* (*eschatos*) Adam, since there can be no need for a further Adam-like figure after him.

The origins of these two men differ, however: Adam is the man of the earth and from the dust; Christ is from heaven. Not only so, but there is a fundamental difference between what they became. In a clear allusion to Genesis 2:7 ('the Lord God formed the man from the dust of the ground and breathed into his nostrils the breath of life, and man became a living being'), Paul says that 'The first man Adam became a living being' (1 Cor. 15:45). But while the first Adam received the breath of God, the last Adam is the One with the very Breath which gives life to his people: 'the last Adam [became] a life-giving spirit' (1 Cor. 15:45).

By this statement, Paul indicates the way in which Christ as last Adam was fully possessed by and came into the full possession of the Spirit in his glorification. Its implication is that the resurrected and glorified Christ, the Adam of the Spirit, now creates life of a new order, life like his own through the power of the Spirit: *eschatological* life whose dominant feature is [S]pirituality. Thus the body that is sown in the grave in death is a natural body (*sōma psychikon*); but in the resurrection-transformation it becomes a S/spiritual body (*sōma pneumatikon*, 1 Cor. 15:44).

The spiritual body

What, though, is a S/spiritual body? It is a body appropriate to the world of the Spirit who is the agent of its transformation. In a series of contrasts with the natural body which is perishable, sown (in the grave) in dishonour and weakness, Paul spells out what this implies: the spiritual body is raised (from the grave) imperishable (*en aphtharsia*), glorious (*en doxē*) and powerful (*en dynamei*; *cf.* 1 Cor. 15:42–44).

The clue to these admittedly enigmatic statements may lie in the contrast between 'dust' and 'heaven' (1 Cor. 15:47). That which emerges from the dust may return to the dust, since it does not possess self-sustaining powers within its own constituent nature. By contrast, that which belongs to the heavenly, *i.e.* to the realm and order of the Spirit, cannot be reduced to anything other than itself. As S/spiritual it is necessarily imperishable. Not only so, but since the heavenly realm of the Spirit is also the realm of the glory of God, and constituted of his glory, the resurrection body is also glorious. Further, since the Spirit expresses the energy of God emanently, the resurrection body is also powerful.

This last contrast between the weakness of the natural body and the power of the resurrection body provides us with an important insight. The energies of God the Spirit are fully released in the resurrection body; those who possess it consequently experience the end of the inertia and lethargy of the flesh, and an ease in serving God to the full capacity of their being.

At present believers are indwelt by the Spirit; the Spirit of

Christ energizes them in the context of their weakness (2 Cor. 12:9–10; 13:4; Phil. 4:13). The present life is lived in the tension between the 'already' and the 'not yet' of grace, where the weakness of the flesh and the energy of the indwelling Spirit coalesce. But in the resurrection body that tension will cease to exist, for this new body is S/spiritually constituted.

In the Old Testament 'Spirit' stands not only for the third person of the Trinity, but, as Geerhardus Vos says, it 'appears as the comprehensive formula for the transcendental, the super-natural'.[12] So here the Spirit is seen not only as the source of the resurrection body but also as 'the substratum of the resurrection-life, the element, as it were, in which, as in its circumambient atmosphere, the life of the coming aeon shall be lived'.[13] Having indwelt the believer in the present age, the Spirit will take absolute possession of the believer's entire being. The body in which the life of the future is lived will be both S/spiritual and glorious in its very constitution.

The resurrection of the body is simultaneously our adoption, the redemption of the body (Rom. 8:23), and our comprehensive vindication ('the crown of righteousness', 2 Tim. 4:8) and glorification. Against the background of the cosmic significance of Adam's fall, the resurrection-transformation also carries cosmic consequences. It brings to pass not only the liberty of the glory of God's sons but the glorification of the whole of creation.

Paul pictures the created order as subject to frustration in the present age; it shares in the consequences of Adam's sin. The very ground is cursed. But this frustration anticipates a day of liberation from the principle of entropy in which it is caught. That liberation involves participation in the 'glorious freedom [perhaps, better, "freedom of glory"] of the children of God' (Rom. 8:21). This is clearly coincidental with 'our adoption as sons, the redemption of our bodies' (Rom. 8:23), *i.e.* the resurrection – which constitutes the final harvest of which the present experience of the Spirit is the firstfruits.

The *indwelling* of the Spirit will then give way to something integrally related to it yet even greater in magnitude, just as the firstfruits share in and point towards the nature of the final harvest. Then the Spirit will not merely indwell mortal bodies, but will 'give life' to them (Rom. 8:11). This will not merely involve restoring the body to the condition experienced by the first Adam; it will mean transforming it ('We will not all sleep, but we will all be changed', 1 Cor. 15:51).

Since Adam was created as the vicegerent of all creation and the head of the entire cosmos under God, when he fell the whole creation fell with him into bondage, frustration and entropy. The resurrection of Christ marks the beginning of the grand reversal of this, the embryonic principle of cosmic transformation which will reach its consummation in the final resurrection. But since the resurrection brings us not only repristinization but eschatologization, it follows that there will be both repristinization and eschatologization of Adam's fallen world. It too will be changed, freed from its frustration and bondage to decay to share in the glorious liberty of God's children (Rom. 8:21).

We are given only faint glimpses of this in Scripture. If, as most commentators believe, the passage in 2 Peter 3:7, 10–13, reflects on the future, the cleansing of the universe will, according to Scripture, take place through judgment (*cf.* the flood).

Lutheran theology has tended to see here the annihilation of the original universe and the creation of a new one. But on the analogy of the 'destruction' of the world by the flood, it is best to see that there will be continuity between the new cosmos and the old, just as there will be between the resurrection body and the present body. Moreover, the vision of the future in Romans 8:20–21 anticipates the liberation and renewal, not the destruction and re-creation *ex nihilo*, of the universe.

From this destructive cleansing-for-glory will emerge 'a new heaven and a new earth, the home of righteousness' (2 Pet. 3:13). Indeed, heaven and earth will, as it were, form one domain of righteousness in which the Spirit of God will be the all-pervasive atmosphere, just as the Lord God and the Lamb will be the temple, the glory of God its light, and the Lamb of God its lamp. As Vos again notes: 'The Spirit is not only the author of the resurrection-act, but likewise the permanent substratum of the resurrection-life, to which He supplies the inner, basic element and the outer atmosphere.'[14]

Then the role of the Spirit of God, who has in history exercised the executive energy of the Father and brought glory to the Son, will be seen in its consummate state. Then that for which the Spirit was given at Pentecost, and with a view to which he seals the church, will be brought to pass in its totality.

Then, at last, the Spirit's work will reach harvest time, and God will be all in all (1 Cor. 15:28). With this in view, both the Spirit and the Bride say, 'Come!' (Rev. 22:17).

Notes

Preface

[1] B. B. Warfield, *Calvin and Calvinism* (New York: Oxford University Press, 1931), p. 21.

Chapter 1

[1] Abraham Kuyper, *The Work of the Holy Spirit*, tr. H. De Vries (New York: Funk & Wagnalls, 1900), p. 118.

[2] Though technically transliterated *rûah*, for convenience the familiar form *ruach* is used throughout this book.

[3] See E. DeWitt Burton, *Spirit, Soul, and Flesh* (Chicago, IL: University of Chicago Press, 1918), p. 113. *Cf.* G. L. Prestige, *God in Patristic Thought* (London: SPCK, [2]1952), pp. 17ff.

[4] All italicization in Scripture quotations is my own emphasis.

[5] Geerhardus Vos, *Biblical Theology* (Grand Rapids, MI: Eerdmans, 1948), p. 257.

[6] *Idem, The Pauline Eschatology* (1930; repr. Grand Rapids, MI: Eerdmans, 1952), p. 300.

[7] See, for example, Irenaeus, *Against Heresies*, 3.24.2; 4.7.4; 4.20.1. The Fathers often viewed biblical references to the activity of Wisdom as references to the Spirit of God. See further, W. H. McLellan, 'The Meaning of *Ruah 'Elohim* in Genesis 1, 2', *Biblica* 15 (1936), pp. 519–520; H. M. Orlinsky defends the rendering 'wind' in 'The Plain Meaning of *RUAH* in Gen. 1:2', in *Jewish Quarterly Review* 48 (1957–58), pp. 174–180.

[8] See B. S. Childs, *Myth and Reality in the Old Testament* (London: SCM Press, 1960), pp. 32–33.

[9] John Calvin, *Commentary on Genesis* (1563), tr. John King (Edinburgh: Calvin Translation Society, 1847), p. 73.

[10] *Cf.* Gordon J. Wenham, *Genesis* (Waco, TX: Word, 1987), p. 16.

[11] Wolfhart Pannenberg, *Systematic Theology*, tr. G. W. Bromiley (Grand Rapids, MI: Eerdmans, 1994), vol. 2, p. 77.

[12] *Cf.* M. G. Kline, *Images of the Spirit* (Grand Rapids, MI: Baker Book House, 1980), pp. 13–15. Gordon J. Wenham provides a *via media* by rendering *ruach Elohim* as 'Wind of God' (note capitalization), but sees this 'as a concrete and vivid image of the Spirit of God. The phrase does really express the powerful presence of God moving mysteriously over the face of the waters' (*op. cit.*, p. 17).

[13] See Kline, *loc. cit.*

[14] John Calvin, *Commentary on Hebrews*, tr. J. Owen (Edinburgh: Calvin Translation Society, 1853), p. 211.

[15] As does L. Neve, *The Spirit of God in the Old Testament* (Tokyo: Seibunsha, 1972), pp. 128–129.

[16] See, for example, Irenaeus, *Against Heresies*, 4.20. Justin makes the more modest and logically accurate proposal in his *Dialogue With Trypho*, lxii, to the effect that there are 'at least two'!

[17] The entail of this is found in the way in which, even for a less radical New Testament scholar like C. F. D. Moule, there is, to say the least, an opaqueness about the hypostatic status of the Spirit: 'threefoldness is, perhaps, less vital to a Christian conception of God than the eternal twofoldness of Father and Son' (*The Holy Spirit* [Oxford: Mowbray, 1978], p. 51). More radically, for G. W. H. Lampe, Spirit is all there is to God. See his *God as Spirit* (Oxford: Oxford University Press, 1977), *passim.*

[18] B. B. Warfield, *Biblical Doctrines* (New York: Oxford University Press, 1929; repr. Edinburgh: Banner of Truth, 1988), pp. 141–142.

[19] Augustine, *Questiones in Heptateuchum*, 2.73.

[20] J. N. D. Kelly, *Early Christian Doctrines*, rev. ed. (New York: Harper Collins, 1978), p. 115. *Cf.* also Prestige, *op. cit.*, pp. 157ff.

Chapter 2

[1] Basil, *On the Holy Spirit*, 16.39.

[2] Abraham Kuyper, *The Work of the Holy Spirit*, tr. H. De Vries (New York: Funk & Wagnalls, 1900), p. 97. A notable exception in English theology is found in John Owen, *Works*, ed. W. H. Goold (Edinburgh: Johnstone & Hunter, 1850–53; repr. London: Banner of Truth, 1965), vol. 3, pp. 152–188. For a recent reworking of this theme, see G. F. Hawthorne, *The Presence and the Power* (Dallas, TX: Word, 1991).

[3] This has been answered particularly thoroughly in J. Gresham Machen, *The Virgin Birth* (New York: Harper, 1930).

[4] See Irenaeus, *Against Heresies*, 3.16.2; 5.1.3. Tertullian accuses the Valentinian Gnostics of corrupting the text. See *On the Flesh of Christ*, 19.24.

[5] *E.g.* T. F. Torrance, writing in the wake of a controversy over the Virgin Birth. *Scottish Bulletin of Evangelical Theology*, 12.1 (Spring 1994), pp. 8ff. He is following the work of A. Harnack and Peter Hofrichter.

[6] Kuyper, *op. cit.*, pp. 81–82.

[7] John Calvin, *The Gospel according to John, 1–10*, tr. T. H. L. Parker, ed. D. W. and T. F. Torrance (Edinburgh: St Andrew Press, 1959), p. 20.

[8] Thus J. Jeremias comments: 'For Jesus to address God as "my Father" is therefore something new' (*The Prayers of Jesus* [London, SCM Press, 1967], p. 57). While some scholars have expressed caution about some of Jeremias' conclusions, his emphasis on the radical distinctiveness of the intimacy to which Jesus gives expression is well founded.

[9] Irenaeus, *Against Heresies*, 2.22.4.

[10] See Nu. 4:3 and *passim*. Nu. 8:24 gives the age as twenty-five, but this may well indicate that some kind of apprenticeship period preceded the full exercise of service.

[11] See A. Feuillet, 'Le symbolisme de la Colombe dans les récits évangéliques du baptême' (*Recherches de Science Religieuse* 46 [1958], pp. 524–544).

[12] Geerhardus Vos, *Biblical Theology* (Grand Rapids, MI: Eerdmans, 1948), p. 358.

[13] K. Rengstorf, in *Theological Dictionary of the New Testament*, ed. G. Kittel and G. Friedrich, tr. G. W. Bromiley (Grand Rapids, MI: Eerdmans, 1964), vol. 1, p. 304.

[14] *E.g.* by A. Bittlinger, *Gifts and Graces* (London: Hodder & Stoughton, 1967), pp. 48–50.

[15] Calvin's comments are particularly striking in this context: 'He now shows clearly how the death of Christ is to be regarded; not from its external act but from the power of the Spirit. Christ suffered as man, but in order that His death might effect our salvation it came forth from the power of the Spirit' (*Commentary on Hebrews*, tr. W. B. Johnston, ed. D. W.

and T. F. Torrance [Edinburgh: Oliver & Boyd, 1963], p. 121).

[16] See H. N. Ridderbos, *Paul: An Outline of his Theology*, tr. J. R. de Witt (Grand Rapids, MI: Eerdmans, 1975), p. 88. *Cf.* Richard B. Gaffin, Jr., *Perspectives on Pentecost* (Phillipsburg, NJ: Presbyterian & Reformed, 1979), pp. 18–19.

[17] The classical distinction between *allos* (distinction of individuals, not distinction in kind) and *heteros* (distinction in kind) is not consistently maintained in the New Testament; but the theology of this section requires us to recognize some such nuance for *allos* in this particular context.

[18] J. D. G. Dunn, *Jesus and the Spirit* (London: SCM Press, 1975), p. 322.

[19] H. Bavinck, *Our Reasonable Faith*, tr. H. Zylstra (Grand Rapids, MI: Eerdmans, 1956), p. 387.

Chapter 3

[1] I. H. Marshall, 'The Significance of Pentecost', *Scottish Journal of Theology* 30 (1977), p. 351 (*contra* J. D. G. Dunn, *Baptism in the Holy Spirit* [London: SCM Press, 1970], pp. 42ff.) regards such a view as 'improbable', arguing that fire is simply the symbol of which the Spirit is the reality, namely power. But the virtual quotation of Lk. 3:16 in Acts 1:5 suggests that the absence of any reference to fire is significant rather than incidental.

[2] I. H. Marshall, *The Acts of the Apostles*, Tyndale New Testament Commentary (Leicester: Inter-Varsity Press, 1980), p. 64. Although he finds no explicit evidence in the text itself for the contrast with Babel, in view of the presence of the table of nations and the speech-phenomenon that Luke records, it is difficult to resist the conclusion that Pentecost is an event of universal proportions which parallels and is set in antithesis to Babel. See especially J. G. Davies, 'Pentecost and Glossolalia', *Journal of Theological Studies*, new series, 5 (1952), pp. 228–231.

[3] See B. Lindars, *New Testament Apologetic* (London: SCM, 1961), p. 44; J. Dupont, 'Ascension du Christ et don de l'Esprit d'après Actes 2:33', in B. Lindars and S. Smalley (eds.), *Christ and Spirit in the New Testament* (London: Cambridge University Press, 1973), pp. 219–228. *Cf.* J. D. G. Dunn, *Jesus and the Spirit* (London: SCM Press, 1975), pp. 48–49.

[4] See especially D. E. Aune, *Prophecy in Early Christianity and the Ancient Mediterranean World* (Grand Rapids, MI: Eerdmans, 1983); W. A. Grudem, *The Gift of Prophecy in 1 Corinthians* (Lanham, MD: University Press of America, 1982); D. Hill, *New Testament Prophecy* (London: Marshalls, 1979); J. Panagopoulos (ed.), *Prophetic Vocation in the New Testament and Today* (*Novum Testamentum* Supplement 45; Leiden: Brill, 1977).

[5] J. Jeremias, *New Testament Theology*, tr. J. Bowden (London: SCM Press, 1971), vol. 1, p. 78.

[6] It ought, perhaps, to be acknowledged here that the view that Jesus' breathing on the disciples is symbolic only, held by Theodore of Mopsuestia (c. 350–428), was condemned by the Council of Constantinople in 553!

[7] This was the Feast of Tabernacles, which celebrated the harvest and God's goodness during the wilderness wanderings. During the seven days of the Feast, the people lived in shelters of leaves, hence the name.

[8] See NIV mg. for the text of John 7:37b–38a.

[9] Abraham Kuyper, *The Work of the Holy Spirit*, tr. H. De Vries (New York: Funk & Wagnalls, 1900), p. 461.

[10] For discussion of the procession formulation within the context of the doctrine of the Trinity as such, see the companion volume in this series, Gerald Bray, *The Doctrine of God* (Leicester: Inter-Varsity Press, 1993), pp. 153–196. For an earlier summary of the issues and the arguments, see P. Schaff, *History of the Christian Church*, 4th ed. (repr. Grand Rapids, MI: Eerdmans, 1981), vol. IV, pp. 484–489. Much of the best work on the doctrine of the Trinity in general and the *Filioque* in particular this century has, in my opinion, been done by Roman Catholic theologians, and here mention may be made of the fine volume by Bertrand de Margerie, *The Christian Trinity in History*, translated from *La Trinité Chrétienne dans l'Histoire* (1975) by E. J. Fortman (Petersham, MA: St Bede's Publications, 1982). See particularly pp. 160–178 for his discussion of the *Filioque*.

[11] H. B. Swete, *On the History of the Doctrine of the Procession of the Holy Spirit* (Cambridge: Deighton, Bell & Co., 1876), pp. 73–74.

[12] See Augustine, *On the Trinity*, 15.17.29.

[13] Cited in J. Neuner and J. Dupois (eds.), *The Christian Faith in the Doctrinal Documents of the Catholic Church*, rev. ed. (New York: Alba House, 1982), p. 110.

[14] See Augustine, *loc. cit.*

[15] Hints of this may be found in de Margerie, *op. cit.*, p. 176.

[16] See, on both sides of the question, Raymond E. Brown, *Gospel according to John* (London: Chapman, 1971), vol. 2, p. 689; M.-J. Lagrange, *Evangile selon Saint Jean* (1924; Paris: Gabalda, [7]1948), p. 413.

[17] See Augustine, *loc. cit.*.

[18] For a landmark exposition of this theme, see John Owen, *Communion With God*, in *The Works of John Owen* (Edinburgh: Johnstone & Hunter, 1850–53; repr. London: Banner of Truth, 1965), pp. 1–274.

Chapter 4

[1] As, for example, J. D. G. Dunn argues in *Baptism in the Holy Spirit* (London: SCM Press, 1970), pp. 55–72.

[2] See C. K. Barrett, 'Apollos and the Twelve Disciples of Ephesus', in

W. C. Weinrich, *The New Testament Age* (Macon, GA: Mercer University Press, 1984), vol. 1, pp. 29–39.

[3] Abraham Kuyper, *The Work of the Holy Spirit*, tr. H. De Vries (New York: Funk & Wagnalls, 1900), pp. 123–126.

[4] Comparing the medieval and the modern church may seem excessive, but there are striking parallels: the presence of miracles, worship which is sense-directed rather than mind-directed, giving Christ or the Spirit by physical means (Christ in the sacramental elements, or the Spirit by the touch of the charismatic leader). This may explain why the charismatic movement has been so capable of appropriation within Roman Catholicism.

[5] Dunn, *op. cit.*, p. 128.

[6] J. R. W. Stott, *The Message of Acts* (Leicester: Inter-Varsity Press, 1990), p. 61. See, in this connection, the brief but stirring section on 'The Spirit in a Religious Awakening', and especially the comments on prayer, in G. Smeaton, *The Doctrine of the Holy Spirit* (Edinburgh: T. & T. Clark, [2]1882), pp. 282ff.

[7] Jonathan Edwards, *A History of the Work of Redemption*, Period I, Part 1, in *The Works of Jonathan Edwards* (London, 1834; repr. Edinburgh: Banner of Truth, 1974), vol. 1, p. 539.

Chapter 5

[1] See Willem A. Van Gemeren, 'The Spirit of Restoration', *Westminster Theological Journal* 50.1 (1988), pp. 81–102.

[2] Robert Bellarmine, *De Justificatione*, III.2.3. Similarly, the Council of Trent declared that 'No one can know with a certainty of faith . . . that he has obtained the grace of God' (Decree on Justification, Session VI, chapter 9).

[3] The expression has been traced back to F. Buddeus, *Institutiones Theologiae Dogmaticae* (1724) and J. Karpov, *Theologia Revelata Dogmatica* (1739), indicating the emergence of the terminology, *but by no means the idea itself*, in the so-called scholastic Protestant orthodoxy of the seventeenth century.

[4] See Thomas Aquinas, *Summa Theologiae*, 1a IIae q.112, 'On the Cause of Grace'.

[5] *The Workes of William Perkins* (3 vols; Cambridge, 1612–19), vol. 1, pp. 11–117.

[6] *Cf.* G. C. Berkouwer, *Faith and Justification* (Grand Rapids, MI: Eerdmans, 1954), pp. 29–33; Karl Barth, *Church Dogmatics*, tr. G. W. Bromiley and T. F. Torrance (Edinburgh: T. & T. Clark, 1958), IV.2, p. 502; Otto Weber, *Foundations of Dogmatics*, tr. D. Guder (Grand Rapids, MI: Eerdmans, 1983), vol. 2, pp. 336ff.

[7] H. N. Ridderbos, *Paul: An Outline of his Theology*, tr. J. R. de Witt (Grand Rapids, MI: Eerdmans, 1975), p. 206.

[8] See R. A. Muller, *Christ and the Decree* (1986; repr. Grand Rapids, MI: Baker Book House, 1988), for a balanced defence of Perkins and other post-Reformation writers with respect to the question of their Christocentricity.

[9] Hendrikus Berkhof, *The Christian Faith*, tr. S. Woudstra (Grand Rapids, MI: Eerdmans, 1979), p. 479.

[10] John Calvin, *Institutes of the Christian Religion*, tr. F. L. Battles, ed. J. T. McNeill (London: SCM Press, 1960), III.1.1.

[11] John Calvin, *Commentary on Romans*, ed. D. W. and T. F. Torrance, tr. R. Mackenzie (Edinburgh: St Andrew Press, 1961), *ad loc.*

[12] John Calvin, *Commentary on 1 Corinthians*, ed. D. W. and T. F. Torrance, tr. J. W. Fraser (Edinburgh: St Andrew Press, 1960), *ad loc.*

[13] Philip Melanchthon, *Loci Communes*, 2.7.

[14] Westminster Shorter Catechism, answer to question 38.

[15] For what follows, see Richard B. Gaffin, Jr., *Resurrection and Redemption* (originally published as *The Centrality of the Resurrection*, 1978; Grand Rapids, MI: Baker Book House, 1987), pp. 114–127.

[16] *Ibid.*, p. 116.

[17] See the landmark essay by Geerhardus Vos, 'The Eschatological Aspect of the Pauline Conception of the Spirit' (1912), originally published in *Biblical and Theological Studies* (New York, 1912), and now reprinted in Richard B. Gaffin, Jr. (ed.), *Redemptive History and Biblical Interpretation* (Phillipsburg, NJ: Presbyterian & Reformed, 1980), pp. 91–125, esp. pp. 103–105.

[18] See John Murray, 'Definitive Sanctification', in *Collected Writings* (Edinburgh: Banner of Truth, 1977), vol. 2, pp. 277ff.

[19] See, for example, Charles Hodge, *I Corinthians* (1857; repr. London: Banner of Truth, 1958), p. 105. Gordon Fee neatly maintains the ambiguity: 'The believer is united to the Lord and thereby has become one S/spirit with him . . .' (*The First Epistle to the Corinthians* [Grand Rapids, MI: Eerdmans, 1987], p. 260).

[20] B. B. Warfield, *Biblical Doctrines* (New York: Oxford University Press, 1929; repr. Edinburgh: Banner of Truth, 1988), p. 451.

[21] *Institutes*, II.16.9.

[22] L. Berkhof, *Systematic Theology* (Grand Rapids, MI: Eerdmans, 1941), p. 451.

Chapter 6

[1] See the striking title of *Institutes*, III.3: 'Our Regeneration by Faith: Repentance', a description which, if written by an anonymous author, would have him branded immediately as theologically Arminian!

[2] Thus, *e.g.*, H. Witsius, *The Economy of the Covenants* (1677), tr. W. Crookshank (London, 1822; repr. San Diego, CA: den Dulk Foundation, 1990), vol. 1, pp. 359–361.

[3] H. N. Ridderbos, *Paul: An Outline of his Theology*, tr. J. R. de Witt (Grand Rapids, MI: Eerdmans, 1975), p. 226.

[4] E. Schweitzer, in *Theological Dictionary of the New Testament*, ed. G. Kittel and G. Friedrich, tr. G. Bromiley (Grand Rapids, MI: Eerdmans, 1971), vol. 7, p. 138. For a modern defence of the older view of the Johannine use of *sarx*, see John Murray, *Collected Writings* (Edinburgh: Banner of Truth, 1977), vol. 2, pp. 184–185.

[5] See the sensitive and wise comments by Archibald Alexander in *Thoughts on Religious Experience* (1844; 3rd ed., repr. London: Banner of Truth, 1967), p. 64.

[6] A similar explanation is worked out in detail by Linda L. Belleville, ' "Born of Water and Spirit": John 3:5', *Trinity Journal* 1 (1980), pp. 125–141, but the general thrust has a long pedigree.

[7] Such language can be found in the European theologians in the 17th century such as Peter Van Mastricht, but also in such English writers as John Owen. While later Reformed theologians understandably expressed grave reservations about this language, its central concern, of course, was to preserve the radical work of the Spirit on the whole individual, affecting not merely mind and will.

[8] Westminster Confession of Faith (London, 1647), X.i. *Cf.* IX.4. Italics mine.

[9] W. G. T. Shedd, *Dogmatics* (New York: 1888), vol. 1, pp. 509, n. 1.

[10] B. B. Warfield, *Biblical Doctrines* (New York: Oxford University Press, 1929; repr. Edinburgh: Banner of Truth, 1988), p. 457; *cf.* C. Hodge, *Systematic Theology* (3 vols., 1872–73; repr. London: James Clark, 1960), vol. 2, pp. 702–703.

[11] *Cf.* Abraham Kuyper, *The Work of the Holy Spirit*, tr. H. De Vries (New York: Funk & Wagnalls, 1900), p. 412; Robert E. Countess, 'Thank God for the Genitive', *Bulletin of the Evangelical Theological Society* 12 (1969), pp. 117–122.

[12] Warfield, *op. cit.*, p. 504.

[13] G. C. Berkouwer, *The Sacraments* (Grand Rapids, MI: Eerdmans, 1969), p. 147.

[14] Otto Weber, *Foundations of Dogmatics*, tr. D. Guder (Grand Rapids, MI: Eerdmans, 1983), vol. 2, p. 261.

[15] *Cf.* NIV. J. R. W. Stott, *Commentary on the Epistles of John* (London: Tyndale Press, 1964), pp. 130–136; Raymond E. Brown, *The Epistles of John* (New York: Doubleday, 1982), pp. 407–416.

[16] Louis Berkhof, *Systematic Theology* (Grand Rapids, MI: Eerdmans, 1941), p. 492.

[17] Westminster Confession of Faith (London, 1647), XIV.ii.

[18] Herman Bavinck, *Our Reasonable Faith*, tr. H. Zylstra (Grand Rapids, MI: Eerdmans, 1956), p. 438.

[19] Artur Weiser, *The Psalms* (London: SCM Press, 1962), p. 403.

Chapter 7

[1] See P. E. Hughes, *Lefèvre, Pioneer of Ecclesiastical Renewal in France* (Grand Rapids, MI: Eerdmans, 1984), pp. 46f., 192ff.

[2] See C. F. D. Moule, *Idiom Book of the New Testament* (Cambridge: Cambridge University Press, 1960), pp. 123–125.

[3] *Cf.*, among others, Robert Haldane, *The Epistle to the Romans* (repr. London: Banner of Truth, 1966), *ad loc.*; C. E. B. Cranfield, *A Critical and Exegetical Commentary on the Epistle to the Romans* (2 vols., Edinburgh: T. & T. Clark, 1975, 1979), *ad loc.*

[4] In this context, the vibrant comments of Anders Nygren are still of value in *Romans*, tr. C. S. Rasmussen (Philadelphia: Fortress Press, 1949), especially pp. 239ff.

[5] Abraham Kuyper, *The Work of the Holy Spirit*, tr. H. De Vries (New York: Funk & Wagnalls, 1900), p. 453.

[6] John Murray, *Principles of Conduct* (London: Tyndale Press, and Grand Rapids, MI: Eerdmans, 1957), p. 205.

[7] Geerhardus Vos, *The Pauline Eschatology* (1930; repr. Grand Rapids, MI: Eerdmans, 1952), p. 300.

[8] A particularly persuasive exposition of this view is to be found in the work of H. N. Ridderbos, in summary form in *Paul: An Outline of his Theology* (1966), tr. J. R. de Witt (Grand Rapids, MI: Eerdmans, 1975), and in greater and more persuasive detail in his *Aan de Romeinen* (Kampen: Kok, 1959).

[9] These include (in chronological order) the major commentaries of John Murray, C. E. B. Cranfield and James D. G. Dunn.

[10] Westminster Confession of Faith (London, 1647), XIII.iii.

[11] Understanding the fall of Adam as a breach of the principles later enunciated in the Decalogue was a characteristic of the Reformed theology of the seventeenth century. It is given fresh impetus in the context of a modern biblico-theological approach to systematic theology in Murray, *Principles of Conduct*.

[12] See Patrick Fairbairn, *The Revelation of Law in Scripture* (Edinburgh: T. & T. Clark, 1868), pp. 82–146, for an extended discussion which, while dated, remains valuable.

[13] For a valuable exposition of this view by a contemporary Old Testament scholar who resists the consensus on the basis of textual considerations, see the contribution of Bruce K. Waltke in W. S. Barker and W. R. Godfrey (eds.), *Theonomy: A Reformed Critique* (Grand Rapids, MI:

Zondervan, 1990), pp. 70–73. For a sympathetic but cautionary note, see Vern S. Poythress, *The Shadow of Christ in the Law of Moses* (Brentwood, TN: Wolgemuth & Hyatt, 1991), pp. 99–103.

[14] *Cf.* G. E. Ladd, *A Theology of the New Testament* (Grand Rapids, MI: Eerdmans, 1974), pp. 509–510.

[15] Quoted from Kuyper in G. C. Berkouwer, *A Half Century of Theology* (1970), tr. L. B. Smedes (Grand Rapids, MI: Eerdmans, 1977), p. 196.

[16] See R. N. Longenecker, *Paul, Apostle of Liberty* (1964; repr. Grand Rapids, MI: Baker Book House, 1976), p. 113.

[17] See Westminster Confession of Faith (1647), ch. XIII.

[18] *Institutes*, III.8.

[19] The argument for understanding the Spirit to be the subject of Romans 8:28 is made by various New Testament scholars. *Cf.* M. Black, 'The Interpretation of Romans 8:28', in *Neotestamentica et Patristica* (Leiden: Brill, 1962), pp. 166ff. Whether exegetically correct or not, the general principle that the Spirit is the executive of the Trinity implies that in this working in the world the Spirit is the agent.

Chapter 8

[1] Geerhardus Vos, *The Pauline Eschatology* (1930; repr. Grand Rapids, MI: Eerdmans, 1952), p. 165.

[2] *Ibid.*

[3] See C. Spicq, *Theological Lexicon of the New Testament*, tr. and ed. J. D. Ernest (Peabody, MA: Hendrickson, 1994), vol. 1, p. 148; H. Balz and G. Schneider, *Exegetical Dictionary of the New Testament* (Grand Rapids, MI: Eerdmans, 1990), vol. 1, p. 116.

[4] *Cf.* W. Bauer, *A Greek-English Lexicon of the New Testament and Other Early Christian Literature*, tr. W. F. Arndt and F. W. Gingrich, rev. F. W. Gingrich and F. W. Danker (Chicago, IL: University of Chicago, [2]1979), sub *aparchē*.

[5] Jonathan Edwards, *Charity and its Fruits* (1852; repr. London: Banner of Truth, 1969), pp. 323ff.

[6] *Cf.* G. W. H. Lampe, *The Seal of the Spirit* (London: Longmans, 1951).

[7] For a sustained rejection of the identification of the seal with baptism or confirmation, see J. D. G. Dunn, *Baptism in the Holy Spirit* (London: SCM Press, 1970), pp. 132–134, 160.

[8] See *The Works of Richard Sibbes*, ed. A. B. Grosart (6 vols., 1862–64; repr. Edinburgh: Banner of Truth, 1979–83), vol. 3, pp. 453ff.

[9] *Ibid.*, p. 456.

[10] I have discussed this at length in *John Owen and the Christian Life* (Edinburgh: Banner of Truth, 1987), pp. 117–121.

[11] *Institutes*, III.1.3.

[12] C. E. B. Cranfield, *A Critical and Exegetical Commentary on the Epistle to the*

Romans (Edinburgh: T. & T. Clark, 1975), vol. 1, p. 403.

[13] B. B. Warfield, *Faith and Life* (1916; repr. Edinburgh: Banner of Truth, 1974), p. 184.

[14] Charles Hodge, *1 and 2 Corinthians* (1857, 1859; repr. in one vol. Edinburgh: Banner of Truth, 1974), p. 689.

[15] Raymond E. Brown, *Gospel according to John* (London: Chapman, 1971), p. 1140.

[16] See Calvin's masterly exposition in *Institutes*, III.20 (a treatise on prayer in its own right). *Cf.* Sinclair B. Ferguson, 'Prayer: A Covenant Work', *Banner of Truth Magazine* 137 (1975), pp. 23ff.

Chapter 9

[1] Livy, *History of Rome*, 2.32.

[2] A. E. Hill, 'The Temple of Asclepius: An Alternative Source of Paul's Body Theology?' *Journal of Biblical Literature* 99 (1980), pp. 297–309; J. Murphy-O'Connor, *St Paul's Corinth: Texts and Archaeology* (Delaware: Michael Glazier, 1983), pp. 161–167.

[3] For a recent discussion, see Gosnell L. O. R. Yorke, *The Church as the Body of Christ in the Pauline Corpus: A Re-examination* (Lanham, MD: University Press of America, 1991).

[4] See G. R. Beasley-Murray, *Baptism in the New Testament* (Grand Rapids, MI: Eerdmans, 1962), pp. 18ff. for discussion.

[5] Robert Barclay, *The Confession of the Society of Friends*, Proposition xii.

[6] See M. G. Kline, *By Oath Consigned* (Grand Rapids, MI: Eerdmans, 1969), pp. 65ff.

[7] John Calvin, *Institutes of the Christian Religion*, ed. J. T. McNeill, tr. F. L. Battles (London: SCM Press, and Philadelphia: Westminster, 1961), IV.17.10.

[8] *Ibid.*, IV.17.4.

[9] *E.g.* by the Mercersburg theologian J. W. Nevins, 'The Doctrine of the Reformed Church on the Lord's Supper', *The Mercersburg Review* (1850), pp. 421–549. *Cf.* T. F. Torrance in his introduction to Robert Bruce, *The Mystery of the Lord's Supper* (Edinburgh: James Clark, 1958).

[10] See Robert Bruce, *op. cit.*, pp. 64, 85.

Chapter 10

[1] Wayne Grudem, *The Gift of Prophecy in the New Testament and Today* (Westchester, IL: Crossway, 1988), pp. 45–63.

[2] The view that Ephesians 2:20 should be taken as a controlling factor in this discussion has been criticized by Grudem and his colleague D. A. Carson. Carson's criticism of this view as represented by Richard B. Gaffin,

Jr., is particularly sharp, not to say acerbic. He argues: 'It is as illegitimate for Gaffin to use this verse as the controlling factor in his understanding of the New Testament gift of prophecy as it would be to conclude from Titus 1:12 ("Even one of their own prophets has said, 'Cretans are always liars, evil brutes, lazy gluttons'") that New Testament prophets were pagan poets from Crete' (D. A. Carson, *Showing the Spirit: A Theological Exposition of 1 Corinthians 12–14* [Grand Rapids, MI: Baker Book House, 1987], p. 97). This is an infelicitious criticism. To regard Titus 1:12 as a controlling statement would be *prima facie* ludicrous. But if, as many commentators have held, Ephesians 2:20 refers to two offices, it inevitably and necessarily exercises a controlling function because it explicitly states that these offices are *foundational.* To regard this as 'an anomalous use of "prophets" in the New Testament' as Carson does is surely misleading, in view of the consistent precedence given to prophecy over the fundamental but non-foundational ministry of pastors and teachers (*cf.* Rom. 12:6–8; 1 Cor. 12:28; Eph. 4:11), as well as over evangelists.

[3] As a representative sample of studies, see Gordon Fee, *The First Epistle to the Corinthians* (Grand Rapids, MI: Eerdmans, 1987), pp. 652–698; A. Bittlinger, *Gifts and Graces: A Commentary on 1 Corinthians 12–14* (London: Hodder & Stoughton, 1967); Gunther Bornkamm, *Early Christian Experience,* tr. Paul L. Hammer (London: SCM Press, 1969); A. A. Hoekema, *What About Tongues-Speaking?* (Grand Rapids, MI: Eerdmans, 1967); Carson, *op. cit.*; O. P. Robertson, *God's Final Word* (Edinburgh: Banner of Truth, 1994); W. J. Samarin, *Tongues of Men and Angels: The Religious Language of Pentecostalism* (New York: Macmillan, 1972).

[4] See Richard B. Gaffin, Jr., *Perspectives on Pentecost* (Phillipsburg, NJ: Presbyterian & Reformed, 1979), p. 57.

[5] Wayne A. Grudem, *The Gift of Prophecy in 1 Corinthians* (Lanham, MD: University of America Press, 1982); *idem, The Gift of Prophecy in the New Testament and Today* (Westchester, IL: Crossway, and Eastbourne: Kingsway, 1988); *idem, Systematic Theology* (Grand Rapids: Zondervan, and Leicester: Inter-Varsity Press, 1994). For a brief discussion, see Roy Clements, *Word and Spirit: The Bible and the Gift of Prophecy Today* (Leicester: UCCF, 1986). Graham Houston, *Prophecy Now* (Leicester: Inter-Varsity Press, 1989; US ed. *Prophecy: A Gift for Today* [Downers Grove, IL: Inter-Varsity Press, 1989]), is a sympathetic assessment of the way in which contemporary prophecy may manifest itself.

[6] See Plato, *Timaeus,* 71e–72b; *Phaedrus,* 244a–d.

[7] Grudem, *The Gift of Prophecy in the New Testament and Today,* p. 90.

[8] See also the appeal to Agabus in D. Hill, 'Christian Prophets as Teachers or Instructors in the Church', in J. Panagopoulos (ed.), *Prophetic Vocation in the New Testament and Today* (*Novum Testamentum* Supplement 45; Leiden: Brill, 1977), p. 124.

[9] Grudem, *op. cit.*, p. 93.

[10] *Ibid.*, p. 94.

[11] *Ibid.*, p. 96.

[12] Grudem, *Systematic Theology*, p. 1052. He appeals to Ignatius' *Epistle to the Philadelphians*, 7:1–2, and *The Epistle of Barnabas*, 6:8; 9:2, 5.

[13] The passages to which Grudem appeals reflect the test of Scripture; it is not possible, on any natural reading of them, to align them with the idea of second-level authority or only relative accuracy.

[14] Grudem, *Systematic Theology*, p. 1052.

[15] Grudem, *The Gift of Prophecy in the New Testament and Today*, p. 96.

[16] John Murray, 'The Guidance of the Holy Spirit', in *Collected Writings of John Murray* (Edinburgh: Banner of Truth, 1976), vol. 1, p. 188.

[17] J. H. Newman, *Two Essays on Biblical and Ecclesiastical Miracles* (London: [3]1873), pp. 261–270.

[18] This is Jon Ruthven's accusation against B. B. Warfield's *Counterfeit Miracles* (New York: Charles Scribner's Sons, 1918; London: Banner of Truth, 1972). His cessationism, Ruthven argues, is based on an Enlightenment-rooted rationalistic view of miracle set within the context of Scottish common-sense realism. See Jon Ruthven, *On the Cessation of the Charismata: The Protestant Polemic on Postbiblical Miracles* (Journal of Pentecostal Theology Supplement Series 3; Sheffield: Sheffield Academic Press, 1993), especially pp. 41–111. Warfield has by no means written the last word on this topic. But, quite apart from other criticisms of Ruthven's arguments, he surely does not want to suggest that it is unadulterated Enlightenment rationalism to query, *e.g.*, the accounts of the miraculous gifts of Gregory Thaumaturgus. In such contexts, is nothing to be said for *Scottish* common sense?

[19] In his critique of Warfield, Ruthven appeals at length to 1 Cor. 4:1–8; Eph. 4:7–13 and a number of other passages in this connection. *Op. cit.*, pp. 123–187.

[20] For the imperfect quality of ancient mirrors, see C. Spicq, *Theological Lexicon of the New Testament* (Peabody, MA: Hendrickson, 1994), vol. 2, pp. 73–76.

[21] Carson, *op. cit.*, p. 70.

[22] Gaffin, *op. cit.*, pp. 109–110.

[23] *Institutes*, Prefatory Address to King Francis I of France.

[24] *Cf.* E. Earle Ellis, 'Prophecy in the New Testament Church and Today', in Panagopolous (ed.), *op. cit.*, p. 53.

[25] Max M. B. Turner contends that to speak in terms of 'the dangerous possibility of new authoritative revelation' is really 'a red herring' ('Spiritual Gifts Then and Now', *Vox Evangelica*, 1985, p. 55). But this ignores the fact that all divine revelation *is* authoritative.

[26] Grudem, *Systematic Theology*, p. 127; *cf. The Gift of Prophecy in the New Testament and Today*, p. 299.

[27] Some voices within Rome have argued, following J. R. Geiselmann, that the formulations of the Council of Trent can be read in a manner which accords with *sola Scriptura*, holding that the Tridentine fathers taught that the tradition does not so much add to Scripture as contain the church's illuminated understanding of the contents of Scripture. *Cf.* J. R. Geiselmann, 'Scripture, Tradition, and the Church: An Ecumenical Problem', in D. J. Callahan, H. A. Oberman and D. J. O'Hanlong (eds.), *Christianity Divided* (London: Sheed & Ward, 1962), pp. 39–72. But see the sharp rejoinder by J. Ratzinger, Cardinal Prefect of the Sacred Congregation of the Doctrine of the Faith: 'as a Catholic theologian, [Geiselmann] has to hold fast to Catholic dogmas as such, but none of them is to be had *sola scriptura* . . .' (K. Rahner and J. Ratzinger, *Revelation and Tradition*, tr. W. J. O'Hara [New York: Herder & Herder, and London: Search Press, 1966], p. 33).

[28] Westminster Confession of Faith (1647), I.vi.

[29] Grudem, *The Gift of Prophecy in the New Testament and Today*, p. 113.

[30] John Owen, *A Discourse of Spiritual Gifts*, in *The Works of John Owen*, ed. W. H. Goold (Edinburgh: Johnstone & Hunter, 1850–53), vol. 4, p. 475; *cf.* p. 454.

[31] Gordon D. Fee, *God's Empowering Presence* (Peabody, MA: Hendrickson, and Carlisle: Paternoster, 1994), p. 890.

[32] *Cf.* the discussion by J. I. Packer in *Keep in Step with the Spirit* (Old Tappan, NJ: Revell, and Leicester: Inter-Varsity Press, 1984), pp. 202–213, especially p. 211.

[33] See Westminster Confession Faith (1647), V.iii.

[34] Owen, *op. cit.*, p. 475.

[35] Fee, *op. cit.*, pp. 96–97.

Chapter 11

[1] Stanley J. Samartha in Emilio Castro (ed.), *To the Wind of God's Spirit* (Geneva: WCC Publications, 1990), pp. 60–61.

[2] This principle, expressed variously, is derived from Cyprian, *Epistles* 73.21.

[3] Karl Rahner, *Theological Investigations*, tr. K.-H. and B. Kruger (London: Darton, Longman & Todd, 1969), vol. 6, p. 391.

[4] For a modern exposition of this, see Bryan Gaybba, *The Spirit of Love* (London: Chapman, 1987).

[5] W. H. Griffith Thomas, *The Holy Spirit of God* (1913; London: Church Book Room Press, 1972), pp. 185–186.

[6] *Ibid.*, p. 187.

[7] Gordon D. Fee, *God's Empowering Presence* (Peabody, MA: Hendrickson, and Carlisle: Paternoster, 1994).

[8] Hendrikus Berkhof, *The Doctrine of the Holy Spirit* (London: Epworth, 1965), p. 102.

[9] Cited in Nicholas Shakespeare's review, *Daily Telegraph*, 9 Dec. 1995, Arts and Books Section, p. 7.

[10] Calvin, *Institutes*, II.2.16. *Cf.* his comments in II.11.12; and in his Commentaries on Gn. 4:20; Ex. 20:4; 34:17.

[11] See Fee, *op. cit.*, pp. 808ff.

[12] Geerhardus Vos, *The Pauline Eschatology* (1930; repr. Grand Rapids, MI: Eerdmans, 1952), p. 162.

[13] *Ibid.*, p. 163.

[14] *Ibid.*, p. 165.

For Further Reading

1. The Spirit and his story

For studies on the Spirit of God in the Old Testament, in addition to the theological wordbooks and Old Testament theologies, see L. Wood, *The Holy Spirit in the Old Testament* (Grand Rapids, MI: Zondervan, 1976); L. Neve, *The Spirit of God in the Old Testament* (Tokyo: Seibunsha, 1972); M. A. Inch, *Saga of the Spirit* (Grand Rapids, MI: Baker Book House, 1985), pp. 1–68; G. Smeaton, *The Doctrine of the Holy Spirit* (Edinburgh: T. & T. Clark, 1843), pp. 9–43; B. B. Warfield, 'The Spirit of God in the Old Testament' (1895), reprinted in *Biblical Doctrines* (New York: Oxford University Press, 1929; Edinburgh: Banner of Truth, 1988), pp. 101–129.

2. The Spirit of Christ

The relationship between the Spirit and the incarnate Christ is a much-neglected subject in systematic theology. A beautiful but all-too-brief summary of the New Testament's teaching appears as early as Basil the Great in his little study *On the Holy Spirit*. Fuller development is found in John Owen, *Works*, ed. W. H. Goold (Edinburgh: Johnstone & Hunter, 1850–53; repr. London: Banner of Truth, 1965), vol. 3, pp. 152–188. Material may be found in, *e.g.*, H. B. Swete, *The Holy Spirit in the New Testament* (London: Macmillan, 1909); C. K. Barrett, *The Holy Spirit and the Gospel Tradition* (London: SPCK, 1947); F. X. Durrwell, *Holy Spirit of God* (London: Chapman, 1986), ch. 5. T. A. Smail, *Reflected Glory* (London: Hodder & Stoughton, 1975) provides an interesting study on the theme of 'The Spirit in Christ and Christians' from a charismatic perspective moulded by a theology influenced by both evangelicalism and Karl Barth. The only available book-length study is G. F. Hawthorne, *The Presence and the Power* (Dallas, TX: Word, 1991). Part One of J. D. G. Dunn, *Jesus and the Spirit* (London: SCM, 1975), is a study of 'The Religious Experience of Jesus'. Dunn sees Jesus' experience of the Spirit as the essential link between doing 'Christology from below' (which he favours) and a 'Christology from above'.

The distinctive eschatological significance of the Spirit's ministry is expounded in the landmark essay of G. Vos, 'The Eschatological Aspects of the Pauline Concept of the Spirit' (1912), reprinted in R. B. Gaffin, Jr. (ed.), *Redemptive History and Biblical Interpretation* (Phillipsburg, NJ: Presbyterian & Reformed, 1980), pp. 91–125. See also N. Q. Hamilton, *The Holy Spirit and Eschatology in Paul* (Edinburgh: Scottish Journal of Theology Occasional Papers no. 6, 1957).

3. The gift of the Spirit *and*
4. Pentecost today?

Studies of Pentecost and the gifts of the Spirit abound. Notable modern works include: J. D. G. Dunn, *Baptism in the Holy Spirit* (London: SCM, 1970); F. D. Bruner, *A Theology of the Holy Spirit* (Grand Rapids, MI: Eerdmans, 1970); R. B. Gaffin, Jr.,

Perspectives on Pentecost (Phillipsburg, NJ: Presbyterian & Reformed, 1979). For a point-by-point critique of the position of Dunn, see H. M. Ervin, *Conversion-Initiation and the Baptism in the Holy Spirit* (Peabody, MA: Hendrickson, 1984). This debate is continued in the context of questions of continuity and discontinuity in L. D. Pettegrew, *The New Covenant Ministry of the Holy Spirit* (Lanham, MD: University of America Press, 1993). For the role of Pentecost as a mission-event, see H. R. Boer, *Pentecost and Missions* (Grand Rapids, MI: Eerdmans, 1961); J. V. Taylor, *The Go-Between God: The Holy Spirit and the Christian Mission* (London: SCM, 1972).

For discussions of the history and theology of the *Filioque* clause, H. B. Swete's long-out-of-print study *On the History of the Doctrine of the Procession of the Holy Spirit* (Cambridge: Deighton, Bell & Coll, 1876), and his later *The Holy Spirit in the Ancient Church* (London: Macmillan) are still of much value. Ecumenical discussions are summarized by the essays in L. Vischer (ed.), *Spirit of God, Spirit of Christ* (London: SPCK, 1981). In addition to his volume on *The Doctrine of God* (also in this Contours of Christian Theology series), Gerald L. Bray's article 'The *Filioque* Clause in History and Theology', *Tyndale Bulletin* 34, 1983, pp. 91–144, provides a helpful and careful survey, and favours the addition. Barth's defence of the *Filioque* appears in his *Church Dogmatics* I.1, tr. G. T. Thomson (Edinburgh: T. & T. Clark, 1936). G. S. Hendry offers a critical discussion in *The Holy Spirit in Christian Theology* (London: SCM, 1965), pp. 11–52. J. Moltmann's exposition can be found in *The Trinity and the Kingdom of God* (London: SCM, 1981).

Broader discussions of the historical development of the doctrine of the Spirit may be found in E. J. Fortman, *The Triune God* (Philadelphia: Westminster, 1972); Bertrand de Margerie, *The Christian Trinity in History*, tr. E. J. Fortman (Petersham, MA: St Bede's Publications, 1982). A. W. Wainwright's *The Trinity in the New Testament* (London: SPCK, 1962) remains a valuable study of the New Testament materials relevant to the doctrine of the Trinity.

5. The Spirit of order *and*
6. *Spiritus recreator*

For a contemporary discussion of *ordo salutis* and the various facets of the application of redemption, see A. A. Hoekema, *Saved by Grace* (Grand Rapids, MI: Eerdmans, 1989; Carlisle: Paternoster, 1994). R. B. Gaffin, Jr., *Resurrection and Redemption* (1978; Grand Rapids, MI: Baker Book House, 1987) is a seminal biblico-theological study with important implications in this area. On union with Christ, see L. B. Smedes, *Union with Christ* (revised version of *All Things Made New*, 1970; Grand Rapids, MI: Eerdmans, 1983). Gordon Fee's *God's Empowering Presence* (Peabody, MA: Hendrickson, 1994), pp. 846–869, contains his summary of the Pauline teaching. For a classical exposition from the Reformed perspective, see John Murray, *Redemption – Accomplished and Applied* (Grand Rapids, MI: Eerdmans, 1955).

On regeneration, the standard, though rather slight, work remains B. Citron, *New Birth* (Edinburgh: Edinburgh University Press, 1951). G. C. Berkouwer's Studies in Dogmatics provide a series of studies correlating faith to various aspects of the application of Christ's work: *Faith and Sanctification* (Grand Rapids, MI: Eerdmans, 1952; Leicester: Inter-Varsity Press, 1973); *Faith and Justification* (Grand Rapids, MI: Eerdmans, 1954); *Faith and Perseverance* (Grand Rapids, MI: Eerdmans, 1958).

For extended studies of the application of redemption in the pre-Reformation church, see Alister E. McGrath, *Iustitia Dei* (Cambridge: Cambridge University Press, 1986), vol. 1, *From the Beginnings to 1500*, and the important work by Heiko Oberman, *The Harvest of Medieval Theology: Gabriel Biel and Late Medieval Nominalism* (Grand Rapids, MI: Eerdmans, 1967).

7. The Spirit of holiness *and*
8. The communion of the Spirit

In addition to the studies on the Spirit in John Owen, *Works*, ed. W. H. Goold (Edinburgh: Johnstone & Hunter, 1850–53; repr. London: Banner of Truth, 1965), vol. 3, and Abraham Kuyper, *The Work of the Holy Spirit* (New York: Funk & Wagnalls, 1900), pp. 431–507, see Owen, *Works*, vols. 6 and 7 for classical evangelical teaching on the ways in which the Spirit develops holiness. Book III of Calvin's *Institutes* is an often-neglected treasure of biblical insight in this area. J. I. Packer, *Keep in Step with the Spirit* (Old Tappan, NJ: Revell, and Leicester: Inter-Varsity Press, 1984), will also be consulted with profit. For an extended treatment of communion with the Spirit, see John Owen, *Communion with God*, in *Works*, vol. 2. A. R. George, *Communion with God in the New Testament* (London: Epworth, 1953), deals with the topic in a more general manner.

9. The Spirit and the body *and*
10. Gifts for ministry

Literature on the ministry of the Spirit within the body of Christ has inevitably tended to focus attention on spiritual gifts. As a representative sample, see A. Bittlinger, *Gifts and Graces* (London: Hodder & Stoughton, 1967); *idem, Gifts and Ministries* (Grand Rapids, MI: Eerdmans, 1973); D. A. Carson, *Showing the Spirit* (Grand Rapids, MI: Baker Book House, 1987). On the theme of prophecy, see in particular: W. Grudem, *The Gift of Prophecy in 1 Corinthians* (Lanham, MD: University of America Press, 1982), and his more popular study, *The Gift of Prophecy in the New Testament and Today* (Westchester, IL: Crossway Books, and Eastbourne: Kingsway, 1988); Graham Houston, *Prophecy Now* (Leicester: Inter-Varsity Press, 1989; US ed. *Prophecy: A Gift for Today* [Downers Grove, IL: InterVarsity Press, 1989]). In defence of the cessationist view, the classical statement in modern times is in B. B. Warfield, *Counterfeit Miracles*, originally published in 1918 as *Miracles Yesterday and Today* (London: Banner of Truth, 1972). Variations of Warfield's view may be found in R. B. Gaffin, Jr., *Perspectives on Pentecost* (Phillipsburg, NJ: Presbyterian & Reformed, 1979); T. R. Edgar, *Miraculous Gifts: Are They For Today?* (Neptune, NJ: Loizeaux Brothers, 1983); O. P. Robertson, *The Final Word* (Edinburgh: Banner of Truth, 1993). The fullest critique of Warfield is Jon Ruthven, *On the Cessation of the Charismata* (Sheffield: Sheffield Academic Press, 1993). By contrast with the issue of spiritual gifts, the role of the Spirit in the ordinances of the church's life has not been well served in theological writing, and is generally treated only as part of broader studies. See H. W. Robinson, *The Christian Experience of the Holy Spirit* (London: Nisbet & Co., 1928), pp. 184–198; J. G. Davies, *Spirit, Church and Sacraments* (London: 1956). See also Calvin's comments in *Institutes*, IV.14.7–13 and IV.17.8–10.

Sadly, little attention has been given in recent literature to the role of the Spirit in relationship to preaching, but there is a stirring account by D. Martyn Lloyd-Jones (after hearing whom Emil Brunner commented that it was the greatest preaching he had ever heard), in *Preaching and Preachers* (London: Hodder & Stoughton, 1971). See also Tony Sargent, *The Sacred Anointing* (London: Hodder & Stoughton, 1994).

11. The Spirit and the world

For discussion of the Spirit's activity in the world, see H. Berkhof, *The Doctrine of the Holy Spirit* (London: Epworth, 1965); J. Comblin, *The Holy Spirit and Liberation* (London: Burns & Oates, 1989), pp. 1–76. For a broader study, see A. Kuyper, *Lectures on Calvinism* (Grand Rapids, MI: Eerdmans, 1898). For the work of the Spirit in the consummation, see G. Vos, *The Pauline Eschatology* (1930; repr. Grand Rapids, MI: Eerdmans, 1952).

Index of Biblical References

279

Index of Names

Index of Subjects